SECRET
ISTANBUL

Emre Öktem

Photos: Letizia Missir de Lusignan and Mesut Tufan

D0095918

JonGlez

Letizia Missir Mamachi de Lusignan comes from a noble Byzantine family: many of her ancestors were among the first dragomans of the Sublime Porte. Amaury II de Lusignan, from whom her family is also descended, was King of Cyprus and King of Jerusalem (1194–1205). A journalist by profession, in 2009 she co-authored (with Melih Ozsöz) a book on Turkey and Europe published in Istanbul by IKV.

Emre Öktem, born in Istanbul, is professor of international law at Galatasaray University (Istanbul). He also teaches at the University of Fribourg (Switzerland) and the Turkish War Academies. The author of books and articles on human rights, freedom of religion, minority rights, the law of armed conflict and the history of law under the Ottoman Empire, he is actively involved in interreligious dialogue. He has served as an expert with the Organization for Security and Co-operation in Europe, the Turkish courts and international investment arbitration.

Mesut Tufan, born in 1953, grew up in Istanbul. In Paris for his graduate studies, he became a photographer, columnist for Radio France Internationale, contributor to Courrier International and documentary filmmaker. On his return to Istanbul in 2006 he continued to take photos, wrote, exhibited and published in Turkey and elsewhere. Specialising in the history and cultures of the Balkans, the Middle East and the Caucasus, he has worked on various programmes of cultural and artistic reconciliation, notably in the Balkans and between Turkey and Armenia.

We have taken great pleasure in drawing up
Secret Istanbul and hope that through its guidance
you will, like us, continue to discover unusual,
hidden or little-known aspects of the city.
Descriptions of certain places are accompanied
by thematic sections highlighting historical details
or anecdotes as an aid to understanding the city
in all its complexity.
Secret Istanbul also draws attention to
the multitude of details found in places that
we may pass every day without noticing.
These are an invitation to look more closely at
the urban landscape and, more generally,
a means of seeing our own city with the curiosity
and attention that we often display while
travelling elsewhere …

Comments on this guide and its contents, as well as
information on sites not mentioned, are welcome
and will help us to enrich future editions.
Don't hesitate to contact us:
• Jonglez Publishing,
  17, boulevard du Roi,
  78000 Versailles, France
• E-mail: info@jonglezpublishing.com

Gümüşkere

Kısırmandıra

Arnavutköy

Göktürk

Habibler

Başakşehir

Sultangazi

Kağıthane

0-2

Esenler

Gaziosmanpaşa

p. 156

0-3

0-2

p. 14

Şişli

0-1

Eyüp

Beyoğlu

Beşiktaş

Bağcılar

0-3

İSTANBUL

Küçükçekmece

Bahçelievler

Zeytinburnu

Fatih

p. 82

D-100

Bakırköy

Atatürk
Havalimanı

D-100

Marmara Denizi

N

0   5   10 km

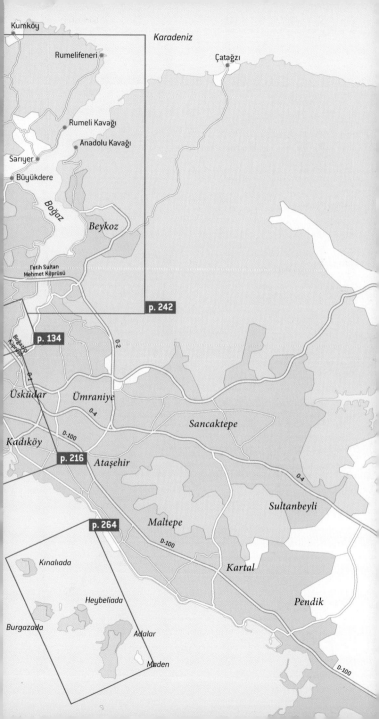

CONTENTS

HISTORIC PENINSULA

FATIH - GOLDEN HORN, WEST

CONTENTS

BEŞIKTAŞ - YILDIZ

BEYOGLU

CONTENTS

NORTH BOSPHORUS

PRINCES' ISLANDS

HISTORIC PENINSULA

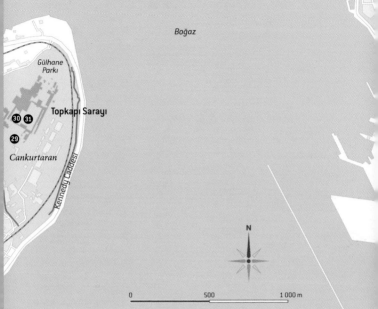

TOMB OF BEKRI MUSTAFA ❶

In front of the apse of the Ahi Ahmed Çelebi Mosque
In the middle of a car park, next to the History Foundation (Tarih Vakfı)
Avenue Ragıp Gümüşpala
Eminönü
• Tram: Eminönü

> *The tomb of a drunkard who became a saint despite himself*

A legendary figure of the early 17th-century, famous for his love of alcohol, Bekri Mustafa lived during the reign of Murad IV (1623-1640), who used physical force to maintain public order in the city. Having observed that the cafes and inns had become the haunts of Janissaries who were indulging in every kind of debauchery and starting fires, the sultan banned the consumption of alcohol, tobacco and coffee. Once apprehended by officers of the law, the transgressors faced the death penalty and were executed immediately by strangulation on-site, by wandering executioners. The sultan often visited inns incognito, accompanied by his henchmen, and oversaw the execution of clients in person, despite being a heavy drinker himself. In the stories attributed to Bekri Mustafa, the latter was caught red-handed many times by the sultan but escaped strangulation through his cunning and pleasant speech.

After his death due to natural causes, no doubt hastened by alcohol, Bekri Mustafa was buried not far from his current tomb. During improvement

work carried out by the city council at the beginning of the 1980s, the tomb was marked for demolition, provoking a strong reaction among his followers and believers. The regulars in the near-by inns would often come to kiss his tombstone at night, crying and pouring out wine or raki. During the day, the wives of drunkards would also sometimes take earth from the grave to mix with their husbands' meals, in the hope of forcing them to give up alcohol.

Due to protests from the innkeepers, opposed to the demolition of Bekri Mustafa's tomb, a compromise was found. The tomb was moved next to that of a genuine saint, Sheikh Abdürrauf Samedani. The devout visitors who came to pray at the tomb of Sheikh Şamadani also began over time to pray for Bekri Mustafa, who started to cure the blind, the lame and squint-eyed. Bekri Mustafa the drunkard thus became a saint, without even wishing it!

At the height of the alcohol ban, Sultan Murad IV and the Grand Vizier travelled incognito in a boat to Üsküdar. As they crossed the Bosphorus, one of the passengers took out a carafe and began drinking without the least concern. "What are you drinking?" inquired the sultan. "A fortifying potion," he replied. "Give me this potion, I want to taste it" said the sultan, taking a sip of the liquid before offering the carafe to the Grand Vizier, who also tasted it. "Infidel! Did you not know that I had forbidden wine?" exclaimed Murad. "Who do you think you are that you can forbid wine?" "Myself? Sultan Murad, and this is my Grand Vizier, Bayram Pasha." "I am certain, gentlemen, that it is not myself but you who should abstain from wine. You have only taken a sip, and you already believe that you are the sultan and the grand vizier. After two sips, you will probably believe that you are the Lord himself."

NEARBY

THEATRE OF THE ALI PAŞA CARAVANSERAI ❷
Avenue Kıbleçeşme Cad., no. 3
Küçükpazar Eminönü
• Tel: 0212 519 00 27 or 0537 523 04 26
• Opposite Istanbul Ticaret Üniversitesi (Istanbul Commerce University)
• Performances Thursday—Sunday at 9pm in summer

Every summer, Genco Erkal, a legendary figure in Turkish theatre (in 1969 he created *Dostlar Tiyatrosu*, the "Theatre of Friends"), carries out a delightful scheme, transforming an 18th-century caravanserai into an open-air theatre. Still partially occupied by metal workshops on the arcaded second floor, covered in vines, the caravanserai contains a veritable labyrinth of abandoned rooms, which the members of the audience/visitors are free to explore prior to the performance.

— THE OTTOMAN MILION

Şehzadebaşı Caddesi
At the southern corner of the Şehzadebaşı Mosque, near the Damat
İbrahim Paşa Mosque
• Tram: Beyazıt or Laleli

The Ottoman version of the Byzantine Milion

In part of the external wall of the Şehzadebaşı Mosque, situated at ground level, a keen observer will notice a rather unique dark green marble column. This column marks the geographical centre of the Ottoman capital, following a tradition inspired by the Byzantine Milion (see p. 67), from which distances were measured.

A century after Constantinople had been captured by the Ottomans, in order to measure distances in the city using a method that no longer relied on the old Byzantine empire, Suleiman the Magnificent (1484-1566) asked the architect Sinan (1489-1588) to determine the centre of the city of Istanbul. Sinan marked the location with a column of green marble, which he placed at the very corner of the Şehzadebaşı Mosque, which was then being built. This column originally swivelled on its axis, as was the case with many such elements in Sinan's works (see p. 24 and 221).

Fate struck during the construction of the mosque, which was almost certainly intended to form part of a huge religious complex dedicated to the sultan, as the sultan's son, Crown Prince Mahmad, died in 1543, five years before its completion. Suleiman therefore dedicated the building to him, and it would be another nine years before he gave his own name ("the Süleymaniye") to another grandiose structure.

For more information on the Byzantine Milion, see p. 67.

WHAT IS THE ORIGIN OF THE TERM "MILION"?
The term "Milion" comes from "Milliarium Aureum", a golden column erected by Emperor Augustus at the Roman Forum to act as a departure point for the roads. The stone markers placed along Roman roads were known as *milliaria* as they marked a distance of one thousand paces. The Milliarium Aureum, the classic *milliarium*, represented the centre from which distances were measured in miles.

TOMB OF LALELI BABA ❹

Courtyard of the Kemal Paşa Mosque
Şirvanzade Street, no. 1
Take the street to the left of the Laleli Mosque, at the first crossroads

A mosque in exchange for a fart

Laleli Baba was an 18th-century holy vagrant who had a reputation for performing miracles. Since 1957, his tomb has held pride of place in the cemetery of the Kemal Paşa Mosque, not far from the Laleli Baba Mosque to which he gave his name, according to legend, in quite unusual circumstances (see opposite). Marked by a flower that was especially dear to him – the tulip (*laleli* in Turkish) –, his gravestone was originally located in the corner of "his" mosque.

"I HAVE BUILT THREE MOSQUES. I WAS OBLIGED TO GIVE THE FIRST TO MY ANCESTOR (FATIH), THE MONKS SEIZED THE SECOND (AYAZMA) AND A VAGRANT TOOK THE THIRD (LALELI)".

The Laleli Mosque, constructed between 1760 and 1763 by the architects Mehmed Tahir Ağa and Hacı Ahmed Ağa, marks a departure from the architectural style adopted by Sinan in the 16th century, with the overall appearance, the style of the minarets and ornamentation displaying a clear European influence. It is one of the three imperial mosques commissioned by Mustafa III, none of which bear his name.

The other two are the Fatih Mosque, rebuilt after the 1766 earthquake, and the Ayazma Mosque in Üsküdar.

Mustafa III, who was not without a sense of humour, was known to have remarked, "I have built three mosques. I was obliged to give the first to my ancestor (Fatih), the monks seized the second (Ayazma) and a vagrant took the third (Laleli)".

"I DO NOT WANT YOUR EMPIRE, WHICH YOU ARE WILLING TO EXCHANGE FOR A FART. YOUR THRONE IS WORTH NO MORE THAN FLATULENCE."

Sultan Mustafa III (1717-1774), whom even Voltaire considered to be a "great ignoramus", wanted to receive the blessing of Laleli Baba (see opposite) for the new mosque that he had commissioned. Laleli Baba was invited to the Topkapı Palace where the sultan sought prayers for his august person. The saint replied to the sultan, "My sultan, throughout your whole life, I have desired that you eat well, drink and fart." Incensed, the sultan rebuked the holy man and threw him out of the palace. As he was being expelled, Laleli Baba uttered a second prayer, "Eat and drink, then, but do not fart!" The next day, the sultan's stomach began to inflate and the best physicians in Istanbul were summoned in the following days to cure the sultan, who suffered cruelly due to the gas that was causing his bowels to swell. Facing the prospect of a slow death, Mustafa saw his error and invited Laleli Baba back to the palace in order to apologise and request prayers for healing. The latter haggled furiously: at first, the sultan offered to name the new mosque after him, but Laleli Baba was not satisfied. He then offered to give him treasures, but this left the saint unmoved. The sultan finally offered his throne to Laleli Baba. The holy man was deeply saddened and said to the sultan, "I do not want your empire, which you are willing to exchange for a fart. Your throne is worth no more than flatulence." He then stroked the sultan's stomach while reciting prayers, which produced an immediate cure. The mosque was finally given the name of "Laleli", which it bears to this day.

RECRUITMENT COLUMN ❺

Süleymaniye Mosque
Avenue Prof. Sıddık Sami Onar cad., nos. 1-46, Süleymaniye
• Visiting between morning and evening prayers
• Metro: Vezneciler

> *A test to determine the physical aptitude of future soldiers*

In the porticoed courtyard of the Süleymaniye Mosque turn your attention to the inside entrance portal. Here, the last column on the left before leaving through the courtyard gateway (on the Golden Horn side) has a little-known but interesting history: legend has it that the column was used to test the physical aptitude of youths wishing to join the Ottoman army. Hopeful recruits were required to put their back to the column and pass from one side to the other without falling from the marble platform, a far from easy feat, and one that would require very strong abdominal muscles.

The worn-down marble on both sides of the column, as well as its proximity to the former Ottoman Ministry of War (which currently houses Istanbul University), makes this legend plausible.

PHRENOLOGY COMES TO SINAN'S AID

The tomb of Mimar Sinan – near the Süleymaniye Mosque, at the intersection of Avenue Mimar Sinan Caddesi and Fetva Yokuşu Street – was designed by the famous architect himself.

On 1 August 1935 (347 years after his death in 1588), three professors from Ankara began digging in Mimar Sinan's tomb, eventually coming across human remains. The skeleton had disintegrated, but the skull was found in excellent condition. It was cleaned by an anthropology professor and measurements were taken using calipers. Greatly relieved, he declared, "Dear friends, Sinan is a Turk".

In order to be understood, this strange story must be situated in its historical context, namely the rise of racism in Europe during the 1930s, which stimulated studies in physical anthropology. European scholars began to devote themselves to the study of phrenology (the science of the study of the skull) which held that the superiority or inferiority of a race could be determined by the proportions of the skull. Since the Aryan race possessed an elongated (or dolichocephalic) skull, they were considered to be superior to the Asiatic races with their short (or brachycephalic) skulls. It was claimed that only a dolichocephal could demonstrate artistic or scientific genius. Since the Turks were of Asiatic stock, and therefore brachycephalic, it was suggested that the great figures of Turkish history could only be of non-Turkish origins. The young, proud Turkish Republic, greatly outraged by these invectives, implemented studies in order to prove that the leading lights of Turkish history were indeed Turks. It therefore had to be proven that they were brachycephals, which inevitably required disinterments. Thousands of skulls were accordingly collected, including those of Seljuk princes and Sinan, which was taken from his tomb. At the time there was even talk of creating a museum of anthropology based on these specimens.

The case of Sinan was especially delicate since he was a Christian-born devşirme. He came from the village of Ağırnas, whose Greek name is Agrianos, or Aghioi Anargiroi. Historians are divided over its origins, which may be Armenian, Greek, or Turkish Orthodox/Karamanli. Prior to the exchanging of populations between Greece and Turkey in 1923, the village of Ağırnas was home only to Muslims and Orthodox Christians, even though Armenians may also have been living there in the 15th century.

A report on Sinan's disinterred skull (which was brachycephalic and therefore Turk) was presented to Mustafa Kemal Atatürk soon after the dig. Realising, no doubt, that the scientific enthusiasm for phrenology was turning sour, the founder of the Republic simply added a laconic note to the report: "Instruction for the Turkish Historical Society: make a statue of Sinan". The latter was unveiled in 1957 in the garden of Ankara University's Faculty of Languages, History and Geography.

Digs carried out during recent restoration work on Sinan's tomb confirmed that the head is indeed missing from the skeleton.

THE BLACK STONE OF THE KAABA OF THE MAUSOLEUM OF SULEIMAN THE MAGNIFICENT

Situated in the cemetery in front of the apse of the Süleymaniye Mosque, the Mausoleum of Suleiman the Magnificent was constructed by the architect Sinan during the reign of Selim II, after Suleiman's death during the Zigetvar expedition in Hungary, in 1566. Although Suleiman's entrails were buried at the site of his death, where his tomb may still be found, his mummified body was transported to Istanbul to be buried in the courtyard of his mosque. A perceptive observer will notice the fragment of the Black Stone (Hajarul Aswad) of the Kaaba inlaid into the top of the arch above the entrance to the mausoleum. When the Kaaba was repaired by the Ottomans in the 16th century, a number of the fragments that had become detached were collected; some of them were placed at this very site, and others in the Sokollu Mosque.

For more information on the Black Stone in Istanbul, see p. 64.

THE BEYAZIT FIRE TOWER ⑥

Istanbul University campus
- Tel: (212) 440 00 00 (10054)
- iubasin@istanbul.edu.tr
- Visiting Friday 2pm and 3pm. Other days: prove professional interest and/or university membership
- For all visits, contact the University Public Relations Department
- Tram: Beyazıt
- Metro: Vezneciler

One of the most beautiful panoramas of Istanbul

Although the Beyazıt Fire Tower itself is well known, many people are unaware that it is possible to go inside on Friday afternoons. After climbing the 180 steps of its spiral staircase, visitors will find superb panoramic views. From this vantage point, surely one of the most spectacular in the city, you can see not only the historic peninsula, but from the mouth of the Black Sea across to the southern shores of the Sea of Marmara in clear weather. The tower platform with its numerous windows was designed as a fire look-out post during the Ottoman period and still fulfils this function today, despite the advance of modern technology.

The ceilings of the platform are decorated with black and white murals which apparently depict the Bosphorus, the Golden Horn, the Kadıköy shore, and the Princes' Islands, perhaps so that the location of a fire seen at night from any of the windows may be determined.

The first (wooden) watchtower was constructed in 1749, on one of the seven hills of the city, on the site of a Byzantine tower designed for the same purpose. It was destroyed in a fire in 1756, rebuilt, then demolished in 1826 following the abolition of the Janissary corps, of which the firemen had previously been members. The current stone tower was erected in 1828 in the Ottoman Baroque style and then gradually enlarged to its present height of 118 metres.

The tower accommodated about twenty firemen in the 19th century. Fires were signalled by hanging baskets during the day and lit lanterns at night. If fire was observed within the walls of the city and neighbouring areas, two baskets or two red lanterns were hung on either side of the tower. For a fire on the Asian side, the tower was hung with one basket on both sides or a green lantern on one side, and for a fire in Pera, a single basket was hung on one side, and two on the other, or a non-coloured lantern on both sides. Using their professional jargon, a fireman who spotted a fire would say to his officer, "Master, you've just had a child." The latter would then reply, "a girl or a boy". "Boy" represented Istanbul *intra muros* while "daughter" referred to the remaining areas of the city.

> Today the tower announces the weather forecast by lighting different coloured lamps: blue for clear skies, green for rain, yellow for fog, and red for snow.

THE STARS OF DAVID OF THE ALI PASHA MOSQUE

❼

Intersection of Mercan Caddesi and Fuat Paşa Caddesi avenues
Opposite the east gate of the Istanbul University Botanical Garden
• Tram: Beyazıt

> *A great Ottoman diplomat under the sign of the Star of David*

Located on the site of the Ağa Mescidi Mosque, constructed by Yakup Ağa in the 16th century, the Ali Pasha Mosque has the remarkable distinguishing feature of being decorated with several Stars of David on the upper windows of its eight facades. As well as being a Hebrew symbol, the Star of David, or six-pointed star, has long had a symbolic role in both the Christian and Islamic religions (see following double-page spread).

The Ağa Mescidi Mosque, used for the funeral prayers of officials from the Old Palace, was destroyed by fire in the 19th century. In 1869 the Italian architect Bariori built the current mosque on the same site, on the orders of the Grand Vizier Ali Pasha, a true genius of Ottoman diplomacy during the period of 19th-century reforms (see opposite). The Palace of Ali Pasha, which no longer exists, previously faced the mosque. The marble inscriptions on the mosque were created by Mustafa İzzet Efendi, a great calligrapher of the period.

ALI PASHA: A BRILLIANT DIPLOMAT, A TESTIMONY TO SOCIAL MOBILITY AMONG THE OTTOMANS

Born in 1815 to a father who was a caretaker at the Egyptian Bazaar (Mısır Çarşısı), Ali Pasha retained the nickname "son of the caretaker" as a reminder of his humble origins. He joined the Imperial Chancery at the age of 15, where he learnt French. At the age of 23, he became First Secretary of the Ottoman embassy in London and ambassador at the age of 26, in 1841.

When Reşhid Pasha, his mentor and protector, became Grand Vizier in 1848, Ali Pasha became Minister of Foreign Affairs, at the age of 33.

He became Grand Vizier in 1852 and, at the apogee of his career, participated in the Congress of Paris in 1856, at the end of the Crimean War. During the conference, he succeeded in securing the Ottoman Empire's recognition as a European power, even though it was in full political and economic decline.

As Minister of Foreign Affairs and Grand Vizier, Ali Pasha faced the 1848 revolutions, Cretan uprisings and the separatist ambitions of the vassal prince of Egypt. Crushed by the burden of his responsibilities, Ali Pasha died of tuberculosis in 1871 and was buried in the Süleymaniye Mosque cemetery.

Sickly, fragile, generous and utterly courteous, Ali Pasha was nevertheless uncompromising where etiquette was concerned and did not hesitate to reprimand the sultan over this issue. He believed that the empire ought to embrace not only European modernity but also its old ceremonial traditions.

At his death, Bismarck declared to a Turkish journalist that, "the Turks have lost a Grand Vizier and Europe, a great man" and showed him a letter signed by Ali Pasha, urging Prussia and France to agree to an immediate armistice during the War of 1870, the first attempt at securing peace between the two countries.

Following Bismarck's advice, Wilhelm I asked Ali Pasha's heirs to sell him the pasha's writing desk as a souvenir. The fate of this precious artefact after the Soviets ransacked Berlin in 1945 is unknown.

As an individual at the apex of government, Ali Pasha is a prime example of the Ottoman Empire's practice of promoting bureaucrats based on their personal abilities alone, regardless of their social origins.

For more information on the history and symbolism of the Star of David (six-pointed star), see following double-page spread.

THE STAR HEXAGRAM: A MAGICAL TALISMAN?

The hexagram – also known as the Star of David or the Shield of David – comprises two interlaced equilateral triangles, one pointing upwards and the other downwards. It symbolises the combination of man's spiritual and human nature.

The six points correspond to the six directions in space (north, south, east and west, together with zenith and nadir) and also refer to the complete universal cycle of the six days of creation (the seventh day being when the Creator rested).

Hence, the hexagram became the symbol of the macrocosm (its six angles of 60° totalling 360°) and of the union between mankind and its creator.

Although present in the synagogue of Capernaum (third century AD), the hexagram does not really make its appearance in rabbinical literature until 1148 – in the *Eshkol Hakofer* written by the Karaite* scholar Judah Ben Elijah. In Chapter 242 its mystical and apotropaic (evil-averting) qualities are described, with the actual words then often being engraved on amulets: "And the names of the seven angels were written on the *mazuzah*: The Everlasting will protect you and this symbol called the Shield of David contains, at the end of the *mezuzah*, the written name of all the angels."

In the thirteenth century the hexagram also became an attribute of one of the seven magic names of Metatron, the angel of the divine presence associated with the archangel Michael (head of the heavenly host and the closest to God the Father).

The identification of Judaism with the Star of David began in the Middle Ages. In 1354 King Karel IV of Bohemia granted the Jewish community of Prague the privilege of putting the symbol on their banner. The Jews embroidered a gold star on a red background to form a standard that became known as the Flag of King David (*Maghen David*) and was adopted as the official symbol of Jewish synagogues. By the nineteenth century, the symbol had spread throughout the Jewish community. Jewish mysticism has it that the origin of the hexagram was directly linked with the flowers that adorn the *menorah***: irises with six petals. For those who believe this origin, the hexagram came directly from the hands of the God of Israel, the six-petal iris not only resembling the Star of David in general form but also being associated with the people of Israel in the *Song of Songs*.

As well as offering protection, the hexagram was believed to have magical powers. This reputation originates in the famous *Clavicula Salomonis* (Key of Solomon), a grimoire (textbook of magic) attributed to Solomon himself but, in all likelihood, produced during the Middle Ages. The anonymous texts probably came from one of the numerous Jewish schools of the Kabbalah that then existed in Europe, for the work is clearly inspired by the teachings of the Talmud and the Jewish faith.

The *Clavicula* contains a collection of thirty-six pentacles (themselves symbols rich in magic and esoteric significance) which were intended to enable communication between the physical world and the different levels of the soul.

There are various versions of the text, in numerous translations, and the content varies between them.

However, most of the surviving texts date from the sixteenth and seventeenth centuries – although there is a Greek translation dating from the fifteenth.

In Tibet and India, the Buddhists and Hindus read this universal symbol of the hexagram in terms of the creator and his creation, while the Brahmins hold it to be the symbol of the god Vishnu.

Originally, the two triangles were in green (upright triangle) and red (inverted triangle). Subsequently, these colours became black and white, the former representing the spirit, the latter the material world. For the Hindus, the upright triangle is associated with Shiva, Vishnu and Brahma (corresponding to the Christian God the Father, Son and Holy Ghost).

The Son (Vishnu) can be seen to always occupy the middle position, being the intercessor between things divine and things earthly.

The hexagram also often appears in the windows and pediments of Christian churches, as a symbolic reference to the universal soul. In this case, that soul is represented by Christ – or, sometimes, by the pair of Christ (upright triangle) and the Virgin (inverted triangle); the result of the interlacing of the two is God the Father Almighty. The hexagram is also found in the mediated form of a lamp with six branches or a six-section rose window.

*qara'im or bnei mikra: "he who follows the Scriptures". Karaism is a branch of Judaism that defends the sole authority of the Hebrew Scripture as the source of divine revelation, thus repudiating oral tradition.
**Menorah – the multibranched candelabra used in the rituals of Judaism. The arms of the seven-branched menorah, one of the oldest symbols of the Jewish faith, represent the seven archangels before the Throne of God: Michael, Gabriel, Samuel, Raphael, Zadkiel, Anael and Kassiel.

THE SEAL OF SOLOMON IN TURKEY

The Seal of Solomon (*Muhr-u Suleyman* or *Khatem-u Suleyman*), or star hexagram, which corresponds to the Star of David in Judaeo-Christian culture (see p. 30), also existed in Turko-Mongol culture: the indigenous cultures of Anatolia and the Middle East made frequent use of it.

The entrance of the Armenian church Surp Asdvadzadzin, for example, is decorated with a beautiful golden relief on which it is visible.

The star hexagram is also used extensively in the decorative Islamic arts, particularly in architecture, but also on paper and textiles, as well as metal, wood, ceramic and glass objects.

As a result of the popular belief that the devil cannot enter places where the Seal of Solomon is visible, this protective symbol was placed on the keystones of domes, arches, doorways and entrances to mosques and dervish monasteries, as well as on fountains, gravestones, kitchen utensils, on helmets, on shirts covered in decorative writing and placed on armour during warfare and on military standards, including that of Barbarossa.

The seal became less common on Ottoman monuments from the second half of the 19th century (marking a break with the old architectural and decorative traditions and the absorption of European style), disappearing entirely in the 20th century, most likely due to it being adopted by the Jews (see p. 30).

SOLOMON AND THE KORAN

The King Solomon of the Old Testament is recognised as a prophet (*Suleyman*) by the Koran. He is praised for his justice (21:78-79) and is said to possess esoteric knowledge: he knows the languages of the birds and other animals (27:16,19), the storm obeys him (21:81, 38:36) and he has control over legions of djinn (31:82, 38:37).

Considering him to be the symbol of a powerful secret knowledge, popular Islamic tradition soon created legends around the character of Solomon that went beyond the verses of the Koran and hadiths of the Prophet relating to him. It was claimed that Solomon wore the star hexagram engraved on his ring, without which he would be deprived of his supernatural powers, giving rise to the Turkish proverb that is still in use today: "Whoever has the seal, is Solomon", which means that the individual's power depends on the authority that s/he is given.

WHERE CAN WE FIND THE SEAL OF SOLOMON IN ISTANBUL?

Ali Paşa Camii Mosque, Mercan - Beyazıt
Old building, Mercan Camii Çıkmazı Street - Beyazıt
Tomb of Lala Mustafa Paşa - Eyüp
Zal Mahmut Paşa Camii Mosque - Eyüp,
Topkapı Palace: Circumcision Room (Sünnet Odası), holy relics entrance (lamps) – Historic Peninsula
Gül Camii Mosque – Historic Peninsula
İstanbul Erkek Lisesi (Ottoman public debt) - Historic Peninsula
Istanbul Postal Museum – Historic Peninsula
Mausoleum of Mehmed the Conqueror - Fatih – Historic Peninsula
Fountain of Sultana Gülnuş Emetullah, hardware market (Perşembe Pazarı) - Karaköy
Kemankeş Mustafa Paşa Camii Mosque - Karaköy
Barbarossa's standard – Naval Museum - Beşiktaş
Barbarossa's coffin - Beşiktaş
Galatasaray University – gate with Star of David motif – Beşiktaş
Atik Valide Mosque - Üsküdar
Emetullah Valide Sultan Mosque - Üsküdar
Armenian church (Surp Asdvadzadzin): entrance, marble relief – Beşiktaş;
Dolmabahçe Palace: marble architectural artefacts from the Çırağan Palace, preserved in the garden - Beşiktaş
Emetullah Valide Sultan Camii Mosque - Üsküdar
Atik Valide Camii Mosque: old lamp under the dome - Üsküdar
St George's church: Christ icon – Heybeliada - Uçurum Manastırı – Princes' Islands

GARDEN OF THE ARMENIAN PATRIARCHATE ⑧

Sevgi sokak Street, nos. 7-9
Kumkapı
• Open 9am-5pm, except weekends

Masonic symbols on Kirkor Agaton's gravestone

Situated immediately to the right on entering the garden of the Armenian Patriarchate, the monumental gravestone of Kirkor Agaton Pasha is decorated with a compass and set square, well-known Masonic symbols indicating his allegiance to Turkish Freemasonry. Kirkor Agaton Pasha's life ended in spectacular fashion: he died of joy on hearing that he had been nominated to the office of pasha (see opposite).

NEARBY

THE MUSEUM OF THE ARMENIAN PATRIARCHATE
Located in the basement of the Armenian Patriarchate of Istanbul, this small museum houses a beautiful collection of objects illustrating life among the Armenian community in Turkey, especially in its ecclesiastical aspect.

SYMBOLISM OF THE COMPASS AND SET SQUARE

Within Masonic symbolism, the compass symbolizes the mind while the set square, symbol of the material, represents "rectitude in action". When both implements are juxtaposed, they express the balance between material and spiritual forces, a necessary condition for obtaining spiritual illumination.

This illumination is represented in the Masonic hierarchy by the third grade of Master Mason, in which the compass is placed on the set square, thereby representing the triumph of spirituality over the material.

KIRKOR AGATON PASHA: A PASHA WHO DIED OF JOY ON THE DAY OF HIS NOMINATION

Before dying at the news of his appointment as the first non-Muslim pasha, Kirkor Agaton Pasha led an extraordinary life.

Prior to the Tanzimat era, inaugurated by the 1839 edict, non-Muslim subjects of the Ottoman Empire were denied access to the civil service, except as governors of certain autonomous regions (such as the Danubian provinces). In 1842, however, all Ottoman subjects were recognised as equal regardless of their religion, after which non-Muslims were granted the right to be promoted up to the rank of colonel in the army. The imperial edict of 1856 finally allowed them to be promoted without restriction within the imperial hierarchy.

It was nevertheless another twelve years before Sultan Abdülaziz decided to appoint a non-Muslim, Kirkor Agaton, as minister of public works. The latter received news of his nomination in Paris, where he was representing the empire at the International Post and Telegraph Conference, from which he sent a telegram expressing his deep gratitude to the Grand Vizier Ali Pasha. This was to be his final act as an official of the Ottoman Empire. The good news had such a strong effect on Kirkor Agaton that it triggered a fatal cardiac arrest.

The tragedy was compounded by the fact that Agaton was a highly prized bureaucrat. Born into a family of poor labourers, he attracted the attention of the Grand Vizier's Armenian banker, Mustafa Reşid Pasha, who sent him to study at the Collège Grignon in Paris. After receiving a strong grounding in agriculture, he was introduced to King Louis Philippe as one of the Ottoman Empire's foremost specialists in this field. On returning to Istanbul, he became a member of the Court of Accounts and represented the empire in several international agricultural exhibitions. He became Chairman of the Post and Telegram Office and it was in this capacity that he was present in Paris in 1868.

In the 1970s, a section of the Hasköy Armenian Cemetery, where Agaton was buried, was expropriated for the construction of the perimeter highway connecting the Golden Horn and Bosphorus bridges. Some of his bones could not be saved and remain under the road; others were buried in a corner of the cemetery, and a third set were buried under his gravestone, which was moved to the Armenian Patriarchate.

THE KADIRGA CAFÉ FOUNTAIN ❾

Havuzlu kahve (the cafe with the basin)
Avenue Kadırga Limanı cad., no. 2
• Tram: Çemberlitaş
• Train: Kumkapı

The last firemen's café

Typically traditional (which means that it is an exclusively male space), the Kadırga Café is the only surviving Ottoman café that was frequented and managed by the local firemen, and whose origins go back to the Janissaries. Its old basin and marble fountain bear witness to its colourful past. The marble fittings spouting jets of water strongly resemble the ends of pump hoses. Following the 1509 earthquake known as the "little apocalypse", it became the custom to build houses entirely out of wood. Although this material was highly resistant to seismic catastrophes, it was hardly fire-resistant. In the absence of a fire brigade, the local inhabitants, equipped with barrels and buckets, had to organise themselves to extinguish the fires that sometimes destroyed entire neighbourhoods. At the beginning of the 18th century, one such inhabitant, Davud Ağa, introduced portable pumps, which were carried by four people on their backs. His team formed the basis of the fire brigade, which was incorporated into the Janissary corps. The policing of the city intra muros was also carried out by the Janissaries and each police station was equipped with a pump and its own dedicated team. It is therefore no coincidence that there is a police station situated near the Kadırga Cafe. Corruption within the Janissary corps also affected the firemen who were part of that body. Houses, evacuated when fire broke out, became opportunities for self-enrichment and were often looted. The Janissary leaders, who were at that time involved in everything except war, began to open cafes, the main venues for socialising in Ottoman society. These became meeting places for the firemen of the Janissary corps, whose culture had begun to influence the former.

When the Janissary corps was suppressed in 1826, the cafes they owned were closed and the firemen's duties were taken over by the regular army, and then by the district authorities. At the same time, young people in these areas organised themselves into groups of volunteers and carried on the work of the firemen as a kind of sport. An *esprit de corps* thus developed, attracting even intellectuals, high-ranking officials and religious dignitaries in the area.

The firemen in the Christian areas, who were numerous and well organised, kept their pumps in their churches. Some of the firemen's groups, however, were religiously mixed. During fights, which were very frequent, solidarity between the firemen prevailed over religious affiliations.

Fires were signalled by one of the city's two fire towers: the Galata Tower or its Beyazıt counterpart located in the gardens of the former war minister, now part of Istanbul University (see p. 26).

— KÂTIP SINAN CAMII

(10)

Mosque entrance on Çoban Çavuş Street
Coffin can be seen more easily from İkbal Street
Soğanağa
• Tram: Beyazıt

The mosque of the flying coffin

A nyone walking along İkbal Street and looking up in the direction of the Kâtip Sinan Mosque will be surprised to see a strange bulge in the roof between the octagonal tympanum supporting the dome and the wall. This coffin-shaped protuberance contains the coffin of the builder who, instead of resting peacefully in the tomb prepared for him in the garden of his mosque, chose to spend the remainder of his days on the roof. The mosque was constructed by Sinan Bey, scribe (or secretary) of the imperial kitchens, in 1496, during the reign of Sultan Bayezid II. When Sinan Bey died, he was, quite naturally, buried in the garden. The day after his interment, the worshippers, who had gathered at an early hour for morning prayer, were terrified at the sight of the corpse, which had left its tomb and settled itself on the dome. The corpse was retrieved for reburial, but the same phenomenon occurred the following night. After a third attempt, the imam of the mosque and the congregation concluded that they had witnessed a miracle and decided to construct a sort of sarcophagus on the edge of the dome. The corpse, inside its coffin, was placed inside this sarcophagus where it has remained for five centuries.

THE FRESCO IN THE UNDERGROUND CHURCH OF THE BODRUM CAMII MOSQUE

⑪

Avenue Mesih Paşa caddesi, no. 25 Laleli
Underground market: open 10am-7pm (depending on season)
Underground chapel: open Friday for midday prayers. On other days, ask
the mosque overseers.
• Tram: Laleli

> *A Christian*
> *princess beneath*
> *a mosque*

Surrounded by modern buildings, the Bodrum Camii Mosque ("Mosque of the Vault") stands on a site once occupied by two churches: the Upper Church, which was converted into the current mosque around 1500, and the Lower Church, which – with its underground cistern that has survived the passage of time – has given the mosque its name. Although the cistern, a real labyrinth of pillars, has become an underground covered market, on the left side of the apse of the Lower Church it is possible to make out a faint mural depicting a princess bringing an offering to the Virgin Mary. The woman in question is Theodora, wife of Romanos Lekapenos, who was buried here.

In the early 10th century, Romanos Lekapenos, droungarios ("admiral") of the Byzantine fleet, purchased the Myrelaion Palace ("myrrh oil" palace). After becoming emperor, he transformed his private residence into an imperial palace and built the Myrelaion Church as a chapel for the monastery of the same name, adjacent to the palace. Romanos Lekapenos also decided that the church should be used as a burial chapel for his family, thereby breaking with a six hundred-year-old tradition according to which members of the imperial family were interred in the crypt of the Church of the Holy Apostles, on the site of the present-day Fatih Mosque.

Following the conquest of the city by the Ottomans, the Myrelaion Church was converted into a mosque by the Grand Vizier Mesih Pasha around the year 1500. The name Mesih, which means "messiah" in Arabic, was sometimes adopted by Greeks named Christos ("messiah" in Greek) after the Ottoman conquest. Mesih Pasha was, in fact, the nephew of the last Byzantine emperor, Constantine XI Palaiologos. The building was thereafter known as the Mesih Paşa Camii or Bodrum Camii. The mosque suffered fires in 1782 and 1911. After the second fire, it was abandoned to its fate until restoration work and excavations were undertaken in 1965, which led to the discovery of the lower chapel. Following insensitive but structurally solid restoration in the 1980s, the mosque was opened to Muslim worshippers in 1986. The mosque's imam will be glad to guide you into the lower chapel, and he also speaks English well. The mosque's small library contains great classics of both Islamic theology and Byzantine history.

Certain commentators claim that the emperor participated in pagan rituals here, although this story seems implausible given that Romanos Lekapenos was well known for his deep religiosity. Towards the end of his reign, he was already spending most of his time with monks. Deposed in 944, he was forced into holy orders and exiled to the island of Proti, modern-day Kınalıada, one of the Princes' Islands. He summoned a council of 300 monks and publicly confessed his sins, in order to obtain absolution before being whipped by a young novice.

THE ÇUKUR MUHALLEBICI MUSEUM ⑫

Avenue Kalpakçılar cad., no. 151
Grand Bazar
Beyazıt
• www.boybeyi.com
• Open daily except Sunday: 8.30am-7pm
• Tram: Beyazıt

***Jewels
in the pudding***

U nder the arches of the Grand Bazaar, the remarkable, tiny wooden structure with its copper dome which takes pride of place by the Mahmud Pasha Gate is known locally as the Çukur Muhallebici ("the ditch pudding shop"). Çukur means "ditch" (the kiosk is situated at the lowest point of the Grand Bazaar) and muhallebi is a typically Turkish dessert, made from milk and similar to a pudding. The kiosk has for many years housed a cake shop which specialises in this type of dessert.

It is said that the Çukur Muhallebici is located on the site of the customs checkpoint of the Byzantine Market, the predecessor of the Ottoman Grand Bazaar, which grew progressively from 1461.

During this period, the Çukur Muhallebici assumed an important role. When the ladies of the harem came to make purchases in the Grand Bazaar, accompanied by their guards and eunuchs, they reached the upper level of the kiosk via the small external staircase, and haggled over jewellery and fabrics in complete safety, away from prying eyes. The guards waited on the ground level while the eunuchs remained next to the women, as in the palace. At the beginning of the 19th century, Sultan Mahmud II (the very same sultan who removed the Janissaries, see p. 56) decided that intimate contact between his concubines and the merchants of the bazaar was indecent; as a result, he prohibited the ladies from visiting the Grand Bazaar and assigned other functions to the kiosk. Thus, the ground floor became a police station and the upper floor was turned into a sort of watch tower for firemen.

In the final years of the empire, the kiosk was sold to private buyers and became the cake shop described above. In 1970 it was sold to the Boybeyi family, jewellers since 1881. Today, the ground floor is used as the Boybeyi showroom and the upper level has been transformed into a small family museum where exhibits include such treasures as: personal jewellery, old calligraphy, antique photos of Istanbul and of Boybeyi family members, weapons inlaid with precious stones, silk scarves embroidered with silver and gold, watches made of precious metals, a miniature carriage encrusted with small stones, prayer beads made of precious stones, and old instruments used for precision navigation.

THE GRAND BAZAAR EAGLE

⑬

İnciciler Kapısı "Gate of the Grand Bazaar"
At the exit to the Cevahir Bedesteni (jewellery market) leading to
Kuyumcular Street, in the direction of Ağa Sokak, towards Mahmutpaşa
• Tram: Beyazıt/Kapalıçarşı

*A historical
and architectural
controversy
over a bird*

ocated within the Grand Bazaar (Kapalıçarşı or "covered market" in Turkish), the İnciciler Gate is, in fact, composed of two consecutive gates. As the inside gate is poorly lit, few visitors notice the bas-relief of a Byzantine eagle gazing out at them from the depths of history. Joseph Hammer (1774-1856), Austrian historian and author of the massive *History of the Ottoman Empire*, considered the presence of this eagle to be sufficient evidence that the Cevahir Bedesteni, the core around which the Grand Bazaar was built, dated from the Byzantine period. Although this conclusion was initially accepted by other historians, both Turkish and foreign, there is now some question as to whether the complex is of Ottoman or Byzantine origin.

Archival research has revealed that the Cevahir Bedesteni and Sandal Bedesteni, which formed the central cores of the Grand Bazaar, were built up from nothing (or almost nothing) by Mehmed the Conqueror, soon after the city had been captured. The original deed of the foundation established by the Conqueror in order to finance the upkeep of Hagia Sophia, which had been converted into a mosque, mentions two new markets whose revenues were said to have been passed on to the foundation in question. The (post-) Byzantine historian Critobulus also provides a very detailed description of the markets built by Mehmed the Conqueror close to his palace, on the current site of Istanbul University. The architecture of the two markets is typical of the 15th-century Ottoman style and exhibits similarities with the markets in Edirne. According to Çelik Gülersoy, to whom we owe many restorations carried out under the auspices of the Turkish Touring Club (including, for instance, the whole of Soğukçeşme Street between Hagia Sophia and the Topkapi Palace, and the Chora/Kariye Camii area), these arguments are far more serious than questions about the origins of a bird.

The solution may be straightforward, however: although the structure of the Grand Bazaar is entirely Ottoman, its infrastructure is Byzantine. Cisterns and underground passages dating from the era of the Basileis abound throughout the site. The Cevahir Bedesteni was probably erected on the site of an open market, or a covered market that had fallen into ruin, and whose ornamentation was "recycled", so to speak, by the Ottomans. This would explain the origin of the eagle and would not be the first example of Byzantine architectural elements being reused by Ottoman builders, in the same way that Byzantine monuments incorporate items from Roman and Hellenistic temples.

ARNAVUT HAN BAS-RELIEF ⑭

Mesih Mehmet Paşa sokak Street, no. 2
Molla Fenari Mahallesi, Beyazıt
• Tram: Beyazıt or Çemberlitaş. Between these two stops, take Kürkçüler Pazarı Sokak Street north towards the Grand Bazaar. The entrance to Arnavut Han is on the second street on the right.

The Albanian nation in search of its own alphabet

Constructed in 1882 as a residential building, the Arnavut Han (*han* designates a former caravanserai) has an attractive pediment above its main entrance depicting its founders. This pediment depicts two Albanian brothers, Lazar (Lazaros) Tanos and Manolis Tanos, surrounded by sheep and holding hands above a writing desk, a probable allusion to bookkeeping in the livestock trade. The brothers are wearing typically Albanian clothes and their names have been written in both the Greek and Cyrillic alphabets. The Albanian language did not actually have its own alphabet when the Arnavut Han was built (it was not codified until 1908).

In Ottoman Albania, the inscriptions on public monuments and buildings were often in different languages and alphabets (Ottoman, Greek, Slavic) so they could be understood more easily by all the ethnic groups in the country. For the Istanbul public, the façade of the Arnavut Han displays, in addition to Greek and Cyrillic, epigraphs in Ottoman Turkish and Armenian, which are visible but indecipherable.

The first attempts at creating an Albanian alphabet were made by Şemseddin Sami (Fracheri) (1850-1904), an Ottoman linguist, writer and encyclopedist of

Albanian origin. In addition to his linguistic work on Albanian, he was also responsible for the first novel written in Ottoman characters (*Taaşşuk-ı Talat ve Fitnat* in 1872), the first encyclopedia in Turkish (*Kamus-ül Alam*, 1889-1898), the first Turkish dictionary meeting European standards (*Kamus-ı Türkî*, 1901) as well as an excellent French-Turkish dictionary (*Kamus-ı Fransevî*, 1905). Buried in Istanbul, Şemsettin Sami's remains were claimed by the Albania of Enver Hoxha, who considered him to be a national hero.

ALBANIA, ISTANBUL, THE OTTOMAN EMPIRE AND TURKEY

Occupied by the Ottoman Empire for more than four centuries, from 1506 to 1912, Albania has developed extremely close links with modern Turkey and many Turks are of Albanian origin, despite having lost the knowledge of their national language.

A few examples include: the son of Şemseddin Sami, Ali Sami Yen, the founder of Galatasaray football club; King Zog of Albania, a former student of Galatasaray High School and the author of the Turkish national anthem; and Mehmet Akif Ersoy, an Albanian on his father's side.

Although the Albanian Muslims have historically been easily absorbed into Turkish culture, the Christian Orthodox Albanians have quickly become Hellenised. Thus, the excellent Baylan cake shop in Kadıköy, which is seen as a reminder of the city's old Greek middle-class traditions, in fact belongs to an old Orthodox Albanian family.

Similarly, although official Greek history portrays the heroes of the Greek revolution as the descendents of Homer revolting against the Turkish yoke, others see them as coming from old Orthodox Albanian families who did not speak a word of Greek. Moreover, the troops sent to suppress the revolt were comprised mainly of (Muslim) Albanians, to the extent that the revolution might as well be described in reality as a civil war between Orthodox and Muslim Albanians.

THE SECRETS OF THE BÜYÜK VALIDE HAN CARAVANSERAI

15

Çakmakçılar Yokuşu, no. 31
Mercan district
• Tram: Beyazıt

A hidden panorama, a Byzantine tower and dome

With its impressive array of features, few buildings testify to Istanbul's diverse cultural history and cosmopolitanism like the Büyük Valide Han. A Shiite mosque sits next to a Byzantine tower that was once used as a treasury by an Ottoman sultana of Greek-Serbian origin who was an expert in palace intrigue and three-time regent.

Büyük Valide Han (literally, "great inn of the mother") is a caravanserai built in the early 17th century by Kösem Sultan in order to fund her charitable foundations. It is comprised of three successive courtyards: the entrance gate leads to a small triangular courtyard, from which another gate provides access to the main courtyard, in the centre of which is a mosque used for worship according to Shiite rites. The caravanserai was more than just a commercial centre. It offered hospitality to merchants of every religion. The Iranians eventually established a permanent presence in the caravanserai and even introduced a printing works, which published books banned by the Sublime Porte, as well as copies of the Koran before the Ottoman spiritual authorities had authorised its reproduction in non-manuscript form.

On the upper floor, ask one of the shopkeepers for the key to the stairs leading to the roof with its several domes. It is possible to walk here if due care is taken. The view, which encompasses the Golden Horn, Galata, the Bosphorus and Asian side, is magnificent.

At the back of the second courtyard, on the left hand side, a dark and narrow

passage leads to a third courtyard, which is flanked by a square tower, twenty-five metres in height. This structure, which predates the caravanserai, was used as a prison during the Byzantine era and, according to certain historians, formed part of the courtroom built by the Emperor Arcadius close to the Macros Embolos (literally, "long portico", a long avenue with porticos on both sides). The top floor of the court housed the silent chamber in which Kösem Sultan stored her treasures. It is now used as a workshop whose owner will willingly open the door to reveal a magnificent ribbed Byzantine dome and Ottoman murals.

A SYNAGOGUE ON THE ROOF   16

The Büyük Çorapçılar Han (caravanserai of the hosiery makers), constructed in the 16th century, has one remarkable feature, which it shares with the Russian lodging houses of Karaköy (see page 191): it has a synagogue on its roof.

The building was built by Piyale Paşa, grand admiral of the Ottoman fleet under Suleiman the Magnificent and Selim II, whose daughter he married. This child of Croat origin, captured after the Battle of Mohács in 1526 and recruited by the palace, ascended rapidly through the military ranks, becoming grand admiral of the fleet in 1553, a position that he would occupy until 1567. In common with many Ottoman statesmen, he built buildings whose income was dedicated to charitable works, as is the case here. Today, the hosiery makers have been replaced by clothes traders of every description and outfits for henna ceremonies.

On the first floor, a metal door marks the entrance to the synagogue. According to certain sources, the synagogue was established by Russian Jews in the 1880s, thanks to generous donations from Camondo. Others maintain that after the Bolshevik Revolution, the Jewish-Russian immigrants in Turkey purchased two shops on the first floor in order to combine them into this synagogue. The interior is not of any particular aesthetic interest.

Avenue Mahmutpaşa Yokuşu, nos. 209-217, at the corner of Fincancılar Yokuşu slope

TOMB OF BABA CAFER

17

Avenue Ragıp Gümüşpala, no. 2
Next to Zindan Han, on Golden Horn side
Eminönü
• Open daily (in theory): 10am-7pm
• Tram: Eminönü

> *Two Islamic saints in the crypt of a Byzantine-Ottoman prison*

Behind the stone tower next to the Zindan Han, a glass door leads to a whitewashed vaulted crypt. Bathed in an almost mystical semi-darkness, the former Ottoman prison of Cafer Baba contains two forgotten saints who are at the centre of a remarkable history: an Abbasid ambassador sent to Byzantium, who gave his name to the place, and Ali Baba, his Byzantine jailer who converted to Islam. Although the pretty grating around the tombs and well winch (all painted dark green, in line with popular beliefs) date from the late Ottoman period, the vault itself dates from the Middle Ages.

In the 9th century A.D., the Abbasid Caliph Harun al-Rashid (786-809) sent two ambassadors to the Byzantine Emperor Nicephorus I (802-811), one of whom, named Cafer, was descended from Hussein, the son of Ali, son-in-law and cousin of the Prophet. During their mission, an intense dispute erupted between the Byzantines and the members of the Muslim colony in Constantinople, who were wiped out. The bodies of the Muslims were denied proper burial and began to decompose in the streets. Cafer appeared before the emperor, whom he severely reprimanded, and was consequently thrown into the dungeon of a tower near the Golden Horn. The other ambassador, Sheikh Maksud, succeeded in convincing the emperor to give the dead a proper

burial, but was unable to save Cafer, who died of poisoning and was buried in his dungeon. During his detention, Cafer is said to have worked miracles, convincing his jailer to convert to Islam. The latter assumed the name Ali, was martyred and buried next to Cafer.

During the taking of Constantinople, Abdürrauf Samedani, who figured among the troops entering the city at this site, discovered Cafer's tomb, declared himself to be his descendent and became his guard.

The Byzantine prison continued to fulfil the same function and its gate was known as Bab-ı Cafer ("The Gate of Cafer"), before later becoming Baba Cafer ("Father Cafer"), with its neighbour assuming the name Ali Baba. Because healing properties were attributed to the earth from these tombs, a ritual developed around them in which pregnant women would come to drink water from the well inside the cell. The presence of another Cafer Baba and other saints associated with prisons, dungeons and cells in the Kütahya Prison suggested the existence of a widespread cult dedicated to prisoner-saints.

The running of Cafer Baba's prison was eventually handed over to the Janissaries, who soon began to abuse their role. The provisioning of the prison was left to the charity of Istanbul residents, who regularly left food, clothing and alms; this practice resulted in the Janissaries extorting commissions for delivering the offerings to the inmates. Bribes were also common currency for softening prison conditions. In 1622, the Janissaries released all the prisoners to celebrate the coming of the new sultan. After the Janissary corps was abolished in 1826, Baba Cafer Prison was used solely for imprisoning prostitutes, and then transformed into a guardhouse. A European-style building was added in the 19th century, but the original tower of the prison, next to the tomb of Cafer Baba, is still intact.

Now restored, Cafer Baba's prison has become a residential building called Zindan Han, which houses a luxury jewellery shop, tourist souvenir shops and a restaurant.

RAILWAY MUSEUM ⓲

Inside Sirkeci Station, on the left after the entrance
• Visiting free 9am — 5pm, except Sun and Mon
• Tram and metro: Sirkeci

In search of lost time

Inside the monumental Sirkeci Station, arrival point of the mythical Orient Express, the little Railway Museum displays a collection of objects that will delight those nostalgic for the railway age. Here you will find many treasures, including: the locomotive of a suburban train whose steering can be manipulated by visitors, model railway installations, one of the Austrian stoves used to heat the waiting room, uniforms, hats, watches, flags and signalling devices, a telegraphic apparatus used by employees, and silverware and cutlery used in the restaurant cars.

Next door, the Orient Express Restaurant is not only a good place to eat, but its walls are covered with old images of the railways. The restaurant is open from 11.30am — midnight and the bistro from 7.30am — 11pm.

"YOU CAN RUN IT ACROSS MY BACK, IF NECESSARY"

Beginning in 1850, railway construction in the Ottoman Empire was also designed as an embodiment of the modernisation programme being implemented at the time. The Sirkeci Station was built to welcome and amaze European visitors with its splendour. With its Seljuk-style portal, its Ottoman-inspired stained glass windows, its granite from different European quarries, ashlar stone from Marseille and waiting room stoves made in Austria, the German architect A. Jasmund (who finished the building in 1890) succeeded in giving the station the appearance of a palace built in an eclectic eastern style.

This magnificent station was built on the site of the first, temporary, station. A line had already reached Sirkeci during the reign of Abdülaziz (1861-1876), a sultan who held a genuine passion for railways. One story claims that when the engineers asked his permission to lay the tracks to Sirkeci through the gardens of the Topkapı Palace, he replied, "You can run it across my back, if necessary". The line was thus laid through the gardens, even though old Byzantine and Ottoman pavilions were sacrificed in the process.

cf. Van Millingen 'Walls'

JANISSARY GRAFFITI ⑲

Yeni Cami Mosque
Eminönü Square
• Tram: Eminönü • Metro: Sirkeci
• Visiting: between morning and evening prayers. Prove professional interest or try to "negotiate" entry with the attendant

The mafia-style threats of the Janissaries

In the stairway leading to the circular balcony inside the dome of the Yeni Cami Mosque (passing under the three tiny domes in the eastern corner), next to the door leading to the dome, we find strange graffiti, carved with daggers in the 17th and 18th centuries by Janissaries of the 56th company. In particular, it is possible to make out carafes and ships.

These were very clear messages to those who knew (and had to know) how to interpret them. Symbol of the 56th company (which supplied arquebusiers for the navy fleet), the galley also, according to experts, indicated that this area was under their control and that everyone must submit to their authority. The carafes (which are actually cruets) signify that the sale of oil for the lamps in this mosque fall under their monopoly and that anyone who attempts to compete with them will be forcibly dissuaded from doing so.

After their years of military glory, the Janissaries had, in fact, become a sort of mafia, engaging in many different types of commerce, with areas of influence divided among the different companies (see page 56). The commander of the 56th company, who was also responsible for overseeing the customs house near the Ahi Çelebi Mosque, had taken up residence close to the Yeni Cami Mosque (1597-1665), from which he extorted money from the entire neighbourhood, including the brothels on the "street where angels fear to tread" (see opposite).

"THE STREET WHERE ANGELS FEAR TO TREAD"

At the beginning of the 19th century, Melekgirmez Street (behind the Istanbul Chamber of Commerce, İstanbul Ticaret Odası) became the main venue for the debauchery of the Janissaries, who entered and used it to hold the women that they had abducted. Its hideous reputation earned it the name "Melekgirmez sokak" (the street where angels fear to tread), the sins committed there being sufficiently heinous to repel the celestial beings.

This street also contained numerous "bekâr odaları" (rooms for single men), city dwellings owned by the Janissaries, outside their barracks. The houses in the street were, in fact, dominated by the 56th company.

Long before the bloody suppression of the Janissary corps in 1826, Sultan Mahmud II used an outbreak of the plague as an excuse to destroy the houses in the area in order to build, in 1813, the Hidayet Mosque (the "mosque of the way of salvation"), an apt description of its purpose. It is said that a number of female skeletons were discovered during excavation work while building the mosque.

The original wooden mosque was replaced in 1887, under Abdulhamid II, by the current ashlar building. It is located at the intersection of Avenues Yalı Köşkü Caddesi and Şeyhülislam Hayri Efendi Caddesi. The architect was the famous Vallaury, who adopted a strange half-Moorish, half-Egyptian style.

THE JANISSARIES

Bodyguards of the Ottoman sultans, the Janissaries (Yeniçeri in Turkish, or "new soldier") developed into a formidable elite infantry who spread terror among the ranks of enemy forces. In the words of the famous Austrian historian Hammer, their invention was, "a thousand times more devastating than that of powder".

In about 1360, Murad I, the third Ottoman ruler, promulgated the penchik law (literally, "the law of the fifth"), which stipulated that one in every five prisoners of war should become a slave and be made to serve in the army. After being captured, these prisoners would spend several years with Muslim families in Anatolia in order to become familiar with Turkish and Islamic culture, before being transferred to the barracks for Adjemis (literally, the "novices" or "unskilful") in Gallipoli (in the Dardanelles strait, to the south of Istanbul), where they would receive military training to become Janissaries.

Among other things, the Janissaries excelled in the use of the arquebus, which played a decisive role in pitched battles, especially at Mohács in 1526, where they defended the Ottoman artillery that destroyed the Hungarian army. They thus acquired a military prestige that they proudly upheld for several centuries.

Although the Janissaries initially did not have the right to marry (a prohibition that went against Islam's promotion of marriage), older, retired Janissaries eventually received this right under Selim I at the beginning of the 16th century. Soon after, the Janissaries began to fill the Adjemi barracks with their male offspring. From this time, the Janissary Corps began to deteriorate into a sort of mafia that anybody could join on payment of a bribe (the corps had as many as 45,000 members who were of little military use).

The Janissaries were also behind the creation of numerous cafes throughout the city, which gave them a considerable degree of control over social and economic life. The Janissaries no longer spread terror among the enemy but among the inhabitants of Istanbul, including the sultan. Over the course of numerous revolts, the Janissaries dethroned sultans and even assassinated Osman II.

It was well over a century before any sultan dared to take on this group that was poisoning Ottoman political, social and military life. In 1826, bolstered by the support of the people and uluma (Islamic scholars), Sultan Mahmud II used the artillery that he had personally accumulated according to European models to crush the Janissaries in their barracks. This operation was known in Ottoman histories as Vaka-I Hayrirye ("the Auspicious Incident"), and any survivors were doggedly pursued and eliminated. Any reminder of their existence was banned, the use of Janissary titles and their own expressions forbidden, their barracks were razed and the hammams that they frequented (symbols of their dubious morals) were dismantled. The sultan even exploited a story about people returning from the dead at Tirnovo, in modern-day Bulgaria, in order to accuse the Janissaries of vampirism (see p. 202).

The Janissary Corps consisted of companies (orta), each with their own symbol. A Janissary's body was tattooed with the symbol of his orta, which also marked documents, seals, standards, weapons, powder magazines, tents, utensils, crockery, lanterns, and, after the corps had become "professionalised", the cafes and other establishments controlled by them. Following the suppression of the corps, Mahmud II had the symbols engraved on buildings and tombs (which also bore the distinctive Janissary hat, the börk) removed, although some of them have survived.

Legend has it that the Janissary corps was created by the holy founder of Bektashism, Haji Bektash Veli (1209 – 1271), despite the fact that he lived a century before the Janissaries came into being. This highly tolerant Islamic religious order, which retains strong traces of shamanism, found fertile ground among the Janissaries, as was the case with many groups that were forced to convert to Islam and found it difficult to adhere to the rigours of Sunni doctrine. The suppression of the Janissary corps heralded the end of the Bektashi: Mahmud II executed the Bektashi leaders, who had acted as spiritual guides in the barracks, and closed their monasteries.

THE HOLY WATER OF ST. THERAPON

Avenue Alemdar caddesi, no. 32
Located directly opposite the Gülhane tram stop, the little *agiasma* of
St. Therapon is sunk into the very ramparts of the Topkapı Palace.
• Tram: Gülhane

> *An agiasma*
> *on the ramparts*
> *of the Topkapı*
> *Palace*

With its well and fountain of intricately carved marble, crowned with a marble icon of St. Therapon, the *agiasma* (holy water fountain, see p. 241) reminds visitors that they must not only wash their faces but must also be cleansed of sin, as in the famous palindrome (which may be read in Greek both from front to back and back to front "Wash the sins, not only the face"). The fountain itself dates from the republican era (1931) and comes from a donation made by the Greek community during the patriarchy of Photios II. In keeping with the miracles performed by St. Therapon and the saint's own name, this *agiasma* is said to have therapeutic qualities. Although the current building dates from the mid-19th century, the legend of St. Therapon goes back much further. Saint Therapon was a bishop who is said to have performed healing miracles in Cyprus in the 6th century. His remains were preserved in a monastery, which has since disappeared, located in the garden of the Topkapı Palace, close to the present-day *agiasma*. Under the reign of Sultan Abdülmecid, a spring gushed out of the palace walls and the Greeks in the city rushed to view the miracle worked by St. Therapon, while others attributed the flowing water to renovation work carried out on the nearby Yerebatan cistern, which was said to have caused a water leak in the vicinity of Gülhane.

The sultan-caliph eventually acquiesced to the requests made by the Greek community and authorised the creation of a new *agiasma* on the ramparts of his palace.

THE MUSEUM OF THE CAĞALOĞLU GERMAN-SPEAKING SCHOOL

㉑

Türkocağı cad., no.4
Cağaloğlu
• Reservations: (0212) 514 1570
• Visiting hours: weekdays 9am- 5pm
• Tram: Gülhane or Sultanahmet

A museum in a strongroom

Formerly the head office of the Ottoman Public Debt (see opposite), the German-speaking Boys' School (İstanbul Erkek Lisesi, which has, in fact, admitted girls for several decades), has occupied this building since 1933. On appointment, it is possible to gain entry to the school in order to visit its small museum, housed in the former strongroom (manufactured by Panzer S.A., in Berlin). Its exhibits include an old fire pump, objects relating to the scouting movement, in which the school was a pioneer, and items that belonged to students of the school who died during the First World War while participating as volunteers.

ONE HUNDRED YEARS TO PAY BACK THE OTTOMAN IMPERIAL DEBT

The Ottoman Empire took on its first external debt in 1854 in order to meet the cost of the Crimean War. The loans policy was also used to fund public works such as railways, ports and new palaces, in conformity with European standards. Unable to control its finances, the empire was plunged into crisis after the Russo-Turkish War of 1877-78. In 1879, it declared itself unable to pay its debts and, for a period of ten years, transferred to its creditors all income from stamps, alcoholic drinks, and taxes on fishing, salt and tobacco, as well as tithes on silk. A decree issued in 1881 institutionalised this practice. The Ottoman Public Debt thus created a sort of private company managed by a board of directors composed of representatives of English, Dutch, French, German, Austrian and Italian creditors, as well as representatives from the Ottoman Bank and bankers from Galata. The institution was initially established in the Celal Bey Han, before the completion of the current building by the architect Vallaury in 1897.

During preparatory work for the 1923 Treaty of Lausanne, which led to the creation of the Turkish Republic, the distribution of the debt proved to be one of the most controversial issues, with the powers present seeking to make the new Turkish state responsible for all the debts incurred under the empire. Ultimately, the debts were fairly distributed between Turkey and the countries separated from the Ottoman Empire following the Balkan Wars of 1912-13 and the Great War. The Turkish Republic finished paying its share in 1954, precisely one century after the first loan made by the Ottoman Empire.

THE WALL OF SEPTIMIUS SEVERUS 22

Avenue Babıali Cad., no. 13
Cağaloğlu
• Tram: Sultanahmet

The remains of the wall built by a Roman emperor, before Constantinople

Walking by Cağaloğlu Anadolu Lisesi College, along Avenue Babıali, it is impossible to miss the long stone wall that stretches for about a hundred meters. Few people know, however, that this wall is a rare and authentic relic of the pre-Constantinople period.

In 196 A.D., Emperor Septimius Severus (193-211) captured the city of Byzantion, a small city of 20,000 inhabitants, which had supported Pescennius Niger, the Legate of Syria who had refused to hail him as emperor. In order to punish Byzantion, which had fiercely resisted him in

a three-year-long siege, Septimius Severus dismantled the city, razed its walls and changed its name to Augusta Antonina.

Byzantion had already acquired its first wall in 657 B.C., which essentially protected the city's acropolis, sited approximately on the hill on which the Topkapı Palace was built (it is also likely that the western wall of the Topkapı follows the line of the first wall of Byzantion).

Although Septimius Severus destroyed the city, he did recognise its strategic importance and shortly thereafter ordered the building of new walls that would significantly increase its area. Beginning on a level with the Yeni Cami Mosque, the new wall then tracked south.

Its only remaining portion is thus said to be this section that is still visible today, even though some historians disagree with the identification, alleging that this wall was, in fact, part of a large cistern, or that it constituted an addition to the old walls of Byzantion. According to this last hypothesis, the wall built by Septimius Severus merely retraced the line of the earlier wall of Byzantion, which the emperor had destroyed.

The third wall was constructed by Constantine the Great (324-337) and the fourth, and final, wall by Theodosius II (408 – 450).

THE FRAGMENTS OF THE BLACK STONE OF THE KAABA OF MECCA ㉓

Sokollu Mosque
Şehit Mehmet Paşa Yokuşu, nos. 20-24
Kadırga area
Also accessible from Su Terazisi Sokak Street
• Tram: Sultanahmet

> **Fragments brought back from Mecca in the 16th century**

A short distance from Sultanahmet, the Sokollu Mosque is a little masterpiece by the architect Sinan that possesses a feature that is almost entirely unique in the Islamic world. Under the entrance door, on the mihrab (recess at the back indicating the direction of Mecca), on the minber (pulpit) and under the dome of the minber, are four pieces of the Black Stone (Hajar al Aswad, Hacer-i Esved in Turkish) of Mecca.

The Black Stone of Mecca is an ovoid sacred stone measuring 30 centimetres in diameter which is situated one and a half meters above the ground in the south-east corner of the Kaaba (the large cube located in the centre of the mosque in Mecca). According to tradition, the Black Stone of Mecca was placed there by Abraham. Legend has it that this antediluvian stone was originally white, but became black following the flood at the time of Noah, as the waters had been polluted by the sins of mankind.

In 605, the Kaaba was damaged in a fire and the Black Stone broken up by the heat. After it had been cleaned up, there were disputes among the chiefs of the tribes of Mecca over the question of who would be given the honour of putting the Black Stone back in its place. The conflict threatened to degenerate into warfare, and so it was eventually decided that the task would be carried out by the young Muhammed, who had not yet become the Prophet but who had already gained the confidence of the inhabitants: Muhammed placed the Black Stone on a large piece of cloth, which the notables of Mecca all gripped at once, returning it to its place. After the arrival of Islam, the Black Stone was preserved in homage to the Prophet Abraham and in memory of the amicable solution found by the Prophet Muhammed, who also kissed it as a sign of submission to the Divine Will. This gesture was subsequently adopted by all Muslims as part of the pilgrimage ritual.

Following the conquest of the Holy Lands of Islam in 1517, the Ottomans found the Kaaba in a state of neglect and requiring renovation. In the late 16th century, the walls were progressively reinforced and the structure repaired. At the same time, the fragments that had become detached were removed to Istanbul and finally inserted into the various locations in the Sokollu Mosque.

Today, the Turkish pilgrims to Mecca who have not succeeded in touching the Black Stone, due to the huge crowds surrounding it, are thus able to complete their rituals and touch a fragment of the stone by visiting the Sokollu Mehmet Paşa Mosque.

Another fragment of the Black Stone can be found inlaid on the exterior of the mausoleum of Suleiman the Magnificent, in the cemetery of the Süleymaniye Mosque.

THE BYZANTINE MILION

㉔

Sultanahmet Square,
On the corner by the Yerabatan Cistern
• Tram: Sultanahmet

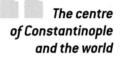

The centre of Constantinople and the world

Located in the northern corner of Sultanahmet Square, on Avenue Divanyolu opposite the entrance to Hagia Sophia, what appears from far away to be a simple upright stone is, in fact, the last remaining fragment of the Great Golden Milion (see below), from which distances were measured during the Byzantine period.

Although it was still intact at the time the city was captured by the Ottomans, the Milion disappeared at an unknown date and was rediscovered during the course of excavations carried out in 1957. Erected shortly after Constantine the Great founded Constantinople in 324, this structure, which was inspired by the Milliarium Aureum in Rome, consisted of four pilasters surmounted by a dome. According to certain historians, the Byzantine Milion was also originally a pagan temple dedicated to Tyche, the goddess of fortune, divine protector of the city. The persistence of polytheism was not in the least surprising, as a climate of religious pluralism reigned in the new capital of the empire, which possessed as many temples as churches. Indeed, Constantine himself was not baptised until he was on his deathbed. It was only later that the Milion was covered in Christian symbols and imagery.

Imperial ceremonies were later conducted under the dome of the Milion, which marked not only the centre of the city, from which distances were measured in Byzantine miles (a Byzantine mile = 1480 m), but also the world, since the whole of the inhabited world (oikoumene) belonged, in theory, to the empire, and its capital was known as the empress of cities, or reigning city (Vassilevoussa).

The Milion also marked the beginning of the great avenue of the Mese (literally, "the middle"), which crossed the city, dividing it in two. The avenue passed through the city walls at the Golden Gate (Porta Aurea) and joined the Via Egnatia, a Roman road built in the 2nd century B.C. which traversed the provinces of Thrace, Macedonia and Illyricum before eventually reaching Dyrrachium (Durrës, in Albania) on the Adriatic.

WHAT IS THE ORIGIN OF THE TERM "MILION"?

The term "Milion" comes from "Milliarium Aureum", a golden column erected by Emperor Augustus at the Roman Forum to act as a departure point for the roads. The stone markers placed along Roman roads were known as *milliaria* as they marked a distance of one thousand paces. The *Milliarium Aureum*, the classic *milliarium*, represented the centre from which distances were measured in miles.

REMAINS OF THE STANDS OF THE ANCIENT HIPPODROME ㉕

Courtyard of the Sultanahmet Mosque, to the right of the main entrance
Sultanahmet Square
• Tram: Sultanahmet

> *The last remnant of the stone benches for Hippodrome spectators*

In the outside courtyard of the Sultanahmet Mosque, few visitors notice the unobtrusive white stone bench situated on the right once you've passed though the entrance. These, however, are the last remains of the stands that once filled the famous Hippodrome used by the Byzantines to watch the extremely popular chariot races.

Begun under Septimius Severus (193-211) following the layout of the Circus Maximus in Rome and finished by Constantine the Great (324-337), the Hippodrome formed the centre of the social and political life of the city. The Hippodrome's Imperial Lodge (Kathisma), located on the current site of the German Fountain, was directly connected to the Great Palace, a vast complex that stretched from the Hippodrome to the sea.

The main racing teams were the Greens and the Blues, perennial rivals, who also formed political factions and acted as police. According to one fanciful story, the Fenerbahçe and Galatasaray football clubs are descended from these teams.

When the imperial residence was moved to the Blachernae Palace in 1264, the chariot races were replaced by chivalric jousts, inspired by the Crusaders who occupied the city from 1204 to 1261.

OTHER HIPPODROME REMAINS

Besides this bench, the obelisks and the Serpentine Column situated in the middle of the *spina* (axis dividing the Hippodrome's two corridors), the *sphendone* is another, less well-known, vestige of the Hippodrome.
This structure was used as a retaining wall for the south-eastern extremity of the Hippodrome.

— REMAINS OF THE PHAROS OF BUCOLEON ㉖

Avenue Kennedy, close to the Çatladıkapı gate, between Cankurtaran and Kumkapı
• Tram: Sultanahmet

> **The remains of an ingenious system of mirrors used to transmit light signals from Cilicia**

Surrounded by Ottoman-era reinforcements, the square tower of the Pharos of Bucoleon formed the end point of an ingenious system of mirrors used to transmit light signals from Cilicia, a southern province of the Byzantine empire, and, in particular, to report Arab incursions. There were eight transmission stations in total, covering a distance of five hundred miles: the castle of Lulum near Tarsus, Mount Argaeus, Isamus, Aegilus, the hill of Mamas, Cyrisus, Mocilus and the hill of Auxentius (present-day Kayışdağı, a suburb on the Asian side of Istanbul), before reaching the Pharos of Bucoleon. This impressive signalling system – genuine wireless telegraphy before its time – had one small defect: it only worked on sunny days.

At night, or on cloudy days, it was therefore necessary to resort to fire signals, which were less visible and less efficient. According to legend, Emperor Michael III (Byzantine ruler 842-867, also known as "The Drunkard"), having been alerted by a message on the eve of important games at the circus, is said to have removed the signals so as not to be disturbed in his pleasures.

The Pharos of Bucoleon, known today as the "Faros", formed part of the eponymous palace, built by Theodosius II (408-450). The name of the palace comes from the word bukolos ("shepherd" in Greek), which suggests that there might have been some kind of pagan shrine dedicated to a pastoral divinity. According to one etymological theory suggested during the Middle Ages, the name Bucoleon comes from bous kai leon ("the bull and the lion").

The port of Bucoleon, located behind the palace, was used by imperial boats, but it isn't the small port you see today. It lies beneath Avenue Kennedy Caddesi, which was built on ground formed when the sea was filled in during the 1950s using debris from the urban construction projects which substantially altered the fabric of Istanbul. The parts of the palace and the Pharos that have survived to the present day probably date from the time of Theophilos (829-849). A Russian pilgrim who visited the city in 1390 and the Florentine traveller Cristoforo Buondelmonti, who passed through Constantinople in 1420, reported that the tower was already a ruin. The original Pharos, circular in design, was surmounted with four columns surrounding the glass walls in the middle of which the lighthouse fire burned. A church located behind the lighthouse and dedicated to the Virgin housed the precious relics, including the garments said to have been worn by Christ on the day of his crucifixion. The church was sacked at the time of the Fourth Crusade in 1204.

THE FOUNTAIN OF THE FOUR SEASONS HOTEL ㉗

Rue Tevkifhane sokak Street, no. 1
Sultanahmet
• Tram: Sultanahmet

> *A fountain designed without a spout, in commemoration of a martyr*

Although the fountain situated in the corner of the main entrance of the luxury Four Seasons Hotel (at the intersection of Tevkifhane and Kutlugün streets) appears to be a classic Ottoman fountain (it dates from 1788), anybody with a keen eye will notice that it does not possess a spout. This has not been stolen, as is the case with other fountains in the city. In fact, the fountain has never had, and was never intended to have, a spout. Indeed, it can be seen that there is no opening in the block of marble to allow water to flow. The inscription found on the fountain provides the explanation for this: the fountain commemorates the thirst of the martyrs of Karbala (a town located in present-day Iraq), a tragedy that goes back to the founding of Islam.

In the year 680 of the Julian calendar and 61 of the Hegira, Hussein, the son of Ali and grandchild of the Prophet Muhammed, was killed along with his close relations at Karbala by an army sent by Yazid, the Umayyad caliph and rival of the house of Ali. This event, which marks the beginnings of Shia Islam, gave rise to the current rituals of Ashura which, in certain regions, includes self-flagellation.

According to legend, Hussein's camp at Karbala was subject to a long siege during which he suffered cruelly due to a shortage of water. Hussein's thirst thus drove him to attempt to break through enemy lines, which led to his martyrdom.

With its missing spout and water, the Four Seasons fountain invites believers to meditate on this suffering.

Although Turkish Islam is Sunni, it maintains very friendly relations with Shiism and commemorates the tragedy of Karbala in prayers and by distributing *Aşure*, a dessert made of boiled wheat and dried fruit, as well as more unusual ingredients such as beans and chickpeas.

NEARBY

REMAINS OF THE GREAT PALACE OF THE HIPPODROME

Upper entrance: Palatium café-restaurant, Kutlügün sokak Street, 31 (opposite the fountain at the Four Seasons Hotel). Lower entrance: Albura Kathisma café-restaurant, Avenue Yeni Akbıyık caddesi, 36-38

Even if Palatium does not initially appear to be any different from the dozens of café-restaurants in Sultanahmet, the two stairways located in its garden provide entry to a labyrinth of corridors and vaulted rooms of impressive size. They are the remains of the Great Palace of the Hippodrome, the residence of the Byzantine emperors until the city was conquered by the Crusaders in 1204 (after Constantinople was recaptured by the Byzantines in 1261, the emperors lived in the Palace of Blachernae, that of Constantine VII Porphyrogenitus).

RUNIC GRAFFITI IN HAGIA SOPHIA   **28**

Hagia Sophia
Sultanahmet area, Ayasofya Meydanı, Fatih
• Open daily: 9am-5pm in winter and 9am-7pm in summer (last entry one hour earlier)
• Tram: Sultanahmet

The little-known history of the Vikings in Byzantium

On the upper level of Hagia Sophia, on the marble balustrade of the upper gallery, there are several examples of runic graffiti which are difficult to decipher. The only legible words are *halvdan* and *are*, which mean "half-Danish" and "eagle," respectively. These inscriptions, written in the language and alphabet of the Vikings, are evidence of a little-known historical institution: the Varangian Guard of the Byzantine emperors. The first Vikings came to Constantinople as traders. The Byzantines called them "Varangians", from the word *vaeringjar*, a term derived from Russian *varyag*, which means "travelling merchant". The Russians and Vikings enjoyed such a peaceful co-existence at that time that the latter were even involved in the creation of the Russian state; a Scandinavian word (*rossmen*, or "rowers") has even been put forward to explain the etymology of the word "Russian". In 830, the Swedish king, Björn, sent an embassy to Emperor Theophilos. In 950, in his *De Administrando Imperio*, Emperor Constantine Porphyrogenitus described the trade route linking Scandinavia and the Black Sea. This route was not used exclusively for commerce, however. Under Romanos Lekapenos, an entire Viking flotilla journeyed across the Black Sea to pillage on the banks of the Bosphorus; the Byzantine fleet used Greek fire to repel the intrepid Northmen.

However, the hostilities eventually turned into collaboration. The Byzantines admired the martial prowess of the Vikings and employed them in the imperial guard from before the year 1000, while Viking troops sometimes fought alongside the Byzantine armies as auxiliary forces. These auxiliaries were stationed intra muros at Saint Mamas (modern Beşiktaş), in the city's inner district and close to the palace of Constantine Porphyrogenitus. The Varangian mercenaries fought under the command of Romanos Diogenes at the dramatic battle of Manzikert (Malazgirt) near Lake Van, in 1071, where the Seljuk army destroyed its Byzantine opponents, thus launching the Turkish conquest of Anatolia. Emperor Alexios III (who reigned 1195-1203) sent embassies to three Scandinavian kings in order to request warriors for his Varangian Guard. The latter bravely defended the Byzantine Emperor during the Fourth Crusade in 1204, which led to the conquest and sacking of Constantinople by the Crusaders. The Varangians, nicknamed "axe-bearing barbarians", remained in imperial service until the beginning of the 13th century, when the golden age of the Vikings came to an end.

The runic inscriptions in Hagia Sophia were almost certainly made by the dagger of a Viking soldier guarding the upper gallery, where men were not admitted, except for certain privileged members of the imperial family. Weary from guarding the empress during a never-ending Byzantine liturgy and certain that he could not be seen from the imperial throne, he probably engraved his name to pass the time, while his comrades-in-arms waited in the marble vestibule, at the exit to the church.

MORE RUNIC INSCRIPTIONS IN VENICE

There are runic inscriptions engraved on a lion now located in Venice, in front of the Arsenal.

Brought back from Athens in 1687 by Doge Francesco Morosini (who is remembered for having been the architect of the explosion at the Parthenon in Athens, which was then used as a powder magazine by the Turks), this lion previously stood guard at the entrance to the Greek port of Piraeus, near Athens. These inscriptions are said to have been engraved in the 11th century on the orders of the future king of Norway, Harald III Sigurdsson (1015-1066). Following the death of his half-brother, Olaf II, Harald left to go into exile in Constantinople. He became chief of the Varangian Guard and conquered Athens, where he had apparently gone to quell an uprising. See *Secret Venice* by the same publisher.

THE FOUNTAIN OF THE EXECUTIONER ㉙

First court of the Topkapı Palace, between Bab-ı Hümayun (the Imperial Gate) and Bab-üs selam (the Gate of Salvation, or Peace) to the right, on the wall
• Topkapı Palace open daily 9am-5pm except Tuesday

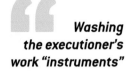

Washing the executioner's work "instruments"

Recruited from its Balkan territories, the Ottoman Empire's executioners reported to the Bostandji-Bachi (Bostancıbaşı in Turkish), literally the "head gardener".

The gardeners were, in fact, responsible for tending the parks as well as maintaining public order and therefore spent their time not only pruning bushes and flowers but also cutting off people's heads.

The legendary master of the corps of executioners was Kara Ali (17th century) who strangled a deposed sultan and a Grand Vizier, among others. Loathed by the people, the executioners were buried in a special cemetery in Eyüp (see page 84), with quadrangular grave markers without inscriptions. Unlike other Ottoman fountains, which are covered in beautiful calligraphy,

the executioner's fountain is also devoid of inscriptions.

The Fountain of the Executioner was moved inside the Bab-ı Hümayun in 1889, on the orders of Abdülhamid II, on the occasion of German Emperor Wilhelm II's first visit. The executioners used to wash their work "instruments" at this fountain and the sultan undoubtedly wished to avoid offending his august friend with this macabre sight.

The fountain was eventually returned to its original position in 1930, under the supervision of Halil Bey, director of the Museum of Antiquities.

The little column in front of the fountain is where the decapitated heads were exhibited.

Strangely, the Jaffa Gate in Jerusalem was also demolished to make way for the imperial procession of the very same Wilhelm II. Its fate was nevertheless less happy than that of the Fountain of the Executioners, as it was never rebuilt and still forms a gap in the beautiful Ottoman wall surrounding the Holy City.

CEVRI KALFA: WHEN THE EMPIRE WAS SAVED BY A HANDFUL OF HOT ASHES

In 1807, the reformist sultan Selim III had been deposed and replaced by the young puppet sultan, Mustafa IV, who was easily manipulated by reactionary factions and the Janissaries.

A year later, Alemdar Mustafa Pasha, who remained faithful to the dethroned sultan, assembled the troops from the Danube and descended on Istanbul to remove Mustafa IV and restore Selim III, imprisoned in the Topkapı Palace, to the throne. When Alemndar Mustafa Pasha's soldiers began to force the doors of the palace, Mustafa IV ordered the execution of Selim III and his nephew Mahmud, who had become the crown prince.

A group of eunuchs attacked Selim with scimitars and daggers, against which the great sultan musician attempted unsuccessfully to defend himself with his ney, the reed flute beloved of Sufi music. With his uncle murdered, Prince Mahmud became the final target of the executioners, who discovered him on a staircase leading to the upper level of his apartments, accompanied by several harem employees and his concubines. As the eunuchs were about to reach the 23-year-old prince, Cevri Kalfa, a Circassian concubine from the harem who was entirely devoted to Mahmud, had a clever idea.

After going down to the hammam furnace, she came back with a bowl of hot ashes, which she threw in large quantities over the assailants and ordered the harem employees to escort the crown prince onto the roof. The prince was then taken down into the inner courtyard of the harem using a makeshift ladder, made to wear shoes abandoned by an official within the inner palace and hidden in rolls of carpet. Alemdar Mustafa Pasha, who had arrived in Istanbul with his troops, had him immediately enthroned in a shortened version of the imperial ritual.

Mahmud II, who reigned until 1838, left his mark on Ottoman history as a great statesman and convinced reformist, pursuing the policy inaugurated by his murdered uncle, Selim III, who had raised him as his own son.

It should be noted that this event probably saved the empire from declining more rapidly than it actually did. Mustafa IV, the reigning sultan (who was also executed several months after being deposed), did not have any male children. Mahmud II appointed Cevri Kalfa to the position of chief treasurer of the harem, a position that the devoted woman held until her death.

After her death in 1819, he had the Cevri Kalfa Primary School (Avenue Divanyolu cad. no. 14 - Sultanahmet) built in her memory. In addition, there is a Cevri Kalfa Mosque in Üsküdar, also constructed by Mahmud II in her honour. In 1858, the primary school became an arts school for girls and then a printing school during the republican era. It housed the courts after the fire at the Palace of Justice in 1933, then became a primary school again in 1945. Since 1985 it has been the main office of the Foundation of Turkish Literature, which contains a bookshop and an attractive cake shop where visitors may enjoy traditional desserts in a period setting.

OTTOMAN INSCRIPTIONS ON BYZANTINE SARCOPHAGI

㉚

Topkapı Palace

> **The memory of Byzantine sarcophagi in an Ottoman palace**

Immediately after the main entrance to the Topkapı Palace, on the right in front of the water reservoirs, you'll find a column in the portico decorated with two superimposed inscriptions. These inscriptions recall the discovery of Byzantine sarcophagi under the roots of the plane tree which still stands in front of the portico.

The first inscription, dating from 1847, explains that two Byzantine sarcophagus covers discovered among the plane tree's roots could not be removed for fear of damaging the tree. The second inscription, from 1919, concludes the story: the covers were dug up and transported to the Archaeological Museum, without causing any damage. This inscription was made by İsmail Hakkı Altunbezer, the doyen of the calligraphers of his time, which illustrates the significance then attributed to archaeological finds.

Although it had been eclipsed by the Dolmabahçe and Yıldız Palaces, the Topkapı Palace had not fallen into disuse by 1919 and continued to be used by the Ottoman dynasty during the twilight of the empire.

The discovery of such sarcophagi is not surprising given that the location of the Topkapı Palace corresponds to the acropolis of the ancient city of Byzantion which is rich in Byzantine remains, including the cisterns that are still visible in the palace garden.

OBELISKS COMMEMORATING
THE "CABBAGES" AND THE "BAMYAS"

③

Topkapı Palace gardens
• Open daily 9am-5pm except Tuesday

> *The memory of exceptional sporting feats*

In the gardens of the Topkapı Palace (after coming in through the main entrance, walk to the right towards the military buildings) and at various sites in Istanbul – in particular at Çengelköy and Paşabahçe (see page 263) on the Asiatic side of the Bosphorus – there are strange little columns in the shape of cabbages or *bamyas*, a vegetable also known as "gumbo" or "okra" in English. The memorial in the Topkapı gardens consists of two columns, one of which, erected by Selim III (reigned 1789-1807), represents a cabbage, in honour of a shooter from the Cabbage team who had succeeded in shooting an egg with a rifle at a distance of 434 paces (see opposite), while the other represents the *bamya*. The *bamya* is an unusual vegetable, unfortunately rare in Europe, which constitutes one of the delights of Turkish cooking and is eaten with lamb or chicken. It is usually dried in the sun during summer before being consumed in winter.

THE CABBAGE AND THE *BAMYA*: VEGETABLES USED AS SYMBOLS BY TWO TOPKAPI PALACE SPORTS TEAMS

The cabbage and the *bamya* were adopted as the symbols of two Topkapı Palace sports teams. According to legend, their origins go back to the 15th century when the future sultan, Mehmed I (who was then governor at Amasya, north-east of Ankara), organised sporting competitions between riders from Amasya, which was known for its *bamyas* (and for being Strabo's birthplace), and from nearby Merzifon, a town known for its cabbages. Encouraged by the palace population, the two teams officially became known according to their respective vegetable symbol. The Cabbage-Bamya rivalry first spread to Edirne (Adrianople) and then to Istanbul, where Mehmed the Conqueror began to hold sports games in the gardens of the newly-built Topkapı Palace. From that time, these Ottoman versions of the green and blue sports teams of the Byzantine era became part of the culture and social life of Istanbul. The colours had changed slightly, however, as the "Cabbages" dressed in green while the "Bamyas" opted for red.

Palace intrigues seeped into this sporting rivalry and, for a period of time, the white eunuchs (who were recruited in the Balkans and served as the palace's internal police) supported the Bamya team while the black eunuchs (who were purchased from merchants in sub-Saharan Africa, sometimes castrated by specialists in Egypt's Coptic monasteries, and occupied important positions within the Harem) supported the Cabbages. The rivalry soon turned into hostility, especially since the violent sporting games, in which archery and rifle shooting were very popular, constituted a sort of preparation for war. In one particularly violent game called *tomak*, opponents would strike each other with a type of club or felt flails. A version of polo was also played, in which riders would throw javelins and wooden skittles at each other. The sultans often attended the games, rewarding the winners generously and even intervening to stop games that had degenerated into actual pitched battles. The games were sometimes followed by concerts, dances and performances by acrobats and conjurers.

Selim III and his nephew Mahmud II (reigned 1808-1839) were the most enthusiastic (and the last) spectators of the Cabbage-Bamya games. In fact, Selim was so fond of the Cabbages that he composed a poem in their honour: "The cabbage, which appears in mid-winter / is like Chosroes' club, and gives vitality to man / for it is like fresh rose petals [...]". His sporting choice had thus been made for him. In 1812, Mahmud II organised games at Büyükdere (north of the Bosphorus, towards Sarıyer) which were attended by European diplomats who had come from their nearby summer embassies. The latter offered fruits and sweets to the Cabbage and Bamya players, whose games had been particularly spectacular and spurred on by the unique slogans of their supporters: "Cabbage Power!" and "Delights of the Bamyas!". Mahmud II, who supported the Bamyas and was a great organizer of the vegetable games, was also the one who put an end to them. After abolishing the Janissaries in 1826, he dissolved the *Enderun*, the palace's internal administration on which the Cabbages and Bamyas depended, and, with the aid of Prussian officers, adopted modern methods of military training. The old war games had lost their reason for being.

FATIH
GOLDEN HORN, WEST

TOMBSTONES OF THE EXECUTIONERS ❶

Eyüp Cemetery
Area around the Karyağdı Baba Tekkesi
Karyağdı Street, behind Pierre Loti Cafe
• Bus: Eyüpsultan (then take the cable car or Avenue İdris Köşkü caddesi)

Remarkable features on the tombstones of Ottoman executioners

Although the tombs of the executioners once formed a specific plot within the immense Eyüp cemetery, there are now only a small number remaining around the Karyağdı Tekkesi. These tombs can be distinguished by the fact that they are the only ones without inscriptions. Despised by the general population in the Ottoman period, the executioners were buried with quadrangular grave markers devoid of inscriptions and carved out of the rough limestone usually used to cover buildings. In contrast, ordinary tombstones were hewn out of Marmara marble, intricately decorated and calligraphed. Perhaps surprisingly, this meant that the executioners were entitled to graves of significantly inferior quality to those of the people they executed. They did, however, have the right to a proper religious funeral.

The Karyağdı Tekkesi (literally, "it has snowed") owes its name to the fact that the slope on which it is situated formed the northernmost point of the ancient city and would receive the first snow of the year.

Other tombstones belonging to executioners may be found in the courtyards of the Zal Mahmut Paşa Mosque (between Avenues Zalpaşa Caddesi and Feshane Caddesi, Nişancı area, Eyüp) and Cezeri Kasım Paşa (junction of Avenue Zalpaşa and Cezeri Kasım Akarçeşme Street, Çömlekçiler area, Eyüp).

Inside the Topkapı Palace, there is also a Fountain of the Executioner (see page 77).

THE MINARET OF THE DEFTERDAR MOSQUE ❷

Avenue Defterdar, Eyüp
Nişancı
• Bus: Feshane

A minaret crowned with an inkwell and pen

lthough the minaret of a mosque is usually crowned with an alem, a crescent-shaped metal ornament, the Defterdar Mosque's alem is composed of six concentric crescents topped by a spherical inkwell and pen, made using a specially selected and treated reed.

The Defterdar Mosque, which was designed by the architect Sinan, was built in 1541 by Mahmud Çelebi, or "Nazlı" ("The Capricious"), minister of finance (defterdar) under Suleiman the Magnificent. Mahmud Çelebi placed these calligraphic instruments on the minaret to remind onlookers of his renown as calligrapher. Indeed, Çelebi had been raised by Sheikh Hamdullah, the true founder of the Ottoman school of calligraphy, and continued to improve his artistic skill in his spare moments as minister of finance, at a time when the empire had reached the apogee of its economic strength.

His nickname, "The Capricious", is said to be the result of the miserliness that he demonstrated while carrying out his duties.

TOMB OF KÖPEKÇI HASAN BABA ❸

Edirnekapı Cemetery
Opposite house at no. 9, Otakçıbaşı Street
Avenue Fethi Çelebi
Edirnekapı.
• Open sunrise to sunset
• Metrobus: Edirnekapı

The patron saint of dogs

n the "Mısır tarlası" ("cornfield") area of the Edirnekapı Cemetery (in the corner near the composer Itri's mausoleum), there is a grave that is often surrounded by a pack of dogs. Although there is nothing exceptional about the tomb itself, it contains the remains of a very colourful figure.

Köpekçi Hasan Baba, sometimes called Ebu-l Kilab ("father of the dogs" in Arabic), was a tramp from the second half of the 19th century who was constantly surrounded by a pack of dogs that would obey him blindly. He would feed his dogs one by one, and when a dog encroached on another dog's portion, he would isolate it from the group for three days, a punishment that was remarkably accepted by the guilty dog. When visiting other

neighbourhoods, he would gather the local dogs together and lead them on a walk through the city. Although he also fed the cats in the streets, the relationships he established with them were not as close.

Regarded as the doyen of the tramps of Istanbul, Hasan Baba slept in front of one of the doors of the Fatih Mosque, where he prayed five times daily.

He also had a reputation for holiness. One day, according to the legend, he stopped a passer-by to ask for alms. While the latter was looking in his pocket for something to give him, a section of a wall collapsed which undoubtedly would have killed the passer-by if Hasan Baba hadn't stopped him. When consulted, Hasan Baba was also able to predict the future by reciting poetry. For instance, prior to the outbreak of hostilities between the Ottoman Empire and Greece in 1897, he predicted the precise day on which the war would begin and its outcome. He was respected by the higher Muslim clerics who allowed him to preach in the mosques.

One day, he is even said to have indirectly influenced the sultan. When the Christians complained to him of the difficulties they were experiencing in obtaining authorisation for the construction of a new church, Hasan Baba quickly wrote down the following words which were addressed to the sovereign: "My sultan! If you do not allow the church to be built, you will offend both Jesus and Moses". Taking account of Hasan Baba's reputation, the sultan granted permission for the building of what is now believed to be the Bulgarian Church of St. Stephen, an entirely plausible story given that this church was erected during Hasan Baba's lifetime, during the reign of Sultan Abdülhamid.

ICONOSTASIS OF THE APOCRYPHAL MIRACLE ❹
OF THE VIRGIN

Agios Dimitrios Xyloportas
12 Kırk Ambar Sokak
Ayvansaray
• Bus: Balat Hastanesi

*Hands
severed
by an angel*

The Dimitrios Xyloportas Church (Aya Dimitri Rum Ortodoks Kilisesi) contains a marvellous iconostasis whose right hand depicts the Dormition of the Virgin in which a rabbi, dressed as an Ottoman dignitary (the church was founded in the 18th century), continues to touch the Virgin's coffin after his hands have been severed by the Archangel Michael's sword. The scene depicts a little-known miracle worked by the Virgin, which is

recounted in a number of texts, including Jacques de Voragine's *Golden Legend*. According to the latter, while the Virgin was sleeping and being transported by the faithful (in Christian tradition, the Virgin did not die prior to her Assumption but only fell asleep), a certain Jephonias approached the body of the Virgin. Seeking to prove that her holiness was by no means certain, he approached the sarcophagus that was being used to transport the Virgin and touched it. His hands were then miraculously cut off and Jephonias fell to the ground. Built on the site of a Byzantine church, Agios Dimitrios "Xyloportas" ("with the wooden doors") also bears the name of a Byzantine aristocrat, Nikolaos Kanavis (Kanavi), who lived through the Latin conquest of the city in 1204. The ancient church was used temporarily as the seat of the Greek Patriarchate, from the conversion of Hagia Sophia into a mosque until the Patriarchate was finally established at its current location in Phanar, at the beginning of the 17th century. The present building was built in 1730 and has been renovated numerous times.

> The Church of San Giacomo dell'Orio in Venice contains a painting depicting the same scene. See *Secret Venice* by the same publisher.

THE DOOR OF THE SURP HREŞDAGABET CHURCH ❺

Kamış sokak Street no. 2
Balat
• Bus: Balat or Köprübaşı

*Inscriptions
in old German*

L ocated in the very heart of the Golden Horn, the Surp Hreşdagabet church is an Armenian church which boasts a magnificent cast iron door with interesting religious bas-reliefs. The door is reputed to have been found during excavations at the Topkapı Palace in 1742 during the reign of Mahmud I and purchased by Babik, chief blacksmith at the palace, who proceeded to place it himself between the nave and the side chapel on the left side of the church.

Although the door was long thought to date from the Roman period due to the "Latin" characters appearing on it, the inscription is, in fact, old German and the door dates from the 18th century. The inscription on the left side, located under the image of Jesus expelling the merchants from the Temple, mentions the relevant verses from the Gospel of John (II:15-17). That on the right praises the victory of St. George in slaying the dragon, with the image it describes above.

The *agiasma* (see p. 241) – a rare feature in an Armenian church – indicates the presence of an old Byzantine sanctuary called Agios Stratios or Taksiarhes ("Archangels" in Greek, thus corresponding with the Armenian name of the church). Reduced to a ruin, the church was given to the Armenians by imperial decree in the 17th century. After suffering damage in numerous fires, the current church dates from 1835 and contains beautiful icons, such as those of Tcharkhapan Surp Asdvadzadzin (Holy Mother of God who prevents evil) and Hyntragadar Surp Asdvadzadzin (Holy Mother who grants all prayers).

The *agiasma* dedicated to Saint Artemios (martyred in 363 by Emperor Julian the Apostate) is reached via the side chapel. Relics are exhibited there, including the bones of St. Peprone, which were discovered here in 2006.

> On the second weekend of September, a strange liturgy used to be celebrated in this church where the faithful from every religion would gather in search of healing, practising a sort of shamanism and sacrificing cocks. The deacons distributed prayer mats to the Muslims who first performed their Islamic ablutions before going down into the *agiasma* to drink the water. Tired of the television companies overusing images of these rituals, the Armenian Patriarchate eventually decided to forbid them.

THE PULPIT OF THE AHRIDA SYNAGOGUE ❻

Between Kürkçü Çeşme Sokak and Gevgili Sokak Streets - Balat
• Tel: 0212 2938794 • www.turkyahudileri.com
• Email: seheratilla@yahoo.com
• Visits by permission of the Chief Rabbinate

O riginally built in the 15th century and burnt down in 1693, the Ahrida Synagogue was reconstructed from 1694 and classified as a historical monument in 1989. It is the largest and undoubtedly one of the oldest synagogues in Istanbul. At its

Noah's Ark or boat that saved the Jews of Spain?

centre is a remarkable *tebah* (a pulpit resembling the altar of the Temple in Jerusalem) shaped as a boat's prow. For some, the ship's prow represents Noah's Ark, while others claim that the prow is simply a reference to the boats of the Ottoman fleet commanded by Kemal Reis, who saved the Jews of Spain and resettled them on Ottoman territory in 1492. The following phrase is attributed to the sultan at the time, Bayezid II: "You venture to call Ferdinand a wise ruler, but by exiling the Jews he has impoverished his own country and enriched mine". Restoration work undertaken in 1992 appears to support an old legend, which says that the synagogue was created by demolishing a wall separating two adjacent synagogues.

Sabbatai Zevi (see p. 224) is alleged to have preached to the Jewish community of Istanbul at Ahrida in order to convince them that he was, in fact, the long-awaited Messiah.

The Spanish Jews, known as "Sephardi", still constitute by far the largest group within the Jewish community of Turkey, which previously included the "Romaniotes", descendants of the Byzantine Jewish community whose origins go back to the Jewish diaspora of the Hellenistic period (between the conquests of Alexander the Great in the 4th century B.C. and the beginning of Roman domination in the 1st century B.C.), and who were eventually absorbed by the Sephardi during the Ottoman era. Although their name describes them as being Jews within the "Roman" Empire, the Byzantines, in fact, called themselves "Romans", the term "Byzantine Empire" being an invention of 16th-century historians. There is also a tiny Ashkenazi community, which is the result of the migration of German Jews fleeing anti-Semitic persecution in 15th-century Bavaria, as well as the emigration of Jews from central and eastern Europe for economic reasons during the 19th century. The Jews of present-day Turkey are still highly attached to Spain and many continue to speak Ladino, a Castilian interspersed with Turkish words, even though its use has declined among young people.

Ahrida owes its name to its founders, who originated from Ohrid in Macedonia and emigrated to Istanbul in the early 15th century. Ahrida is the Greek pronunciation of *Ohrid*; the Jews of Byzantium used a particular Greek dialect (Yevanik) at that time.

THE PIERCED STONE OF THE TAXIARCHIS CHURCH

❼

Taxiarhis Church - Ayan Caddesi 25 - Balat

> *A reminder of the ancient cults of "pierced stones"*

In the garden of the Taxiarchis Church (also called Agios Stratios in Greek or Aya Strati in Turkish), a building houses an *agiasma* (holy spring) dedicated to the Archangel Michael. In the middle of the internal wall, which cuts the building roughly in half, a large stone at ground level is said to have been pierced by the Archangel's spear.

According to tradition, mentally ill individuals who passed through the hole would be healed and children would be spared from childhood diseases. Prayers would also be granted to the faithful. These sorts of pagan rituals were practised in the heart of the Orthodox church from the earliest times.

In antiquity, passing through a hole was often an act of initiation. The hole symbolised the maternal uterus and passing through the hole was taken as a sign of spiritual rebirth.

In ancient texts, the Taxiarchis pierced stone was known as Zurlopetra or Zolohopetra, which is said to have signified "the stone of the madmen" and to have given its name to the nearby district of Zuropetra. Although the church's existence has been documented since the 16th century, the current building dates from 1833. Despite the complete disappearance of Greek churchgoers from the area, the church is perfectly preserved and holds a large collection of ancient icons.

MORE PIERCED STONES IN ANATOLIA

Anatolia boasts many pierced stones. For example, in the village of Solfasol (now lost among the suburbs of Ankara), there's a pierced stone in the basement of a saint's mausoleum; only the innocent are permitted to pass through its hole, while sinners, however thin, remain stuck. At Nallıhan and close to Gaziantep, children suffering from whooping cough are passed through a pierced stone. At Mudurnu and Isparta, anorexic children are passed through a pierced stone for healing. At Erzurum, passing through a stone in a windmill is said to cure squints, coughing and aphonia, while at Alaşehir (the "Philadelphia" of the Apocalypse of St. John), the passing is meant to cure coughing. Near Selçuk, young people pass through a pierced rock in the act of marriage. At Karaman, this ritual is observed by those wanting children. The most famous example of a pierced stone can be found three kilometres from Hacıbektaş, at the site of the mausoleum of Haji Bektash Veli, founder of the Bektashi Sufi order and venerated by the Alevis, who hold a great annual festival centred on his tomb. The Hacıbektaş pierced stone is located at the back of a cave where the saint is said to have withdrawn for contemplation and meditation. Here again, only the innocent are able to pass through, while the sinner who remains stuck must make a pledge to the saint in order to be set free.

There are also pierced stones in southern Italy, with similar rituals. In Apulia, for example, the Sacra Roccia di San Vito in Calimera is also found in the middle of a church. The faithful pass through the hole in the rock once a year, on Easter Monday, in order to purify themselves from their sins, ask for fertility and be healed of sickness.

MASONIC SYMBOL ON THE FENER GREEK ❽ ORTHODOX SCHOOL

Sancaktar Street, no. 36
Fener
• Visiting is sometimes possible if one asks the school caretakers politely

> **A patriarchal school with a Masonic symbol**

The magnificent building that can be admired today at number 36 Sancaktar Street, in Fener, dates from the 1880s. With its scarlet-coloured bricks from Marseille, imposing size and eclectic architecture reminiscent of a fairy tale castle, the Fener Boys' School (Fener Rum Erkek Lisesi, often confused with the Greek Patriarchate) dominates the view of the Golden Horn. Those fortunate to gain entry marvel at its beautiful interiors, its intelligently arranged rooms and high-quality neoclassical ornamentation. The school authorities have traditionally placed photos of all its former teachers on the walls of the spacious main meeting room. Among them is Kenan Rifai, a major figure within the Rifai order at the beginning of the 20th century, who taught French to the students of the patriarchal school, which is indicative of the openness and intellectual level of the institution, and of Sufism at the beginning of that century.

Those fortunate individuals given permission to climb up the lantern tower on the college dome, which was used as an astronomical observatory, will be astonished by the breathtaking view they find there. After visiting the interior of the college, a tour of the exterior is highly recommended. On the rear façade of the building you will find the signature of the architect, Konstantinos Dimadis, who had studied at the Fener school.

Strangely, Konstantinos Dimadis's signature is surrounded by Masonic symbols, which leaves no doubt concerning his allegiance. Although the Fener school is not a seminary for training the clergy, it is nevertheless an ecclesiastical institution, at least in its origins, and the Orthodox Church has never been entirely sympathetic towards Freemasonry.

Moreover, the building was inaugurated at the beginning of the reign of Abdülhamid II, who attempted to dismantle a network of Freemasons. Among its members was his predecessor, Murad V, who was dethroned and incarcerated for mental health problems, but also to keep him from regaining power.

Continuing the traditions of the "Patriarchate Academy" of the Byzantine era, the Greek Great School (Rum Mekteb-i Kebiri) was founded by the Patriarch Gennadius Scholarius, in accordance with privileges granted by the firman ("imperial edict") of Mehmed the Conqueror in 1454, one year after the city had been captured.

A number of dragomans and Greek clergymen of the Ottoman era came from this institution. The Great School also trained the governors of the empire's two Danubian principalities, Wallachia and Modavia, who were usually selected from among the "Pharnariotes", the Greek aristocracy of Phanar (an area neighbouring the Patriarchate in which the merchant class and Greek bureaucrats settled). The curriculum was based on theology but also encompassed ancient and modern philosophy, as well as ancient philology and literature. The school relocated to Kuruçeşme (Xriokrinis) at the beginning of the 19th century and subsequently returned to Fener sometime in the 1850s. From the 1860s, it became a college providing a classical education.

THE BLOCKED DOOR OF THE GREEK ORTHODOX PATRIARCHATE

9

Avenue Sadrazam Ali Paşa Cad., no. 35
From Eminönü or Unkapanı, take bus/taxi towards Eyüp
Not to be confused with the Patriarchal School on the heights of the
Golden Horn, which local shopkeepers may identify as the Patriarchate

A patriarch hanged

Strangely, the entrance to the Greek Orthodox Patriarchate of Constantinople is actually the door to the left of the main entrance. The central door is, in fact, closed and has been blocked by a gate in memory of the 1821 hanging of the Patriarch Gregory V at this very place. He, along with the bishops of Nicomedia, Anchialos and Ephesus), was accused of supporting the Greek uprising, which had broken out in the Peloponnese. Gregory V was eventually canonised as a martyr for Greek independence, while Turkish historiography took an opposing view, representing him as the archetype of the treacherous Greek who betrays "the Empire", his benefactor. The Orthodox Church remained wary of the French Revolution as well as the nationalist ideology it had begun to export throughout the world, and especially in the Balkans. The Greek clergy responded against the "impious ideas" of the revolution with pamplets to which Gregory V probably contributed. In fact, the Patriarchate had no interest in allowing the emergence of nation states in the Balkans, which would have led to their separation from the Mother Church. In addition to his privileges dating from the Byzantine period, the Patriarch enjoyed political authority over the faithful, combining in his person both the religious and political power of the Byzantine Emperors, whose symbols (including the double-headed eagle) and titles he adopted. The Patriarch had become so well integrated within the administrative structures of the Ottoman state that the non-Greek-speaking orthodox communities in the Balkans protested that they were being forcibly Hellenized by the Greek clergy, in collusion with the Sublime Porte. After a century of self-censorship on all sides, the eminent politician Eleftherios Venizelos broke the silence at the Lausanne Conference in 1923, during which the Patriarchate's presence in Istanbul was called into question. According to Venizelos, Gregory V had remained faithful to the Sublime Porte during the Greek uprising and had, in fact, threatened Ottoman nationals who participated in the insurrection with excommunication. However,

as the symbolic head of his community, he was held responsible for the actions of his co-religionists and was executed on the gallows.

An enduring legend states that the blocked door will be reopened when Istanbul becomes Constantinople again and is liberated from Turkish rule.

THE GREEK ORTHODOX PATRIARCHATE OF CONSTANTINOPLE

With its status of primus inter pares in relation to the other Orthodox Patriarchates (Alexandria, Antioch, Jerusalem, Moscow, Belgrade, etc.), the Patriarchate of Constantinople/Istanbul today represents the 2000 Orthodox believers in Istanbul.

As an ecclesiastical institution, the Orthodox Patriarchate of Istanbul is recognised as being "ecumenical" and holds direct administrative authority over the Orthodox churches of several other countries, including the Orthodox communities of Western Europe, North America and South America. It is also recognised as an ecumenical spiritual authority by the other autonomous or autocephalous Orthodox churches.

THE BAS-RELIEF OF THE HAND OF MUHAMMED

⑩

Agiasma of St. Charalambos
Garden of the Greek Orthodox Patriarchate
35, Sadrazam Ali Paşa Cad.

A mong the icons and remains of Byzantine architectural ornaments populating the small *agiasma* dedicated to St. Charalambos in the garden of the Greek Patriarchate, a marble bas-relief depicting a hand, flanked by a sort of mitre, often goes unnoticed. Located next to the library stairway, at the end of the path that runs to the right (along the wall of the Patriarchal Church of St.

*An
Orthodox
monastery
protected
by the Prophet
of Islam*

George), this symbol is highly unusual. Not only is this bas relief of Muhammed, the Prophet of Islam, located in what one might assume to be an exclusively Christian location, it depicts him protecting the ancient Orthodox monastery with his hand. This hand previously adorned the gate of a monastic building attached to the nearby church of St. John Prodrome (134 Mürsel Paşa Caddesi, Balat). The latter had the peculiarity of being a metochion (embassy) of the Monastery of St. Catherine on Mount Sinai in Egypt.

In common with its parent monastery, it is exceptional in that it enjoys the personal protection of Muhammed. Mount Sinai is indeed recognised within Islam and venerated as the site where Moses received the revelation of the Ten Commandments: the Koran refers to this in Sura 52 At-Tur ("The Mount"). From its early days, Islam has accordingly maintained friendly relations with the monastic community of St. Catherine. In 623, for instance, a document signed by the Prophet himself is said to have exempted the monks of St. Catherine from tax and urged all Muslims to come to their aid, when necessary. Out of gratitude, the monks gave permission for a chapel to be transformed into a mosque during the Fatimid era, in order to make life easier for the Muslim travellers who enjoyed the monks' hospitality during their dangerous crossing of the Sinai Peninsula.

The origins of the Church of St. John Prodrome can be traced back to the 14th century, at which time it was called "St. John of the Hunters". Following its restoration in the 17th century by virtue of an Ottoman imperial edict, the church was attached to the Patriarchate of Alexandria, and then, on request by the Russian ambassador, transferred to the (Orthodox) Monastery of St. Catherine on Mount Sinai, for political reasons. It was considered appropriate to remind passers-by of the protection accorded by the Prophet, which extended to the dependencies of the Sinai monastery, by installing a bas-relief of a hand. When the bas-relief recently fell from its position, the decision was taken to preserve it in this small *agiasma* belonging to the Patriarchate.

THE MANTLE OF THE PROPHET IN THE HIRKA-I ŞERIF MOSQUE

⑪

Muhtesip İskender Mahallesi
Akseki Caddesi
Fatih
• Open between morning and evening prayers
• Relic on display during Ramadan
• Metro: Emniyet/Fatih

A holy relic ironed with a clothes iron

The Hırka-I Şerif Mosque was built by Sultan Abdülmecid in 1851 specifically for the purpose of housing and protecting one of Islam's holiest relics – the Mantle of the Prophet.

Nevertheless, it has recently been the victim of over-zealous devotion: it has been ironed with a clothes iron.

The Prophet's cloak was given to Uways Al Qar(a)ni ("Veysel Karani" in Turkish), a man who converted to Islam during the Prophet's lifetime but whom he never met personally. In Islamic tradition, however, he is venerated as a "*sahabi*", a term applied to the Prophet's immediate companions, due to his burning desire to see Muhammed and the spiritual bond established between himself and the Prophet. More than just a straightforward gift, this cloak, given to Qarani by Ali, the fourth caliph and son-in-law of the Prophet, symbolises the transmission of spiritual knowledge, the true gnosis. Al Quarani's descendants, the Uwaysi family, preserved the cloak and brought it to Istanbul in the early 17th century under an imperial decree issued by Ahmed I. The Uwaysi family continues to hold the privilege of guarding this relic, which is extremely precious both because it is one of the Prophet's personal effects and because it embodies the continued communication of his esoteric tradition. In Islamic tradition, putting on someone else's clothes signifies that one identifies with them. Thus, even today, sheikhs wear robes that have been worn by generations of religious leaders.

The buildings designated for conserving the Holy Mantle include a mosque, a place of residence for the oldest representative of the Uwaysi family, and a small barracks for the company of guards charged with protecting the relic, which has been turned into a primary school. The highly eclectic architecture of this ensemble, in which Doric columns mingle with the Baroque and the neo-Gothic, also features wonderful calligraphy created with a reed pen by Kazasker Mustafa Izzet Efendi.

Ever since it was moved to Istanbul, the mantle has been greatly venerated by the city's residents. Previously displayed during the last two weeks of Ramadan, due to the large crowds of visitors it may now be viewed by the faithful throughout the whole of Ramadan.

The cloak, which is 120 centimetres long, is beige in colour and composed of eight pieces of fabric woven from the hairs that grow under the throats of young camels.

In 2009, viewings of the mantle were suspended for quite mysterious reasons. It is said (although denied by the religious authorities of the city), that the relic's last curator hired an employee in 2002 who was a little too zealous and devout. The latter is said to have ironed the mantle several times. After a while, the conservator became concerned by its rapid and unusual deterioration and, horrified, entrusted the relic to an expert in the restoration of ancient fabrics.

Another cloak belonging to the Prophet, woven from goat hair, is preserved in the Chamber of the Sacred Relics in the Topkapi Palace, and has given the chamber its more familiar name of "Pavilion of the Holy Mantle" ("Hırka-i Saadet Dairesi"). The poet Kâ'b Bin Zuheyr received this cloak from the Prophet and it was later removed to Istanbul by Selim I after the conquest of Egypt under the Mamelukes, who had taken possession of the holy relics of Islam.

THE SULTAN'S CISTERN

Avenue Yavuz Selim, Ali Naki Street, no. 4
Fatih
• Tel: 0212 521 07 20
• www.sultansarnici.com
• Bus: Çarşamba

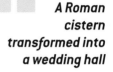

Located in the heart of the conservative Islamic area of Fatih, "the sultan's cistern" (Sultan Sarnıcı) was, in fact, constructed during the reign of the Roman Emperor Theodosius (378-395). Although it is significantly smaller in size than the Yerebatan cistern at Sultanahmet, its volume

A Roman cistern transformed into a wedding hall

still remains impressive with its 28 columns (21 of which are marble and 7 granite) on which many Christian crosses can be seen. The construction

techniques and ornamentation used here mark the period of transition towards a Byzantine style. The cistern, which was one of the largest covered water reservoirs in the city, was emptied during the Ottoman period (as was the case for several other cisterns) so that it could be used as a workshop for spinning textiles, due to the high level of humidity required for spinning. Since its restoration in 2007, the cistern has been hired out for dinners and marriage celebrations to those looking for a delightfully mysterious atmosphere.

OTHER MONUMENTAL CISTERNS IN ISTANBUL

Cisterns dating from the Romano-Byzantine period are so numerous in Istanbul that it is not rare for one to be discovered during new constructions or renovation works on the Historic Peninsula. Here are three of the most important:

The most famous is Yerebatan Sarnıcı with its 336 columns (Avenue Yerebatan, no. 1/3 Sultanahmet), which dates from the time of Justinian (527-565). Also in Sultanahmet, the Binbirdirek cistern (also known as Philoxenos) rests on 224 columns (Avenue İmran Öktem cad. No. 4). Constructed by Theodosius II (408-450), the cistern of Şerefiye, at Çemberlitaş (Avenue Pierre Loti) has 32 columns.

THE ROSE MOSQUE

Gül Camii
Gül Camii sokak Street, nos. 2-6
Küçükmustafapaşa area
On the Golden Horn, behind the Greek Church of Saint Nicholas, to the
west of the Unkapanı Bridge, following the Golden Horn upstream
• Bus: Kadir Has/Unkapanı

Tomb
of an apostle

In the pilaster situated between the apse and the right nave of the Rose Mosque, a narrow staircase leads to a tiny cell housing a typically Islamic tomb. The entrance is crowned with an Ottoman inscription which reads, "the tomb of an Apostle, a companion of Jesus".

Since both Byzantine and Ottoman sources are silent regarding the name

of this apostle, the inscription might refer to a little-known Byzantine saint buried in the church, whom the Ottomans then adopted as one of the apostles, as the latter are acknowledged within Islamic tradition and are therefore more compatible with an Islamic sanctuary.

> The Rose Mosque also attracts attention because of the profusion of Seals of Solomon, which decorate nearly all the walls and arches (see p. 32 on the symbolism of this device).

> The little gate in the Byzantine walls, right next to the Rose Mosque, is still known as "Aya Kapı", or "Gate of the Saint", in a mixture of Turkish (kapı: gate) and Greek (agia/ayia: holy), most likely in memory of the church dedicated to St. Theodosia.

WHY IS IT CALLED THE "ROSE MOSQUE"?

Orginally built as a church dedicated to St. Euphemia, the current Rose Mosque was renovated by Basil I (867-886) and dedicated to St. Theodosia, a saint martyred in about 729 by the Iconoclasts for opposing the removal of the icon of Christ hanging from the Chalke Gate of the Great Palace of the Hippodrome. The saint's relics were placed in this church, which became a sort of funerary chapel for the family of Basil I.

The feast day of St. Theodosia is celebrated on 29 May. According to legend, when the Ottoman army conquered the city on 29 May 1453, the soldiers who entered the church found it covered in roses. The feast of St. Theodosia had been celebrated the previous evening, because, according to the Byzantine calendar, the new day begins at dusk. As the roses that had been used to decorate the building were still fresh, the converted church was called The Rose Mosque.

The story is disputed: the inhabitants of the besieged city undoubtedly had more important things to do than search for fresh roses to decorate the church on the eve of the fall of the Byzantine Empire. The Church of St. Theodosia long served as an arsenal for the fleet after the conquest and was only converted into a mosque towards the end of the 15th century. Would the mosque really have been named in memory of an event that had occurred dozens of years earlier?

The mosque assumed its final form under Selim II (1566-1574). It was probably his chief architect, the great Sinan, who renovated the building, which had been damaged in the earthquake of 1509. The current dome rests directly on the pendentives and arches, whereas the original structure probably had a tholobate under the dome and pierced by windows, a typical feature of Byzantine architecture.

REZAN HAS MUSEUM ⓮

Kadir Has University
Avenue Kadir Has Caddesi, Cibali
• Tel: 0 212 533 65 32 or 0 212 534 10 34
• Open daily: 9am-6pm (except national and religious holidays, and New Year's Day)
• Bus: Unkapanı-Kadir Has

> *A museum in a former hammam which became a tobacco factory and then a university*

Located inside the private Kadir Has University, the Rezan Has Museum, named after the wife of the industrialist who founded the university (see opposite), was created when the former tobacco factory that now houses the university was restored in 2002.

The remains of the Ottoman hammam and Byzantine cistern under the building have accordingly been transformed into a museum with an archaeological collection of artefacts dating from as far back as 7000 B.C., as well as archives and objects from the tobacco factory.

The hammam's central stonework, as well as the steam pipes which probably date from the 17th century, are well preserved. The cistern, known as "Seferikoz", in reference to the adjacent neighbourhood, is from the 11th

century and has 48 arches, 15 pillars and 20 columns. It was used as a warehouse for the tobacco factory and a supply store during the Second World War.

A corner of the museum is also devoted to mementos and personal objects belonging to Kadir Has. He is represented by a wax statue dressed in his original clothes and seated at his actual work desk. The statue is very effective: from a distance in the subterranean half-light, Has appears to be absorbed in his work.

The museum exhibition hall also hosts temporary exhibitions devoted to specific archaeological periods, as well as art exhibitions, especially of Turkish painting.

The prestigious private Kadir Has University occupies the restored premises of a factory that belonged to the Régie Company, a business created in 1884 that held a monopoly over tobacco and which began to produce cigarettes in 1900. At that time, the factory constituted a sort of city within the city, with its own police, hospitals, grocers, schools, firemen, restaurants and unions. The collaboration between men and women, who were, moreover, of diverse origin, was a noteworthy first in Istanbul.

The factory, nationalised in 1925, soon became a centre for left-wing movements that organised strikes and helped to increase awareness among the working classes. As a consequence, in the 1960s the Cibali district became one of the bastions of the Workers' Party of Turkey (Türkiye İşçi Partisi, TIP), one of whose objectives was the adoption of the principle of free public education. As a result, it fought against the creation of private universities.

It is ironic then, that after many decades, a private university should take possession of this former TIP stronghold. Disused, the tobacco factory was sold in 1997 to the Kadir Has Foundation (1921-2007), a manufacturer that had formerly been the main distributor for Michelin tyres in Turkey. After four years of restoration work supervised by Mehmet Alper, Kadir Has University was inaugurated on 13 February 2002 by its benefactor. The building renovation received the Europa Nostra Award in 2003.

THE *AGIASMA* OF SAINT MARY OF VEFA ⑮

Ayın Biri Kilisesi
Avenue Unkapanı, behind the buildings of Istanbul Manifaturacılar
Çarşısı
Vefa area
• Bus: Unkapanı

O n the first day of every month, the
Orthodox Church of Saint Mary of
Vefa is the venue for an *agiasma* (a
celebration associated with a holy water
spring - see p. 241), which has given the
church its Turkish name: Ayın Biri Kilisesi
("church of the first of the month") or Ayda Bir
Kilisesi ("once monthly church").

A "once per month" miraculous water spring

On this day, a never-ending queue of visitors (mostly Muslims, even though
the church is Christian) participate in a ritual in which the participants buy
a key, make vows, recite prayers of thanksgiving (each according to their
own religion and confession), and then throw the key into a sea, lake or river.
Although there has likely been a church on this site since the time of the
conquest, the current building was restored in the 18th century by an Epirote
(a Greek native of Epirus) whose daughter had seen the church's holy spring
in a dream. Excavations then led to the discovery of the *agiasma* and an 11th-
century marble icon, now conserved in a bronze case. The family subsequently
sold the church to the Macedonian Educational Confraternity.

CONSTANTINE PALAIOLOGOS AND THE ORIGIN OF THE NAME OF THE VEFA NEIGHBOURHOOD

The Church of Saint Mary of Vefa is alleged to have been built close to the
lost tomb of Constantine Palaiologos, the last Byzantine emperor, who died
defending his capital against the Turks. According to legend, after the city
had fallen on 29 May 1453, Constantine Palaiologos continued to fight in
the streets until he was killed by an Arab slave owned by Sultan Mehmed
II. At the moment he died, Constantine is supposed to have said to his killer,
"M'ephages!" ["You have eaten me"], thus giving the area its name: firstly
Mefa, and then Vefa. A more plausible etymology might be that Sheikh
Vefa (Muslihiddin Mustafa) built a religious and educational complex in
this area in the years following the conquest, although this does not rule
out the possibility that the tomb of Constantine Palaiologos, "invisible and
insignificant" as described in the legend, is to be found somewhere near
the Church of Saint Mary of Vefa.

THE GLASS OF MUSTAFA KEMAL ATATÜRK ⑯

Vefa Bozacisi shop
Avenue Katip Çelebi Cad., no. 104/1
Vefa
• Tel:+90 212 519 49 22
• www.vefa.com.tr
• vefa@vefa.com.tr
• Metro: Vezneciler

The Survivor of Boza and Şıra

Both a cafe and a shop, the beautiful Vefa Bozacisi establishment offers a number of typically Turkish drinks. Boza is served there between October and April and şıra from April to October.

Vefa Bozacısı ("house of Boza in the Vefa area") was founded by an Albanian family originally from Prizren, who emigrated to Istanbul in the 1870s, just before the Balkans became the setting for the Russo-Turkish War. Finding it difficult to establish themselves in the boza sector (where the Armenians had gained the upper hand over the Albanians), this family introduced a new way of producing boza that allowed them to make their fortune in a neighbourhood where many high-level bureaucrats resided. Instead of conserving the boza in wooden barrels, which encouraged the spread of bacteria and rapidly spoiled the precious liquid, they used enormous marble jars, which were both hygienic and decorative. The establishment quickly became renowned and attracted clients as illustrious as Mustafa Kemal Atatürk, the founder of the Republic, a great Vefa regular whose personal glass is still proudly exhibited in a bell jar.

There were previously hundreds of family-run boza bars in Istanbul, a practice that is now disappearing (though several boza producers can still be found in Turkish Thrace, another reminder of its Balkan origins). That the Vefa Bozacisi establishment continues to thrive is a testament to its consistent quality.

Şıra, which is served during the summer season, is a refreshing drink made from grape juice, or occasionally from dried grapes soaked in water. It has suffered more violently from religious controversy than boza, since şıra, if fermented too long, turns into wine.

Apart from the traditional manufacturing of boza and şıra, Vefa also sells classic vinegar and Italian-inspired balsamic vinegar, both of which are highly sought by food-lovers. All of these products can be taken away in elegant glass bottles. In summer, their homemade ice cream is excellent.

BOZA: A CONTROVERSIAL DRINK

Boza is a slightly fermented beverage made from millet and sugar. Very rich in carbohydrates, vitamins and lactic acid, it is recommended for serious athletes and pregnant women. Boza was also previously made from wheat, maize and other crops.

The origins of boza can undoubtedly be found in zythum, a fermented drink produced by the Egyptians in antiquity. Xenophon's *Anabasis* refers to a similar drink consumed in an area corresponding to modern-day eastern Anatolia. During the Ottoman period, the manufacturing of boza was the privilege of the Balkan peoples, especially the Albanians. The army consumed large quantities, as prior to the discovery of the extraction of beet sugar at the beginning of the 19th century, cane sugar was expensive and the carbohydrate-rich foods helped soldiers against the cold of the Balkans. The consumption of boza was subject to continual theological controversy, since the delicious drink contained a small amount of alcohol. The legal experts distinguished between "acidic" boza, rich in alcohol, and "sweet" boza, which good Muslims could drink without any crises of conscience. However, certain sultans such as Murad IV (1623-40) or Selim III (1789-1807), who were more devout, strictly forbade all varieties of boza, acidic or sweet. This prohibition is also explained by the fact that the boza establishments had become places where political plots were hatched.

Boza was previously served sprinkled with cinnamon, ginger and finely grated coconut. Today, boza is decorated with cinnamon and roasted chickpeas, called leblebi.

THE INDIAN SHRINE ⑰

Horhor Caddesi
Guraba Hüseyin Ağa area
On Aksaray Square, at the start of Horhor Caddesi, near Murat Paşa Mosque
• Open weekdays 9am-5pm
• Metro: Yusufpaşa. Tram: Aksaray

An embassy of Indian Sufism in the heart of the city

Amid the noise and activity of Aksaray Square, a stone fountain with a pyramidal roof goes almost unnoticed despite its impressive size. This fountain forms part of the Hindiler Tekkesi (or "Indian shrine") complex, erroneously described as the "Hindular" Tekkesi ("Hindu" refers to the religion, and "Indian" to the nationality), even on the official signs. In reference to its fountain, it is also called the "Horhor" Tekkesi, an onomatopoeia attributed to fountains whose flowing water makes a loud noise.

Inside, there are a number of graves protruding from a little garden in front of a wooden house. In keeping with Ottoman custom, the Indian dervishes are buried with tombstones imitating the shape of their head coverings, some of which are typically Indian, such as the hats shaped like an upturned boat or those of the pointed, asymmetrical variety, very different from the Ottoman turbans (usually round or spherical) or the classic fez.

Founded in the 15th century by order of Mehmed the Conqueror, this monument is among the oldest belonging to the Sufi Naqshbandi brotherhood. Still linked to the Indian branch of the order, whose visitors it welcomed, the shrine became a genuine home for Indian dervishes in the 19th century. In addition to its role as a bridge between the branches of Ottoman and Indian Sufism, the Horhor Indian shrine also became a centre of political activity. Imam Mehmed, who is buried in the shrine's cemetery, was a member of the delegation sent to Istanbul in 1787 by Tipu Sultan, ruler of Mysore, to request help from the Ottoman Sultan Abdul Hamid I in his struggle against the English colonisers. At the beginning of the 20th century, a sheikh at the shrine, Riyazeddin Babür Efendi, became the superior of the Indian shrine in Jerusalem (Tekye-t-ul Hunud), where he joined the Ottoman army in its fight against the English during the First World War. Once Jerusalem had been lost, he returned to Istanbul to become head of the Horhor Tekkesi. He could not, however, escape the English, who came to arrest him during the Allied occupation of Istanbul. There is also an Indian shrine in Üsküdar, and in Jerusalem as well.

— REMAINS OF THE COLUMN OF ARCADIUS ⑱

Haseki Kadın Sokak Street
Right next to the famous cake shop Cerrahpaşa (Avenue
Kocamustafapaşa Cad, no. 16)
Cerrahpaşa Mahallesi
• Tram: Yusufpaşa or Haseki

A forgotten relic of Byzantium

Not far from the Cerrahpaşa Medical Faculty Hospital, between two houses on Haseki Kadın Sokak Street, you will see a remarkable pile of stones reaching almost as high as the house to its right. These remains, located right next to the famous cake shop Cerrahpaşa, are none other than the remnants of the plinth for a gigantic Byzantine column (47 metres high), which was erected to celebrate the victories of the Emperor Arcadius (395-408) and his son, Theodosius I (379-395). This column was formerly located in the middle of the Forum of Arcadius, which was situated on this very site (and of which no further traces remain), and rested on a square plinth which is still preserved today. The column recounted the victories of the imperial armies with bas-reliefs spiralling upwards along its shaft, probably based on the columns of Trajan and Marcus Aurelius in Rome, which also inspired Napoleon to build the Vendôme Column in Paris. Inside was a spiral staircase that went up to the balcony at the top of the column. The statue of Arcadius was added to it in 421, under Theodosius II.

The column survived major earthquakes, including that of 740, which nevertheless got the better of the statue of Arcadius, which was destroyed. During the Ottoman era, the site was visited by European travellers in the 16th and 17th centuries, whose descriptions allow us to reconstruct the design of the monument. On the verge of collapse, the column was finally demolished at the beginning of the 18th century, leaving only the pile of stones visible today.

Evliya Çelebi, the great traveller and Ottoman historian (1611-1682), recalls in his wonderful *Seyyahatname* (Book of Travels) that there was also a statue of a girl at the top of the column. According to legend, this statue would come to life once a year and cry out, causing the birds flying over the column to fall. The local inhabitants eventually turned this day into a feast day. Evliya Çelebi also recounts that, at the moment the Prophet Muhammad was born, a major earthquake shook the city and destroyed the column, after which, legend says, the column rebuilt itself of its own accord.

During the Ottoman era, the column was known as Avrat Taşı (the stone of the lady), as a market for women was held there on Sundays. In classical Ottoman society, in which men and women were relatively segregated, the women found it difficult to go to the weekly markets, whose merchants were usually men. Special markets were thus organised exclusively for women where the female merchants were able to show their goods to their customers.

A DREAM THAT TRAVELLED THE WORLD

On the night of 19 August 1630 (1040 Hegira), a palace official, Evliya Çelebi, was sleeping peacefully at home when, in an intermediate state "between sleeping and waking", he saw himself seated near the minbar of the Ahi Çelebi Mosque. In his dream, a radiant crowd of believers, composed of Islamic saints and prophets, entered suddenly, led by Muhammed. The assembled had come to provide spiritual support to Khan Giray of Crimea, who was then at war and was preparing to perform the morning prayer.

One of the saints instructed Evliya Çelebi to participate in the prayer and to then kiss the hands of the Prophet Muhammed, addressing him with, "Şefaat ya resulallah!" ("Intercede with the Lord – O Prophet of God!").

Evliya Çelebi was happy to obey, but when introduced to the Prophet so that he could kiss his hands, he was seized with awe and mixed up the ritual formula, saying, "Seyahat ya resulallah." ("Travels, O Prophet of God.").

According to the legend, this mistake pleased the Prophet, who replied, "I have interceded on your behalf: go on your travels in good health and peace!" When he awoke, Evliya Çelebi went to speak to two dream-interpreting mystics, who both declared that he would undertake long journeys in this world and enjoy a happy life in the next.

Evliya Çelebi's many travels resulted in the *Seyyahatname* (Book of Travels), a ten-volume work in which acute real-life observation is occasionally mixed with fantastical imagery (women give birth to elephants, cats are frozen while jumping from one roof to another in winter, only to be thawed in summer).

The books describe a rich panorama covering the history, economics, geography, ethnology, sociology and folklore of the many places he visited, as well as life under the Ottomans during that period.

Evliya Çelebi first travelled to Istanbul, describing the dervish lodges, the mosques and madaris he visited, as well as inns, concerts, places of entertainment and the many vices, such as drink and drugs. From 1640, he accompanied dignitaries on their journeys through Anatolia, Syria, Palestine, Iraq, the Hejaz, Egypt, Sudan and the Balkans. He also participated in missions sent to places such as Iran, Azerbaijan, Georgia, the Caucasus, Crimea, Hungary, Austria, Germany, the Netherlands, Poland, Sweden, and Russia, and participated in the conquest of Crete as a genuine war reporter *avant la lettre*.

Located next to Istanbul Commerce University (Istanbul Ticaret Üniversitesi), on the banks of the Golden Horn, Ahi Çelebi Mosque was built in the 15th century by Ahi Çelebi Tabib Kemal, director of the great hospital created by Mehmed the Conqueror and personal physician to Bayezid II. A specialist in urology, he authored a treatise on kidney and bladder stones. Although the mosque was long deserted due to subsidence, it has recently been restored.

REMAINS OF AN OBELISK ⑲

Faculty of Medicine Campus, Cerrahpaşa Hospital
Visible during the day (open evenings but without illumination)
Avenue Koca Mustafa Paşa Caddesi, no. 53
• Tram: Fındıkzade

The third
obelisk
of Byzantium

When the city of Constantinople was founded, Constantine the Great (324-337) ordered an Egyptian obelisk from Karnak to be transported to the "Second Rome", as there were already several in the original Rome. This giant mass of granite (from the reign of Thutmosis III, 1502-1488 B.C.) was eventually erected in 390, under Theodosius I, on the site of the Hippodrome, where it may still be found today.

Discovered during archaeological excavations at Sarayburnu, the second obelisk is currently on display in the garden of the archaeological museum.

Written sources mentioned a third obelisk, of which all traces had been lost. Restoration work recently undertaken on the Esekapı Mosque uncovered a piece of pink granite – rectangular, slightly pyramidal in shape and measuring 80×90×300 centimetres – which appears to have come from this obelisk.

This section of obelisk was discovered in the courtyard of the Esekapı Mosque and Ibrahim Pasha Madrasa. The Esekapı Mosque – originally a Byzantine church built between the end of the 13th century and the beginning of the 14th century – was located near a city gate known as the Gate of Christ (hence the Turkish name Isakapı, which became Esekapı).

Between 1551 and 1560, Vizier Hadim Ibrahim Pasha (the eunuch) transformed the church into a mosque and the architect Sinan supervised the construction of the madrasa incorporated into the building. The obelisk fragment was almost certainly visible at that time, but it is thought that it was not moved due to its enormous weight. The granite fragment remained hidden under the floor of the mosque for centuries. The latter collapsed during the earthquake of 1894 and the entire complex fell into ruin, before becoming part of the campus of the Faculty of Medicine in the 1960s.

THE MARTYRIUM OF THE ST. MENAS CHURCH ㉛

Avenue Nafiz Gürman Cad. Bestekâr Hakkı Bey sok. Street
Kocamustafapaşa/Samatya
Church open Sunday
• On other days: telephone (0212) 5861650 or (0212) 5889296
• Train: Koca Mustafa Paşa

A forgotten Roman building in Istanbul

O
ne of the least well-known Roman monuments of Istanbul is located under the St. Menas Church (Agios Menas). Almost completely forgotten, it may be visited depending on the willingness of the owner of the garage located below the church, on Avenue Nafiz Gürman.

If you visit on the right day, you will be able to enter the martyrium dating from the early years of the Christian era. This is the small catacomb in which the martyrs Papylos and Karpos were buried; their names were later contracted to Papylokarpos, and then to Polykarpos.

According to the ancient sources, the martyrium was constructed in the 4th or 5th century according to the same plan as the Dome of the Rock in Jerusalem. Although poorly maintained, the martyrium, with its high vaulted ceiling and dark interior, is still impressive.

The church above the martyrium has been rebuilt several times and dates from 1833. Its name was probably changed to St. Menas as the local inhabitants preferred this saint, who is highly revered by the Orthodox, to St. Polycarp, whose *agiasma* (holy water spring) is located underneath.

THE CYPRESS OF THE SÜMBÜL EFENDI MOSQUE ㉑

Avenue Kocamustafapaşa cad.
Kocamustafapaşa Medresesi sokak Street - Fatih
• Train: Koca Mustafa Paşa. Bus: Kocamustafapaşa line

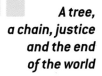

A tree, a chain, justice and the end of the world

Located near the Kocamustafa Paşa Mosque, the Sümbül Efendi Mosque (Sümbül Efendi Camii) is a former monastery dedicated to St. Andrew and built in 1284. It was converted into a mosque in 1486 and became the main location of the "Sünbüli" order of dervishes. The tomb of Sheikh Yusuf Sinan Efendi, known as Sünbül Efendi, the founder of the order, may be seen there.

In the courtyard there are two more tombs, built in 1813, which are said to be for the daughters of Hussein, grandson of the Prophet and son of Fatima and Ali (the fourth Islamic Caliph). Next to their tombs stands a parched cypress tree. Previously this tree was encircled by a large chain, one end of which hung some distance from the ground. According to popular legend, Hussein's two daughters were captured by the Byzantines and forced to renounce their faith. Imprisoned close to the cypress, they had forty days in which to convert. When the period of deferment expired, they were killed under the cypress tree and buried nearby. Later, the cypress was also used to dispense justice. The alleged perpetrator of a crime was placed under the tree and if the chain hanging from the cypress touched the suspect's head, he or she was deemed guilty. Conversely, if the chain did not move, the man was innocent.

According to another legend, if the chain were to break of its own accord and fall to the ground, it would signify the end of time. In order to avoid unnecessary risks, the city authorities removed the chain, the traces of which have now disappeared.

FOR CHILDREN WITH READING AND WRITING DIFFICULTIES

According to an old tradition, children with a stammer or reading and writing difficulties could be cured by going up onto the circular balcony (şerefe) of the minaret and walking around it several times.

THE MOSQUE HYACINTH

Sün(m)bül means "hyacinth" in Turkish. Sheikh Sünbül Efendi liked to put hyacinths in his turban when they were in season. This symbol is found throughout the religious complex and permeates every aspect of the aesthetic life of the Sünbüli order: calligraphy, ornamentation, gravestones, clothing, etc.

In front of the mosque, one of the tombs is reputed to be that of a daughter of the last Byzantine Emperor, Constantine Dragases. She is alleged to have converted to Islam and to have been buried in this very place.

THE SILIVRIKAPI CLUB ㉒

Silivrikapı Gate (inner gate in the Byzantine walls)
Avenue 10. Yıl Caddesi
Bus: Silivrikapı (Zeytinburnu line)

*A club
in memory
of a sporting
achievement*

Hidden inside the Silivrikapı Gate (the inner gate in the Byzantine walls), a remarkable club of colossal dimensions hangs from the wall. Contrary to what you might expect, it was not used to knock out opponents during ferocious battles in the Middle Ages, but was used simply for sports training by warriors.

Among the Ottomans (and in particular the Janissaries – see p. 56), when a record was broken in a sporting competition, it was customary to hang the record-breaking objects (javelin, bow, club, etc.) on the wall of either a mosque or monumental gateway.

Although the clubs regularly used for training soldiers (instead of dumbbells) weighed 25-30 kilograms, Sultan Murad IV (reigned 1623-1640), who was known for his Herculean strength and imposing stature, used to train

with a club weighing 102 kilos, which he held with just his little finger.

The inscription accompanying the club hanging at Silivrikapı reveals the identity of the hero, "Whoever beholds the club of Idris the wrestler, native of Rize, member of the corps of halberdiers of the Old Palace, and recites the Fatiha (first chapter of the Koran, recited for the departed) will give up his soul in the faith, 1090 of the Hegira -1679 of the Julian Calendar".

Until a few years ago, the club was crowned with two large whalebones, whose disappearance remains as great a mystery as their origins.

The clubs used for training in the Topkapı Palace are conserved in the weaponry section in the Palace museum.

— SILIVRIKAPI HYPOGEUM ㉓

Next to the Silivrikapı Gate in the Byzantine walls
Avenue 10. Yıl Caddesi
• Bus stop: Silivrikapı (Zeytinburnu line)
After taking the outer gate at Silivrikapı, turn immediately left, without
passing through the inner gate. The hypogeum can be reached by
walking fifty metres along the wooded path running between the
external wall (exoteichos) and the main inner wall (esoteichos).

" A family vault wedged between two Byzantine walls

Situated in the space between two Byzantine walls (peribolos), the Silivrikapı family vault remained undiscovered until restoration work carried out on the walls in 1988 revealed this pleasant surprise. *(my 'Little Tomb')*

The hypogeum, which was apparently part of a larger necropolis, probably dates from a period before the reign of Theodosius II (408-450), who was also responsible for these great walls, known as the Theodosian Walls. It provides evidence of a period in which the ancient style was moving towards Byzantine art proper.

The marble and limestone sarcophagi found on the site bear bas-reliefs depicting scenes from the Old and New Testament, decorated with peacocks, pigeons and creepers. Among the bas-reliefs that are still reasonably well preserved, it is possible to make out Jesus surrounded by his apostles, the saints, as well as monograms of Christ.

Other tombs, visible through their broken covers, are located under the paving of the hypogeum.

This remarkable monument has unfortunately suffered from, and is still subject to, vandalism: in 1989, the bas-reliefs were removed by thieves. Fortunately though, they were seized by police before they could be sold on the international black market in antiquities. The bas-reliefs are currently being conserved in the Archaeological Museum and have been replaced in the hypogeum by cast models.

The murals on the interior walls, which were still partially visible when the hypogeum was discovered, have also disappeared due to the effect of the fires lit by tramps who have sought refuge here.

Although the area around the Silivrikapı Gate is busy at all hours, it is advisable to go there only in a group and in broad daylight.

AGIASMA OF BALIKLI ㉔

Church of St. Mary
Church also called Zoodochos Pighi ("life-giving spring") and Balıklı Rum
Kilisesi ("Church of the Fish")
Silivri Kapı Street no. 3, Zeytinburnu
Not to be confused with Balıklı hospital, located further south
• Open daily: 8.30am-4.30pm
• Bus stop: Silivrikapı

> **Fried fish leaping in a holy spring**

Next to the entrance to the Church of St. Mary (also known as Zoodochos Pighi, "the life-giving spring"), a steep and narrow stairway descends into an underground *agiasma* (see p. 241), a genuine aquatic chapel where even the iconostasis is made from marble to withstand the ubiquitous dampness. Indeed, there is a large basin here fed by an abundant spring in which fish swim in beautiful clear green water. The holy water is offered by the nuns free of charge in small plastic phials. The nuns you will meet here do not speak because they have taken a vow of silence.

The Turks who devotedly visited this spring to plead for healing named it Balıklı Kilise ("Church of the Fish"). The origins of this church can be traced back to a very strange legend: on 29 May 1453, at the time when the city was captured by the Ottoman armies, a monk was busy frying fish close to the holy spring, located within the monastery. When he was told that the city had fallen, he said he would only believe it if the fish he was frying were to jump into the water of the sacred spring. The partially-burnt fish did just that, and its descendants have been dark on one side ever since.

The origin of this great complex – with its church, cemetery, *agiasma*, monastery and hospital – can be traced back to Justinian, whose gallstones are alleged to have been cured due to the healing properties of the spring. The current structure was built in 1833. The hegumen of this church is traditionally the Ecumenical Patriarch, who has a small lodge at his disposal on site. The cemetery is also home to the graves of the patriarchs and important aristocratic Greek families. A number of the gravestones in the churchyard bear epigraphs in Karamanli.

The large icon of the Prophet Elijah on the wall to the right of the church iconostasis owes its existence to Sultan Mahmud II, who visited the church after its opening in 1833 and observed that there were no icons of the Old Testament prophets on display, some of whom are recognised and venerated in the Islamic tradition. The result was this icon, in which the bright red of the prophet's clothing stands out elegantly against the dark background.

FISH MUSEUM (25)

Fatih Seafood Products Cooperative
Kenedi caddesi
Next to the sea, near the Narlıkapı Armenian Church
Yedikule
• Open weekdays 9am-5pm

A surprising atmosphere

The Seafood Products Cooperative of the Fatih quarter (Fatih Su Ürünleri Kooperatifi) has, since 1994, boasted an astonishing collection of fish preserved in formaldehyde-filled jars. The noticeably subdued lighting and sometimes frightening nature of the collections create a wonderful, and mysterious, atmosphere.

Visitors can also enjoy a cup of tea in the little Fishermen's café in a rustic and pleasant ambience. Cut off from the bustle of the city, one feels as though one could be in a fishing village by the Aegean.

The collection originated in Instanbul University's decision to locate part of its Faculty of Fisheries on the deserted island of Hayırsızada (Oxia), among the Princes' Islands, 11 kilometres south of Istanbul, along with its fish collection. Transporting the students and supplying the institution proved so difficult (in particular due to the terrible southwest wind, the "Lodos", a hazardous nightmare for those attempting to navigate the Sea of Marmara) that the faculty was eventually moved back to Istanbul. For reasons unknown, the fish collection remained on the island and was later given as a gift to the Fatih Seafood Products Cooperative by the dean of the faculty.

The oldest specimens date from the 1970s and sometimes represent species that have long since disappeared from the Sea of Marmara, which has seen significant levels of development since the 1980s. Over the last few years, due to an increase in ecological awareness, some of these species have returned while others are still only visible in the cooperative's jars. Other species, however, are new, having arrived from tropical regions, and are now able to survive here due to the increased temperature in the Sea of Marmara, as is the case elsewhere in the world.

In an act of seafaring solidarity, fishermen from other areas have gradually contributed other types of fish. The museum now includes several species from the Aegean and Black Seas, as well as from seas further removed. The slender conger ‹ els that greet the visitor, and the impressive variety of octopuses and squid, are also species unknown in the Sea of Marmara.

There are also shellfish, including snails the size of a melon, but these have not been assigned dates, unlike the fish, whose date of capture and Latin names have been carefully recorded.

Due to a lack of space and funds, only a part of the collection is on display.

THE GOOSE FOUNTAIN OF KAZLIÇEŞME (26)

Halfway along Demirhane Caddesi, next to the Erikli Baba Tekkesi
(1 Zakirbaşı Sokak)
Zeytinburnu area
• Metro: Marmaray line, Kazlıçeşme station

> *The geese*
> *that helped*
> *to capture*
> *Constantinople*
> *in 1453*

Kazlıçeşme (literally, "the fountain of the geese" in Turkish) is an old neighbourhood of tanneries which owes its name to a fountain decorated with a bas-relief of a goose, whose legendary origins may be traced back to the discovery of abundant water sources by the Turks during the siege of the city. While the besieging army was suffering greatly due to a shortage of water in May 1453, the Sakabaşı ("master of the water carriers") is said to have seen some geese in flight and ordered his aides to find out where these birds were landing, in the certain knowledge that he would find a spring there.

The goose bas-relief on the Kazlıçeşme Fountain, which dates from 1537, clearly originates from an older monument, as in the case of the Byzantine eagle of Kapalıçarşı (see p. 45). What was the identity of the Ottoman sculptor who created a three-dimensional work of this nature in an era when even two-dimensional images of living creatures were barely tolerated?

It is, in all probability, an artefact from the temple of Juno whose existence in this area is attested by historical sources. Temples dedicated to Juno were, in fact, often built near major water sources. As the goddess of marriage, Juno was associated with fertility and abundance.

The ivy leaf bas-relief placed next to the goose appears to come from a Dionysiac temple.

Close to the fountain, there is a drinking trough, which was, almost certainly, originally a sarcophagus, and the Roman columns located immediately behind the fountain are similar to ones found in the courtyard of the Bektashi shrine of Erikli Baba.

GEESE: FROM THE FIRST TO THE SECOND ROME

The Kazlıçeşme geese bear a striking similarity to the foundation myth of the city of Rome. In the legend of the "Capitoline geese", the birds, who were dedicated to Juno, saved the city by warning the Romans that the Gauls had tried to climb the walls of the Capitol during the night. One of history's great ironies is thus that the geese saved the First Rome but also contributed to the fall of Constantinople, known for centuries as the Second Rome.

KAZLIÇEŞME: AN OLD NEIGHBOURHOOD OF TANNERS

Due to its particularly abundant groundwater, during the Ottoman period Kazlıçeşme became the neighbourhood of tanners, who were heavy consumers of water, which they used for soaking their hides. The leather industry grew to such an extent in the 20th century that any tourist who travelled to Istanbul was greeted at the entrance to the city by the nauseating and unbearable stench typically associated with the tanneries. When Kazlıçeşme's 350 tanneries were closed in 1993, it was feared that there would be an invasion of rats caused by the departure of the area's rodents who, it was thought, might board the boats in nearby ports. This did not, in fact, happen. Along with the tanneries, historic buildings in the neighbourhood were also demolished. Remaining in this area now are only a few abandoned old factories and mosques, the St. Paraskevi Church, the Bektashi Erikli Baba Tekkesi, a small cemetery for soldiers who died during the siege, and several fountains, including that of Kazlıçeşme.

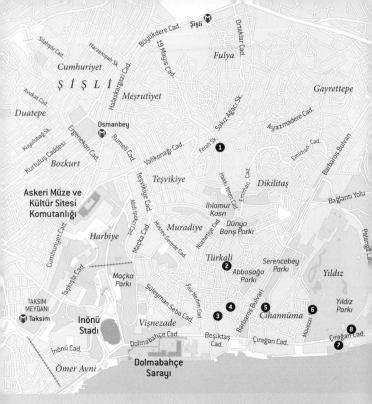

BEŞIKTAŞ - YILDIZ

TOMB OF BARDAKÇI BABA ❶

At the entrance to the Fulya Terrace Residence complex
11 Hakkı Yeten Caddesi
Fulya İstanbul

A monumental hoax

At the entrance to the Fulya Terrace Residence complex, the gleaming new tomb covered in dark green marble and protected by a large glass case belongs to one Bardakçi Baba, the "Father of glass manufacturers". Although the inhabitants of the nearby Beşiktaş neighbourhood say this saint's tomb has been an object of veneration since time immemorial, in reality the "cult" has been completely fabricated by a local dentist and his friends.

In the early 1970s, H. D. was a student at the faculty of dentistry, located near Bardakçi Baba's tomb. He and his friends would often take a path through a small wood where students had placed a table so they could study outdoors and occasionally drink wine. This table was always covered in drinking glasses. One day (no doubt under the inspiration of the alcoholic vapours), they decided to paint the inscription "Bardakçi Baba" on the table in capital letters. They then improvised a rudimentary tomb in which they buried a genuine human skull they had been using for their studies. One day, a bottle of water they had left empty the night before had been filled by a visitor wanting to pay his respects to the saint. And so the cult was born. At the end of the 1970s, while construction work was being carried out on Hakkı Yeten Caddesi, workers discovered the skull and buried it on the other side of the avenue, including on the tomb the inscription which had been painted on the table. This modest tomb soon attracted a crowd of visitors, who came to ask for healing and a blessing for their

marriages, children, jobs and so on. A ritual then developed whereby a glass would be broken when making a request to saint Bardakçı Baba. A few charitable individuals then had the tomb enclosed with iron railings and the religious authorities even installed the notices that read, "Pray for the soul of Bardakçı Baba. The man who lies in this tomb is a friend of God. Do not attach bands to his tomb, do not break glasses, do not light candles. These are superstitions and sinful. Pray for his soul and address your requests directly to the Lord."

In 2009, the Fulya Terrace Residence luxury complex was constructed opposite the tomb of Bardakçı Baba. The developers, who believed that this derisory tomb was not in keeping with their residence, decided to update it and came up with the current design. Now the tomb is protected by a glass case which evokes the ritual peculiar to Bardakçı Baba, and the notice (which was undoubtedly seen as too long and complicated) was replaced by a much shorter version: "Bardakçı Baba – pray for his soul". The tomb is now illuminated at night and Istanbul has acquired its first modern residence with a patron saint.

The dentist's disclosure in 2002 was devastating for everyone, although this did not prevent the works from being carried out in 2009. H. D. defended his silence by claiming that he wished to protect the wood surrounding the tomb, which, he hoped, would benefit from the saint's immunity. This, however, was not the case and the dentist broke his silence when the trees were cut down. He invited the authorities to carry out an excavation in order to locate the skull, which was still wearing the plastic dental and palate prosthesis that had been fitted by the young student himself. The cemetery authorities stated that they did not have any historical records referring to Bardakçı Baba and that if the archaeological excavations confirmed the dentist's revelations, the tomb of Bardakçı Baba would be demolished. It should also be noted that the saint's body is not oriented towards the Qibla, which is usually required of an Islamic tomb. The tomb remains in situ for the time being, and the older inhabitants of the area continue to believe strongly in the veracity of Bardakçı Baba.

اللّٰه

SULTAN FATİH'İN
TUZCUBAŞI'SI

TUZCUBABA HZ.
1420-1500

RUHUNA FATİHA

THE SALT MILL OF TUZ BABA ❷

22 Avenue Uzuncaova
• Beşiktaş, Türkali area

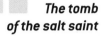

The tomb of the salt saint

Not far from the Yıldız Mosque, devout Muslims can sometimes be seen praying fervently in front of an ornamented marble niche, on which small salt sacks have been placed. Although the marble plinth supporting the recess has been eroded by ancient deposits of salt, it is nevertheless clear that this is an architectural fragment of Byzantine origin.

Behind this niche lies the tomb of Rum Ali Ağa, who was in charge of salt supplies under Mehmed the Conqueror (1432 – 1481), which explains his nickname, "Tuz Baba" (literally, "Father Salt"). Unfortunately, the tomb is barely recognizable due to subsequent renovations and later additions.

Next to the tomb there is also a hand-operated salt mill. Legend has it that by turning this mill Tuz Baba was miraculously able to produce salt for the Ottoman army, of which it was in desperate need during the siege of Constantinople.

Today, the tomb of Tuz Baba is still the centre of devotions associated with salt. Hence, visitors leave their sacks of salt while offering prayers and passers-by dip their fingers in the salt and eat a little in order to receive the saint's favour.

The name of the mosque located behind the tomb (Rum Ali Ağa) bears witness to the unusual level of social mobility present at the time of the conquest, as "Rum" means "Greek". Tuz Baba was undoubtedly one of the many converts who took up service with the sultan in roles as diverse as secretaries, bureaucrats, architects, and diplomats.

According to tradition, Rum Ali Ağa joined the Rifai Brotherhood and became a saint. Founded in the 12th century by Seyyid Ahmed Rifai, the Rifai Sufi Brotherhood is guided by three principles: do not ask, do not refuse and do not accumulate wealth. Certain followers of this order were known to have stuck pins in their cheeks, in a state of mystical ecstasy, in order to demonstrate their insensitivity to pain.

THE PORTRAIT IN THE YEDI SEKIZ HASAN PASHA BAKERY ③

Beşiktaş Market
Şehit Asım Street, no. 12
Near the fish market

> **The bakery of the skull-smashing pasha who could neither read nor write**

At the entrance to the Yedi Sekiz Hasan Pasha bakery, the portrait of a sinister-looking man provides a stern welcome to the customers who come here to purchase one of the delicious pastries. Depicted in his uniform, with a thick Ottoman-style moustache, Hasan Pasha is the ancestor of the cake shop owner from whom this venerable establishment takes its name, which means literally "the Seven-Eight". Pasha earned this title after smashing the skull of a revolutionary.

An ordinary policeman, the young Hasan had secured the favour of Sultan Abdul Hamid who appointed him to the position of commander of the Beşiktaş bodyguards. On 20 May 1878, Ali Suavi, a young revolutionary accompanied by Balkans volunteers, attacked the Çiragan Palace, with the intention of freeing Sultan Murad V, who had been imprisoned there on mental health grounds since his dethronement in 1876.

A member of the higher Muslim clergy, Ali Suavi was a complex individual. Although he had spent a long period as an exile in Europe, marrying a beautiful English woman and adopting a "Frankish" lifestyle, he remained deeply Islamic and wished to establish a constitutional government in the Ottoman Empire. The restoration of Sultan Murad V would have allowed him to realise his ambitions, all the more so given that they were both Freemasons. But Commander Hasan blocked his way and broke his skull with his club, thus thwarting the revolution.

In order to thank him for saving his throne, and indeed his life, Abdul Hamid awarded Hasan the rank of pasha. The new pasha, however, was not able to read or write, much less sign his name. How then would he be able to authenticate official documents? Ottoman pragmatism came to the rescue: he would simply draw the Arab figures 7 (٧) and 8 (٨) and join them with a horizontal line to create a symbol that sufficiently resembled the name "Hasan".

Emboldened by his new title, the all-powerful ruler of Beşiktaş maintained order by brute force. With the club he used to kill Ali Suavi, he personally beat drunks and anybody who publicly violated Ramadan or mistreated dogs in the street.

THE DOME OF THE CHURCH OF ST. MARY OF BESIKTAS ❹

Church of the Holy Mother of God (Surp Asdvadzadzin)
20 İlhan Sokak
Beşiktaş
• Open for mass on Sundays and Armenian religious feast days
• Bus stop: Beşiktaş

> **Surp Asdvadzadzin's (Saint Mary's) forbidden, hidden dome**

Invisible from the outside, the dome of the Armenian Church of St. Mary, constructed between 1836 and 1838, has an astonishing history. In the wake of the Ottoman conquests, Christians were allowed to keep existing domes but prohibited from building new domed churches, a prohibition that lasted until the reforms (Tanzimat) that started in 1839 and ensured equal rights for the Ottoman Empire's non-Muslim subjects.

In the major religious traditions, the dome symbolizes the sky. This is particularly true for Islam since the Prophet Muhammed, at the time of his Ascension, or Miraj, describes the sky as a pearly dome resting on four pillars. In esoteric traditions, however, the dome is an initiatory symbol. Examples of this include the first Ottoman mausolea at Bursa whose domes are pierced with a circular hole, and the Pantheon in Rome, which was used as a model for Hagia Sophia. This central hole, often identified with the polar star or sun, corresponds to the initiate's flight from the conditioned world. The four walls of the building thus symbolise the finite, temporal world, while the dome symbolises initiation and elevation, and the summit, freedom and the infinite.

The church was built and funded by the architect Garabed Amira Balyan (1800 – 1866), who belonged to the famous Balyan family of architects, to whom we owe the great majority of public buildings (palaces, barracks, and also mosques) erected between the mid-18th and late 19th century. The building, which is covered by a roof with a triangular cross-section, follows a cruciform plan. This design, conceived for the express purpose of hiding the dome, inspired the layout of the great reception hall of the Dolmabahçe Palace, also built by Amira Balyan.

The icons of St. Mary of Beşiktaş are the work of Umed Beyzad (1809 – 1874), who also painted the palace. Relations between the palace and the Armenian community were extremely close at that time. Moreover, the church was built during the reign of Mahmud II, who had entrusted the imperial finances to Armenian experts.

At the entrance to the church, there is a marble relief depicting the Seal of Solomon (see p. 32).

THE ŞAZELI TEKKESI

⑤

14 Mehmet Ali Bey Sokak
Between the beginning of Yıldız Caddesi and the Serencebey slope
(Serencebey Yokuşu) - Beşiktaş
• Open during hours of prayer

*A Sufi
centre in art
nouveau style*

"**A** Muslim brotherhood adopting the latest art nouveau style: the perfect symbol for the reign!" exclaimed François Georgeon, the great biographer of Sultan Abdülhamid, builder of the Şazeli Tekkesi. Constructed in 1903 by the Italian architect Raimondo d'Aronco in the purest art nouveau style, which was then in vogue in Europe, the Şazeli Tekkesi (Ertuğrul Tekkesi) abounds with floral architectural details and other decorative features typical of this style. The spiritual retreat was built at the request of Sultan Abdülhamid II in homage to Sheikh Hamza Zâfir Medeni, head of the Şazeliye Brotherhood[1] (*Chadhiliyya* in Arabic), which has given its name to the institution. The tekke is also known in Turkish as *Ertuğrul*, from the name of the father of Osman Gazi, founder of the Ottoman dynasty. The shrine's mosque was used principally as a place of worship for the Ertuğrul regiment, an elite corps responsible for protecting the sultan, whose troops were recruited from Turkoman groups in the Domaniç region, birthplace of the imperial dynasty. This represented a nostalgic, but significant, return to Turkish sources, which had often been neglected or ignored by the House of Osman in previous years. The tekke was also an instrument in the pan-Islamic policy of the sultan, whom Bismarck, by no means a Turkophile, considered to be the greatest diplomat of his time. Sheikh Zâfir originally came from Tripolitania, in Libya, and was held in great esteem in North Africa. The tekke thus welcomed sheikhs and ulema from many Muslim religions and, through the connections that it established between the capital and spiritual centres on the periphery, helped to increase the influence of the caliphate's institution, which was held by the Ottomans. The European art nouveau style used here, in an Islamic country, was therefore perfectly in accordance with the philosophy of cultural mixing to which the tekke bore witness.

AN ITALIAN IN ISTANBUL

Based in Istanbul from 1893 to 1909, the Italian architect Raimondo d'Aronco was one of the favourite architects of Sultan Abdülhamid, during whose reign he built numerous public and private buildings still admired today: a myriad of buildings and lodges within the enclosure of the Yıldız Palace, including the Chalet Pavilion (Şale Köşkü), which was used to accommodate Wilhelm II during his visit in 1898; the Huber family palace in Yeniköy, now the president's summer residence; and the Italian summer embassy in Tarabya. He also designed the building of the Ministry of Agriculture, Forests and Mines on Sultanahmet Square, opposite the Hagia Sophia.

[1] A brotherhood founded in the early 13th century in Egypt by Abul Hasan Taqiyuddin Ali bin Abdullah ash-Shadhili, a Sufi master of Morrocan origin. Scattered throughout North Africa, the Shadhiliyah reached Istanbul and were able to flourish there due to Abdülhamid's special interest in the brotherhood, whose sheikh became the sultan's spiritual guide. In gratitude, and remaining faithful to their benefactor and fellow member, the Shadhiliyah dervishes celebrated their special rituals at Abdülhamid's funeral.

THE RAISED WALLS OF YILDIZ ⑥

Lower end of the Müvezzi Caddesi slope, Çırağan
Beşiktaş
• Bus: Çırağan

> *A relic of the 21 July 1905 assassination attempt on Sultan Abdülhamid*

An attentive observer will notice that the wall surrounding Yıldız Park (formerly the garden of the Yıldız Palace) is curiously uneven in the vicinity of the Yıldız Mosque and the main entrance to the palace. The walls in this area have been carefully constructed up to a certain height using large ashlar blocks while the upper part has been further raised with small, hastily-stacked bricks. This increased height bears witness to the extraordinary security measures taken following the assassination attempt of 21 July 1905 against Sultan Abdülhamid, with the first recorded use of a time bomb in history. Depending on the terrain, the sultan had the walls raised by 5 to 10 metres.

On that day, the diplomatic corps, state dignitaries, the imperial guard in its ceremonial dress, numerous interested parties and journalists were preparing to take part in the selamlık ceremony (an exchange of greetings between the sultan and his subjects), as was customary after all Friday prayers. Once the prayers were finished, the sultan, in a departure from his usual practice, did not leave the mosque immediately but instead embarked on a theological discussion with Sheikh-ul-Islam (the Grand Mufti, the highest religious authority at the time). A deafening noise was then heard as a bomb placed under a carriage exploded, killing twenty-six people and wounding a further fifty-eight. The investigation led back to Édouard Joris, a Belgian anarchist who had been won over to the Armenian cause. The conspirators had meticulously calculated the length of time usually taken by the sultan to reach his carriage after leaving the mosque. The reason why Abdülhamid lingered to

speak with Sheikh-ul-Islam is still unknown. Although he was deeply devout, Abdülhamid was suspicious of this dignitary whom he had placed under close surveillance. Indeed, the two preceding sultans had been deposed as the result of legal decisions issued by the Grand Mufti of the time.

Abdülhamid behaved in an unusual manner after the attack. The emperor, who lived in constant fear of assassination and dethronement, showed remarkable courage and fortitude: he continued with the selamlık ceremony as if nothing had happened, reassured the terrified people and continued his daily activities in the usual way.

After ultimately being deposed in 1909 (following a legal opinion given by none other than Sheikh-ul-Islam), he spent the last nine years of his life in perfect peace, without bearing any resentment or hard feelings, having previously pardoned Édouard Joris and employed him as his own intelligence agent.

THE ÇIRAĞAN PALACE HAMMAM

Çırağan Palace Kempinski Hotel
Avenue Çırağan cad., no. 32
Beşiktaş
• Visiting by appointment: meetings.istanbul@kempinski.com
• The hammam may be hired for dinners or cocktails
• Bus: Çırağan. Pier: Beşiktaş

The sultan's personal hammam which miraculously escaped the flames

Inside the magnificent Çırağan Kempinski Hotel, the Çırağan Palace hammam is the only part of the historical palace which escaped the fire that devastated the premises in 1910.

Although it is no longer used as a hammam, it may be visited by appointment or hired for private events.

Built by Sarkis Balyan (son of Garabed Balyan), Çırağan Palace was completed in 1871 for Sultan Abdülaziz, who was only able to make use of the building until he was dethroned in 1876. From 1878 to 1904, Sultan Murad V was held prisoner there after being dethroned several months after Abdülaziz, allegedly for mental health reasons. In 1909, the Ottoman Parliament left its site close to St. Sophia and moved into the palace, where it was only able to operate for two months. On 6 January 1910, a fire caused by a short-circuit destroyed almost the entire palace, with the exception of the walls and hammam.

The hammam, which is made of intricately carved marble, is a delightful mixture of Moorish and classic Ottoman styles. The second chamber, at the back, is crowned with a dome whose window, shaped as a twelve-pointed star and surrounded by twelve hexagonal windows, allows a soft white light to filter through. Given that Abdülaziz was sympathetic to the "Bektaşi" Sufi brotherhood, was this intended to serve as a reminder of the stone of submission (*teslim taşı*), which members of the brotherhood wear as a necklace in memory of the twelve imams revered within Shiism and certain Sunni mystical traditions?

The narrow entrance to the second chamber leads us to believe that a gate may have disappeared in the fire, perhaps one similar to that in the hammam of the sultans in the Topkapı Palace. This gate would have allowed the sultan to shut himself away in complete tranquility during his most vulnerable moments, in particular when he was washing his head with soap, with his eyes closed.

The hammam may be hired for dinners or private cocktail parties.

THE CYPRESS IN THE YAHYA EFENDI SUFI SHRINE   **8**

Çırağan Caddesi./2 Yahya Efendi Sokak
• Bus: Yahya Efendi
• Open between morning and evening prayers

> **The cypress where the sheikh met the "Green Man"**

Located on one of the busiest streets in the city, the Yahya Efendi shrine overlooks the Bosphorus and is one of the few Sufi shrines in Istanbul that has managed to preserve its original structure and contemplative ambience. Behind the small marble fountain (named the Hamidiye Fountain after its donor, Sultan Abdülhamid) on the left-hand side of the building, you will find a five-hundred-year-old cypress which commands special respect. It is here, at the foot of this cypress, where the sheikh who founded the shrine is said to have met Hızır (*Khidr* in Arabic), a mythical figure within the Islamic tradition.

Although Hızır is not mentioned in the Koran, it is thought that he is referred to in verse 65 of Sura 18 (the Cave), "[...] a servant from among Our servants to whom we had given mercy from us and had taught him from Us a certain knowledge". Hızır's prophetic status has generally been accepted: he has therefore been granted immortality until the Last Judgement, and is able to aid those in distress, sometimes by disguising himself as another person, often a dervish. Nobody has guessed his true identity as he has not revealed it, and he often subjects individuals to tests. He begs for food and rewards those who answer his request, while punishing those who refuse him.

According to a Hadith, when Hızır sits in a desert, the ground becomes covered with verdant grass when he leaves. The word "Hızır" (Khidr) means "green" and he is accordingly depicted dressed in green. In popular tradition, the faithful must call upon him three times for protection against theft, drowning, tyrants, demons, snakes and scorpions. He is also associated with the figure of Ilyas (Elijah) whom he is believed to have met on 6 May to regenerate nature. That is why this date marks the beginning of summer and the festival of Hıdırellez (Hızır+İlyas).

It is thought that this is the very cypress tree under which Hızır met Sheikh Yahya Efendi (1495-1570), the founder of the shrine run jointly by the Naqshbandi and Qadiri brotherhoods during the Ottoman period, which has served as an ordinary mosque since 1925. The room containing the tombs, located before the main nave of the mosque, houses the sheikh's tomb, as well as those of his family members and the Ottoman dynasty, including Sultana Raziye, daughter of Suleiman the Magnificent and spiritual daughter of Yahya Efendi.

The leafy cemetery surrounding the shrine holds the tombs of important religious dignitaries and also army generals, judges, governors and members of families belonging to the imperial dynasty.

OFFICE OF THE HEADMASTER OF KABATAŞ COLLEGE ❾

Former Feriye Palace - 40 Çırağan Caddesi - 34349 Ortaköy Beşiktaş
• www.kabatasel.com
• Bus: Kabataş Lisesi
• It is sometimes possible to visit on weekdays 9am-5pm by asking permission at the college entrance. Permission is usually granted

Sultan Abdülaziz: suicide or murder?

Visitors who ask permission at the entrance to Kabataş College are sometimes permitted to visit the principal's office. The room occupies a special place in the history of the Ottoman Empire as it was here that Sultan Abdülaziz was discovered dead after being deposed (see opposite). The former students of Kabataş College and neighbouring Galatasaray College relate how during the night, when the north wind (*Poyraz*) was blowing very hard and coming through the cracks in the old buildings, Abdülaziz's ghost would roam through the dormitories in search of his assassins. In the mid-1990s, there was a rumour circulating in one of the hotels in the neighbourhood that a member of staff had been slapped in the middle of the night by an old gentleman wearing an Ottoman uniform and a fez, who then disappeared without a trace.

THE CONTROVERSIAL LAST DAYS OF SULTAN ABDÜLAZIZ

Sultan Abdülaziz was deposed for his allegedly authoritarian rule on 30 May 1876, after initially being imprisoned in the Topkapı Palace, in the apartments of Sultan Selim III, who himself had been dethroned in 1807 and then assassinated in 1808. Of a melancholic disposition, Abdülaziz was devastated by the jail selected for him. Several days later he was transferred to the Feriye Palace (now occupied by Kabataş College), in Ortaköy. On 4 June 1876, he asked the Sultana-Mother for a pair of scissors with which to trim his beard and then shut himself in his room. Groaning was soon heard and the guards decided to break down the door. Abdülaziz was found lying in a pool of blood, with the veins open at the wrists. His corpse was carried to the palace police station (which is now the excellent Feriye Restaurant) and after consultation among the doctors it was decided that the cause of death had been suicide. His successor, Murad V, reigned only for a few months before he was also removed in a coup d'état. Suspecting that his uncle, Abdülaziz, had been the victim of a political assassination, Abdülhamid, the succeeding sultan, created a special court which condemned the accused – the former Grand Vizier Midhat Pasha, two of the sultan's brothers-in-law, various officers and a chamberlain – to death. (These sentences were then commuted to banishment for life.) From that moment on a controversy has obsessed and divided public opinion in Turkey: did Sultan Abdülaziz commit suicide or was he murdered? There is no reason to doubt the scientific accuracy of the medical report. The possibility that someone entered from outside using a ladder may also be excluded: the guards would almost certainly have noticed, especially given that Abdülaziz's room was located on the second floor. However, there are reasons to believe that the special court (convened five years after the event) secured confessions using torture. Other elements also suggest that the sultan was murdered: the cries and wailing of the sultan's concubines had only just been heard when Hüseyin Avni Pasha, the main instigator of the coup d'état, arrived at the scene of the tragedy, already in full dress uniform and with his official boat, whose rowers had been in a state of readiness. The story of how the body was discovered also seems highly suspect. Why, for example, was it deemed necessary to break down the main door to the room, when the small service door leading from the sultan's room to the neighbouring room was available? Moreover, the latter possessed a window that opened directly onto the sultan's room. Finally, both of the sultan's wrists had been cut, despite the fact that when someone cuts their wrists, the tendons are cut along with the veins, so that the hand is paralysed. Over time, the debate acquired political overtones. Abdülhamid, Abdülaziz's successor, was demonised by progressive, secularist and left-wing groups. Conversely, conservatives adopted him as a symbol of traditional wisdom and a martyr to the conspiracies that ruined the empire. Anyone who supports the thesis that he was murdered thus risks being called a reactionary and obscurantist fanatic, while supporters of the suicide thesis risk being branded, among other things, as infidels and traitors.

THE HOLY SPRING OF THE CHURCH OF ST. DEMETRIOS

⑩

52 Kırbaç Sokak
Kuruçeşme
• Blessing from the spring during Sat morning mass approx. 10am-12 noon
• Duration of mass varies depending on time of year
• Bus: Kuruçeşme

> **A spring for healing, marriage and exorcisms**

To reach the underground basin where the waters of the *agiasma* (holy spring) of the Church of St. Demetrios (*Agios Dimitrios Ksirokrinis* in Greek, *Aya Dimitri* in Turkish) flow, the visitor must walk along a long and very damp brick-vaulted Byzantine tunnel studded with centuries-old stalactites. On the walls are rings that must be moved to produce the "apotropaic" sounds which are said to ward off evil and malevolent spirits.

The water from the *agiasma* is said to cure diseases, chase away demons and bring good luck. It is advisable to go to St. Demetrios on a Saturday morning, when crowds of people queue to ask the priest to bless the spring water to heal diseases, bless marriages and carry out exorcisms. The priest then dispenses his services indiscriminately, without regard for religion or confession. The majority of these pilgrims are upper-middle-class Muslims who come down from Ulus and Etiler, residential areas on the hills overlooking the Bosphorus. The ladies who sport the latest fashions in this place of such Byzantine, spiritual origins offer a great spectacle.

During the Ottoman era, the Church of St. Demetrios served as the parish church for the Greek area, which was a sort of summer residence for the Greek aristocracy of the Fener/Phanar district. The original Byzantine church, which dates back to the 15th century, was built on the site of a pagan temple dedicated to Demeter, and perhaps Isis. After falling into ruin, it was rebuilt by Sultan Selim III in 1789, and then underwent numerous renovations.

The Kuruçeşme area of the Bosphorus has been inhabited since ancient times Legend has it that, in antiquity, Medea's laurel was located here, known as Bithias, Kalamos or Amopolos. During the Byzantine period, Simeon Stylites and Daniel the Stylite spent respectively twenty-seven and thirty-three years on top of a column here.

BEYOGLU

KARAITE CEMETERY ①

Avenue Halıcıoğlu Yanyolu caddesi no. 1/1
Çıksalın
• Open from sunrise to sunset
• Bus: Çıksalın (take 54Ç from Taksim or 77Ç from Eminönü)

> *The memory of a forgotten Jewish confession*

As the Karaite synagogue (Kahal ha Kadosh Bene Mikra Mahlul sokak, no. 4 in Hasköy) is no longer open to visitors, the little Karaite cemetery of Çıksalın is the last concrete evidence of a once thriving Jewish community now reduced to a handful of families (see below).

Open from sunrise to sunset, the cemetery is scattered with old tombstones which are completely covered in Hebrew inscriptions. Strangely, these tombs take the form of Ottoman sarcophagi, which is most likely an expression of the historical affinities between the Karaites and Turks.

Examples of these Karaite graves can sometimes be found in Muslim cemeteries (close to the tomb of Hasan Baba, for example – see p. 86). This form is extremely rare in traditional Jewish cemeteries, however .

WHO ARE THE KARAITE JEWS?
Once a flourishing community, the Karaite Jews have now been reduced to a few families. Services are now only held on holidays in the sole Karaite synagogue (Mahlul sokak Street, no. 4, Hasköy), built in 1842 with the authorisation of Sultan Abdülmecid on the site of an older synagogue dating from the Byzantine period (whose wall still exists today). This synagogue was built below ground level as an expression of the faithfulness of the Karaites to Sacred Scripture ("Out of the depths I cry to you, Lord", Psalm 130).
The Karaites represent a little-known Jewish movement considered to be heretical within rabbinical Judaism, since they reject the oral law codified in the Talmud and only observe the written law, the Torah.

Although Karaism came into existence between the 7th and 9th centuries in Baghdad and Cairo, its origins may possibly be found in the ancient anti-rabbinical sects, such as the Sadducees. There were, in any case, earlier movements which rose up against the authority of the rabbinical traditions and advocated a return to the letter of Sacred Scripture. The Karaites, who are sometimes called Bene Mikra ("Sons of Scripture") are, literally, the "readers" of the Hebrew Scriptures. Originating from the same Semitic root, the word qara'a ("read" in Arabic) is related to "Koran".

The role played by Islam in the emergence of Karaism is disputed, but its influence on Karaite philosophy and rituals seems less in doubt: the Karaites, for instance, remove their shoes at the synagogue entrance and prostrate themselves during certain prayers.

Anan ben David (715 – 795), often viewed as the founder of the movement, was rescued from the prisons of Baghdad by his fellow prisoner, Abu Hanifa (699-767), the great Islamic theologian and founder of Hanafism, one of the four schools of Sunni jurisprudence, to which the majority of Turks belong. He was given permission to settle in Jerusalem, where his community prospered until the First Crusade. Karaism subsequently spread throughout Syria and into Egypt and Eastern Europe.

The history of the Karaites appears to parallel that of the Turks themselves: numerous Karaite communities in Russia, the Crimea, Lithuania and Poland are or were Turkish-speaking.

According to some historians, they were, in fact, the descendants of the Khazars, a Turkic people around the northern part of the Caspian Sea, who adopted Judaism as the state religion in the 8th century. We owe the rediscovery of this fascinating history to Arthur Koestler, who considered the Khazars to be "The Thirteenth Tribe" of Israel, the title he gave to his famous book.

Contemporary historians are grateful to Koestler for rescuing the Khazar Empire from the depths of the past, but criticise him for assuming that the entire Khazar population converted to Judaism (likely only the ruling class converted). The Jews of Eastern Europe were therefore unlikely to have been exclusively of Khazar origin, as Koestler claims. However, as far as the Turkish-speaking Karaites in particular are concerned, the hypothesis of Khazar origins is certainly plausible.

The presence of Karaites in Istanbul has been attested since the 12th century by Jewish travellers. At the time when the city was captured by the Turks, a large community was living in Karaköy, which almost certainly gave its name to that area (Karay-Köy: Karaite village). The Karaite synagogue at Karaköy has unfortunately since disappeared.

The period that followed the Turkish conquest saw attempts at reconciliation between the Karaite and mainstream Jewish authorities. The Ottoman government respected the autonomy of the Karaite community, whose institutions were strictly separated from those of the rabbinical Jewish community.

Mixed marriages, for example, were not recognised. Curiously, use of the Greek language persisted among the Karaites after the fall of Byzantium.

⌐ CAFÉ SAFIYE SULTAN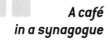

Avenue Hasköy Cad. no. 1
Hasköy
250 metres from Rahmi Koç Museum, in direction of Karaköy
• Open daily 9am to midnight
• Bus: Hasköy

*A café
in a synagogue*

Built at the beginning of the 19th century, the extremely beautiful Esgher (Ezger) Synagogue, which was linked by tunnels to other Jewish institutions in the area, was closed down in the 1940s. Sold to private owners, it was turned successively into a tar depot, a foundry, a vinegar warehouse and then a pottery workshop. Following a meticulous restoration – in which old tiles from Çanakkale and leftover ashlar blocks from Istanbul University (Ottoman Ministry of War

building) were used – the synagogue reopened in 2003 as the Safiye Sultan Café-Restaurant. Out of respect for the sacred nature of the original building no alcohol is served, but it is possible to smoke nargile in a spectacular location full to bursting with old artefacts. In summer, a vast shaded garden is open to patrons.

Unusually, the café is dedicated to Safiye Sultan, alias Sofia Bellicui Baffo (1550-1605), daughter of a patrician Venetian family who was kidnapped by Ottoman corsairs while travelling to meet her father, the governor of the island of Corfu. She was then sold to the palace as a concubine before becoming the wife of Sultan Murad III. Sofia went on to play a significant political role, corresponding with European sovereigns, such as Queen Elizabeth I of England (1558 – 1603).

The choice of the name Safiye Sultan probably came about due to confusion between this sultana and Sultana Nurbanu (1525 – 1583), alias Rachel Maria Nassi, mother of Sultan Murad III, whose Jewish and/or Venetian origins, and also relationship with the Baffo family of Venice, are disputed.

CAMONDO VAULT ③

Hasköy Jewish Cemetery
Avenue Okmeydanı cad. Avenue, no. 20
• May be visited at any time
• Metrobus: Halıcıoğlu

> *The neo-Gothic mausoleum of a Jewish Ottoman family which has left a Parisian legacy*

Contrary to appearances, the small ashlar building on the hillside, to the right of the perimeter road when descending towards the Haliç Bridge, is not a military munitions store. This neo-Gothic structure is, in fact, a family vault located in the middle of the Hasköy Jewish Cemetery, where Count Abraham Salomon de Camondo was buried on 14 April 1873, following his death in Paris on 30 March 1873. Count Abraham was the patriarch of this famous Jewish family whose members were bankers to the upper echelons of the Ottoman bureaucracy and also major patrons. The Camondo eventually settled in Paris at the Hôtel Camondo, built in 1912 on the edge of Parc Monceau. This building is now the magnificent and little-known Musée Nissim de Camondo, which houses a collection of French furniture and works of art from the 18th century. The Camondo family line has since died out.

The Hasköy Jewish Cemetery was largely demolished during the construction of the perimeter roads between the 1950s and 1980s. Left to decay, the Camondo Mausoleum was vandalised and even rented out by an unknown party to tramps as a night shelter. It was not restored until 2010 when measures to protect it were also introduced. Today, the entrance to the building is protected by a thick glass door that allows the sepulchre inside to be seen.

PANGALTI CATHOLIC CEMETERY

Tayyareci Fehmi Sokak Street, 3/1
Pangalti
• Metro: Osmanbey

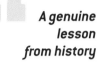

A genuine lesson from history

With its vaults of differing styles (Roman, neo-Gothic, Renaissance, Ottoman), the Catholic cemetery of Istanbul (Pangaltı Fransız Latin Katolik Mezarlığ - "French Latin Catholic") is a real lesson in history. There are inscriptions, often with fanciful spellings, in many different languages (French, Italian, Latin, Armenian and Croat for instance). Catholics of Greek, Syrian, Chaldean, Melkite and Albanian origin can also be found buried here, as well as Poles, Germans, Croats and Czechs. Some of the deceased have Arab first names with Slavic-sounding surnames and grandparents whose names sound Italian or Greek or French.

The cemetery was founded in 1853 by bringing together the bones exhumed from the Christian cemeteries of the Grand Champs des Morts ("Great Field of the Dead") next to the present-day Taksim Square and the Petit Champs des Morts ("Little Field of the Dead"), close to Tepebaşı, as a result of urban developments in these areas, which explains the large number of victims of the great plague epidemics of the beginning of the 19th century. (It is worth remembering that plague bacilli are able to survive for millennia…)

The cemetery then grew rapidly in size to accommodate Catholic soldiers who had died in the Crimean War (1853-1856), including the Italian soldiers (subjects of the Kingdom of Sardinia) now lying in the remarkable pyramidal ossuary. Napoleon III, a great friend of the Ottoman Empire, also had a chapel constructed here.

More human remains arrived during the First World War.

THE BYZANTINE CHAIN IN THE MILITARY MUSEUM

⑤

Harbiye Askeri Müzesi
Avenue Valikonağı Cad.
Harbiye
• Visiting: 9am-5pm, except Mon and Tues
• Metro: Osmanbey

The chain that blocked entry to the Golden Horn

The enormous pile of scrap metal which fills an entire hall of the Military Museum is just one section of the chain used to block the entrance to the Golden Horn in 1453 in an effort to prevent the Ottoman fleet from entering. Forged by the Genoese engineer Bartolomeo Soligo, the chain was stretched out and floated on wooden buoys between the Tower of Eugenius, in present-day Sirkeci, and the Kastellion Tower, whose cellars became an underground mosque (Yeraltı Camii) in the 18th century.

The chain consists of rings shaped like flattened figures of eight, S's with closed ends, or flattened circles, each weighing 10 to 20 kilos and measuring more than 50 cm in length. The ends are capped with pincers which were attached to a giant ring affixed to each tower. This section of chain is so well preserved because of a layer of black patina formed by metallic oxidation.

Installed in April 1453, the chain functioned as intended: it succeeded in preventing the Ottoman fleet from bombarding the sea walls facing the Golden Horn.

In order to bypass the chain, Sultan Mehmed the Conqueror was forced to

come up with an alternate route; on the night of 21-22 April, 67 ships were hauled over boards coated with tallow from Tophane up to the heights of Pera/Beyoğlu and down to the Golden Horn at Kasımpaşa. The sultan was inspired by his true passion, ancient history, which recounted similar subterfuges undertaken by Hannibal in the Gulf of Taranto and the Emperor Augustus on the Isthmus of Corinth.

In a manner reminiscent of the film *Fitzcarraldo*, the sultan transported his whole fleet over a significant stretch of high ground. When the city finally fell on 29 May, Alvise Diedo, commander of the Venetian auxiliary fleet stationed in the Golden Horn, broke the chain to allow his ships to flee in the opposite direction.

Further sections of the chain are housed in the Beşiktaş Naval Museum, the Archaeological Museum and the fortress at Rumelihisarı (see p. 261). The total length of the four pieces is 115 m.

PLAQUE IN HONOUR OF BASIL ZAHAROFF ❻

Kurtuluş Sports Club Iraklis ("Hercules")
Ateş Böceği sok. Street
Kurtuluş
• Metro: Osmanbey or Taksim

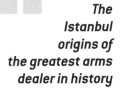

I nside the head office of the sports club in the old Greek neighbourhood of Tatavla (Kurtuluş), several items recall the life of Sir Basil Zaharoff, the greatest, and undoubtedly the most mysterious, arms trafficker in history. Thus we find portraits and inscriptions (in particular, above the basketball hoop in the main sports hall) which serve as reminders that Zaharoff was one of the club's major sponsors.

The Istanbul origins of the greatest arms dealer in history

Official biographies tell us that Vasilios Zacharias, alias Zaharoff, was born in 1849 in Muğla (Turkey). However, during the course of testimony given in a London trial, the young Zaharoff confirmed that he had been born in Tatavla (Greek name for the Kurtuluş area in Istanbul) and that the information regarding his birth in Muğla came from a statement made by an Orthodox priest with memory problems. Zaharoff therefore had good reason to express his gratitude towards the institutions in his childhood neighbourhood.

BASIL ZAHAROFF IN *THE BROKEN EAR* TINTIN ADVENTURE

Basil Zaharoff has inspired several fictional heroes, including the arms trafficker Basil Bazaroff who appears in *The Broken Ear*, a Tintin adventure. Bazaroff, whom Hergé portrays with the same characteristics as Zaharoff, fosters disagreement between the Republic of San Theodoros, ruled by General Alcazar, and the neighbouring state in order to sell identical weapons to both South American countries. It is interesting to note that the first edition of *The Broken Ear* appeared in black and white in 1937, one year after Zaharoff's death.

For more information about Basil Zaharoff, see following double-page spread.

BASIL ZAHAROFF: "A MAGNIFICENT ADVENTURER, SECRET KING OF EUROPE"

The great polyglot Vasilios Zacharias, alias Zaharoff, started earning money working as a tourist guide in Istanbul. However, instead of taking his clients on visits to the historical monuments, he led them straight to the brothels of Galata. Unable to compete with the career sex traffickers, he moved on to the badly-paid career of fireman before becoming a broker, exchanging fake money to tourists. His fraudulent transactions forced him to flee to London, and then to Athens, which paved the way to his fortune.

At the age of 24, he met a Swedish captain who gave him a position as a representative for Thorsten Nordenfelt, an arms manufacturing company. Zacharias soon took advantage of the age-old antagonisms and expansionist goals of the Balkan states to become rich by selling arms simultaneously to both sides of a conflict.

The success of this method depended solely on the seller's discretion, a quality which Zaharoff had in abundance. In Athens, Zacharias also changed his name to Zaharoff, inspired no doubt by his parents' extended residence in Odessa during the tumult of the Greek Revolution.

While in Greece he began to sell the first submarine capable of firing torpedoes when submerged. Denouncing the Greek threat, he subsequently sold two of these vessels to the Ottoman navy, which he would later also present as a genuine danger in the Black Sea, in order to sell two more to Russia.

After organising the alliance between Nordenfelt and the famous Maxim machine guns, Zaharoff left the former for the latter when the agreement ended in 1886. Maxim then entered into partnership with Vickers, whose board of directors welcomed Zaharoff in 1911.

Following the Japanese victory over Russia in 1905, Zaharoff reorganised the Russian arms industry. Meanwhile, Vickers had begun to manipulate the European newspapers with a view to exposing the danger which the various neighbours represented towards one another.

Zaharoff's experience proved to be excellent preparation for the First World War, during which his investments extended to the banking sector and press. Vickers made a fortune by selling arms to England and France. In order to perpetuate his influence, Zaharoff knew that he had to find favour with politicians.

Thus, he established a retirement home for French seamen, a chair in aerodynamics at the Sorbonne and made significant donations to war widows, which earned him French Legion of Honour membership and the rank of officer and commander. In time Zaharoff became good friends with Lloyd George, Clemenceau and Aristide Briand. A marble plaque at the entrance to the Sorbonne, in Paris, pays tribute to this benefactor.

Zaharoff's most significant conspiracy during the war – he attempted to push Greece into entering the war on the Allied side – had dramatic consequences both for the country of his birth and his first adopted country. Since King Constantine was against such an action, Zaharoff participated in the plot that led to the former's deposition in 1917.

Greece, now led by Prime Minister Venizelos, joined the Allies in the Great War. In 1919, at the instigation of Zaharoff, Venizelos invaded the eastern part of Anatolia. The king returned to power in 1920, but Zaharoff did his best to convince him to launch a new offensive.

The subsequent Greek invasion led to the emergence of the Kemalist movement in Ankara, which successfully repelled the Greek forces in 1922. What the Greeks call the "Asia Minor Catastrophe" and the Turks the "War of Independence" marked the end of Anatolian Hellenism and the birth of a new state: Turkey. Would it be an exaggeration to say that Zaharoff contributed to its creation?

At the end of the war, Zaharoff was knighted. He was now known as "Sir Basil Zaharoff" and began to invest in sectors just as lucrative as arms dealing: casinos and oil.

Zaharoff also had a romantic side which survived the vicissitudes of his professional life. In 1924, at the age of 75, Zaharoff married Maria del Pilar, Duchess of Villafranca de Los Caballeros, who was close to the Spanish royal family.

Zaharoff had fallen in love with the duchess in 1886 on board the Orient Express and waited decades (until the death of her first husband in a mental hospital) to marry the love of his life.

On 27 November 1936, Zacharias Basileios Zaharopoulos, alias Sir Basil Zaharoff, died at the Hôtel de Paris in Monte Carlo, at the age of 87.

SAINT MARY CHURCH OF THE SYRIAC ORTHODOX ❼

Karakurum Sok. Street, no. 10 - Tarlabaşı Beyoğlu
• Tel: 0212 238 54 70
• Mass: Sun 9.00am—10.30am in summer and 9.00am—11.00am in winter
• Metro: Taksim or Şişhane

A mass held in the "language of Christi"

Although the Saint Mary Church of the Syriac Orthodox (Süryani Kadim Meryemana Kilisesi) – the spiritual centre of the Syriac community in Istanbul – does not hold any particular historical interest, it does provide a rare opportunity: once a week, mass is held here in Aramaic, a Semitic language that was widely spoken in the Middle East in antiquity and which was also the language of Jesus of Nazareth (Hebrew being restricted to liturgical use).

Inside the church, take note of the altar curtain covering the iconostasis, which is typical of Syriac art. Finished in a naive style, it depicts the crucifixion along with its trappings, including the cock (which testified to the treason of St. Peter, a rarity in eastern churches).

Although its orgins go back to 1844, the present building dates from 1963. The ashlar stone chiselled by the Syriac masons, which cover the building façade, are a gift from one "of our brother Muslims from Mardin" (a town in southeast Turkey).

WHAT HAS BECOME OF THE ARAMAIC LANGUAGE?

Aramaic is the historic language of the Arameans, an ancient people of the Near and Middle East whose name comes from Aram, an ancient region in the centre of modern-day Syria. In the 8th century B.C., Aramean was spoken widely from Egypt to Asia Major (as far as Pakistan) and Aramaic was the main language of the Assyrian, Babylonian and later Chaldean Empires as well as that of the imperial government of Mesopotamia. In the 6th century B.C., Aramaic was also the administrative language of the Persian Empire. Aramaic was also used widely throughout Israel, supplanting Hebrew as the most widely spoken language between 721 and 500 B.C. Jesus would have spoken what we now describe as Western Aramaic, the dialect of the Jews at that time. From the 3rd century B.C. until the 7th century A.D., Aramaic was the principal written language of the Near East. Over time Aramaic developed into numerous dialects and is still spoken today by its current heirs (about 400,000 people), known as Syriacs (and also sometimes called Assyrians, Chaldeans or Assyro-Chaldeans), in forms which are relatively close to the original.

There are three main variants in existence today:

Western Aramaic (mainly in the Anti-Lebanon, Lebanese-Syrian border)

Eastern Aramaic (mainly in the north of Iraq and Caucasus)

Central Aramaic (mainly in the Turkish region of Tur Abdin, in the south-east of the country – about 25,000 speakers)

For more information, see the excellent work by Sébastien de Courtois, *Les derniers Araméens, le peuple oublié de Jésus*.

THE FORGOTTEN STATUES OF GENERALS FRUNZE AND VOROSHILOV ❽

Taksim Square
• Metro: Taksim

The Soviet generals who helped to create Turkey

Unveiled in 1928 in the centre of Taksim Square, the Republic Monument represents the birth of the young Turkish Republic. The northern façade depicts the founders of the republic in military uniform, at the time of the War of Independence. The southern façade depicts them in civilian clothes, heralding a new political era.

On the southern façade, behind Atatürk, there are two forgotten figures: Mikhail Vasilyevich Frunze, an outstanding figure of the Bolshevik Revolution, and Kliment Yefremovich Voroshilov, who defended Leningrad against the Nazi invaders.

Lenin had sent Frunze to Ankara as a special ambassador. In his speeches, he showed strong support for the Turkish nationalist movement during the War of Independence (1920 – 22) and visited the Sakarya front.

Voroshilov, for his part, was sent specifically as a military advisor to the Turkish army. The advice offered by Frunze and Voroshilov had an undoubted influence on Turkish strategy, to the extent that the Battle of Sakarya seemed to have been inspired by the "scorched earth" policy beloved of Peter the Great, and used against Napoleon and Hitler. It consisted, in brief, of allowing the enemy to advance as far as possible, separating it from its base and destroying its supply sources. Thus weakened and cut off from its main forces, the enemy would be forced to withdraw.

The Soviet government, which supported the Turkish cause as an anti-imperialist struggle, offered vital economic and military support. The very first documentary films on the Turkish War of Independence were even shot on Soviet cameras.

Turko-Soviet relations nevertheless deteriorated rapidly, in particular due to the methods used by Frunze to suppress the revolts of the Turkic peoples in Central Asia. The two Soviet generals of Taksim were thus forgotten and only "rediscovered" after the fall of the Berlin Wall.

Although the plinth and layout of the surroundings are the work of the Italian architect Giulio Mongeri, the statues were created by another Italian, the sculptor Pietro Canonica.

TOMB OF HAGOP IV

9

Üç Horan Armenian Church
Fish market (Balıkpazarı)
Sahne Sokak Street, no. 24
Galatasaray
• Metro: Taksim or Şişhane

An Armenian saint venerated by the Ottoman army

In the courtyard of the Armenian Church of the Holy Trinity (Üç Horan /Yerrortutyun), an unusual miniature church made of metal bars draws the attention.

This remarkable tomb contains the remains of Hagop IV, Patriarch of Etchmiadzin (spiritual capital of Armenia), an Armenian saint who was surprisingly venerated by the Ottoman army.

Born in Chouha in 1598, Hagop was renowned for his kindness and piety. Enthroned as Patriarch of Etchmiadzin in 1655, in 1680 he journeyed to Istanbul, where he died at the age of 82.

He was buried in the Armenian cemetery of Pangalti, far away from his current tomb. According to legend, the Ottoman soldiers in the barracks to the east of the cemetery noticed one night that a beam of light was

shining miraculously from the sky onto the patriarch's tomb. An oil lamp was then placed on Hagop's tomb and refilled regularly by the Taksim barracks, in keeping with a tradition that would continue until the latter was demolished in the 1940s, when the area was urbanized. Hagop's remains were then transported to the courtyard of the Üç Horan Church, where they were buried in a marble sarcophagus bearing his episcopal crown and patriarchal sceptre. Every Tuesday after mass, Hagop's tomb, nicknamed "Spiritual Father", is visited by both Christians and Muslims (a regular practice in Istanbul), who recite prayers for healing beside it.

NEARBY

THE PLAQUE OF THE CONSTITUTION HAMMAM
Rue Gölbaşı Sokak Street no. 80
- Women: morning and early afternoon
- Men: late afternoon and early evening
- Taxi recommended (area not always safe)

Anybody able to read Ottoman Turkish, Greek and Armenian will notice that Freedom Hammam (Hürriyet Hamamı) has one special characteristic: on its façade, we find its old name written in three languages and in three different alphabets: Ottoman Turkish, Greek and Armenian. All three inscriptions refer to the same building: the Constitution Hammam, or *Paghnik Sahmanatragan* in Armenian and Ο λουτρος του συνταγματος (O loutros tou syntagmatos) in Greek; and Constitutional Monarchy Hammam, or *Meşrutiyet Hamamı* in Ottoman. Built by the Armenian Levon Aga Kapoyan, the hammam was opened in 1908, the same year in which Sultan Abdülhamid established a constitutional monarchy due to pressure from the Young Turks. In reality, this was a reinstatement of the constitution, suspended since 1878. The hammam was reopened following a fire in 1923, the year in which the Turkish Republic was proclaimed. It was then renamed Freedom Hammam, a name it continues to bear proudly today.

MARIA CALLAS' PIANO ⑩

Pera Museum
Meşrutiyet Caddesi No.65 Tepebaşı
Beyoğlu
• Tel: + 90 212 334 99 00 • info@peramuzesi.org.tr
• Open Tuesday-Saturday: 10am-7pm; Sunday: 12-6pm. Closed Monday
• Metro: Şişhane

The wanderings of La Callas' piano

The Pera Museum holds a piano that is said to have belonged to Maria Callas. Its acquisition by the museum is the result of an incredible combination of circumstances. Sometime during the 1990s, İnan Kıraç, the future founder of the museum, was hosting friends for dinner, including the lawyer and novelist Yiğit Okur and Mordo Dinar (1918-2004), lawyer, famous music lover, musical patron and Chilean Honorary Consul over several decades. The latter declared that he was in possession of a piano that was reputed to have belonged to Maria Callas and Elvira de Hidalgo. Constructed in New York, the piano initially crossed the Atlantic in 1940, during the war, to be unloaded at Piraeus and then Athens, where it awaited its owner, the very young Anna Maria Cecilia Sofia Kalogeropoulos (1923-1977) who would become the celebrated Maria Callas. At the Athens Conservatory, Callas attended courses given by the Opera's prima donna, Elvira de Hidalgo (1891-1980). After the war, Callas returned to New York, her birthplace, but left her piano with Elvira de Hidalgo as a token of her gratitude.

In 1949, Hidalgo arrived in Istanbul with Callas' piano. She had been invited by Carl Ebert of the Ankara Opera, where she also taught at the conservatory until 1954. On her departure for the Milan Conservatory, she was unable to take the Callas piano and entrusted it to her friend, Mordo Dinar, who kept it in his apartment until he grew tired of maintaining it, at which point he sold it. One evening though, he saw by chance a recording of Callas on television and was gripped by guilt. After a sleepless night, he went to the piano purchaser and bought it back for double the price.

Yiğit Okur, who listened to the piano's story with wonder, used it as the inspiration for his 2003 novel *The Piano*, which became a commercial success and made the Callas piano famous in Turkey. Following Dinar's death in 2004, his daughter, who lived in Madrid, contacted İnan Kıraç and asked if he'd be willing to take the piano. When he asked for her selling price, she answered that a glass of raki and the taste of some fresh fish eaten beside the Bosphorus on her next visit to Istanbul would be enough, provided the piano was well taken care of. Kıraç offered a significantly more generous sum and the piano was subsequently moved to the Pera Museum.

Some have argued that Callas did not have the money to purchase a piano when she was studying in Athens and that it was, in fact, Elvira de Hidalgo who first bought it.

THE ATATÜRK CARPET

Atatürk Museum in the Pera Palace
Meşrutiyet cad. no. 52
Tepebaşı Beyoğlu
• Museum open 10am—11am and 3pm—4pm
• Metro: Şişhane

*A carpet
that foretold
the death of Atatürk*

After the First World War, Mustafa Kemal rarely stayed with his mother, who lived at Akaretler/Beşiktaş, since the apartment was under surveillance by the Allied occupation forces who suspected this young Ottoman army general of scheming against their interests, suspicions which were entirely correct.

The future founder of the Turkish Republic thus often stayed in room 101 at the Pera Palace where he met his friends to assess the political situation. In 1981, on the occasion of Atatürk's 100th birthday, the room was transformed into a museum in which 37 of his personal effects were put on display, including: binoculars for military exercises, glasses, toothbrush and toothpaste, crockery, a clothes brush, tea and coffee cups, spurs, suits, branded underwear, hats, pyjamas and slippers. The most interesting and enigmatic of these objects is a prayer mat (*seccade*) made of silk and embroidered with gold thread, which was given to Atatürk by an unknown maharaja.

In 1929, an Indian prince presented himself to the Secretariat of the Presidential Office of the Republic to request an audience with Atatürk, a request which was granted immediately. Though the purpose of their meeting and the identity of the maharaja is still a mystery today, we do know that when he took his leave, the maharaja gave Atatürk a prayer mat woven in India as a present. This mat was then was then sent to room 101 at the Pera Palace, where Atatürk still stayed on occasion.

No attention was paid to the mat until 1938, the year in which Atatürk died. It was then noticed that the design on the mat depicted a clock 20 centimetres in diameter showing the time as 9.07am. The time shown is unsettling, in fact, since Atatürk died on 10 November 1938, at 9.05am. The surprise does not stop there: the design also depicted ten chrysanthemums. Given that "chrysanthemum" is *kasımpatı* in Turkish and that the month of November is called *K ısım*, we might begin to wonder whether the mat predicted the time of Atatürk's death in coded fashion.

COULD THE SECRET OF AGATHA CHRISTIE'S ELEVEN MISSING DAYS BE IN THE PERA PALACE?

Agatha Christie stayed in the Pera Palace in 1924 and 1933, and it was here that the famous writer is said to have written *Murder on the Orient Express*.

Between these dates, in a mystery worthy of one of her novels, Agatha Christie disappeared on 3 December 1926. Her car was found the next day at Newlands Corner, by a chalk pit near Guildford, along with her coat and driving licence. The surrounding area was searched thoroughly by 15,000 volunteers and several aircraft. In an attempt to locate the missing novelist, Sir Arthur Conan Doyle, author of the Sherlock Holmes series, worked with a medium to whom he gave Christie's gloves. The latter was found ten days later in a hotel in Yorkshire, which she had booked into under the name Mrs Teresa Neele (her husband's mistress). She showed signs of amnesia, although some people continue to believe that she was faking this condition. Although her autobiography passes over these eleven days in silence, a note discovered among her papers after her death in 1976 states that, "the key to the mystery of my disappearance is located in my room in the Pera Palace in Istanbul".

After her death, Warner Bros wished to make a film about the eleven days of Agatha Christie's disappearance in which Vanessa Redgrave would play the role of the writer, and Dustin Hoffman that of an American reporter on her trail. In order to find out information that could not be obtained by traditional means, they called upon the services of a famous Los Angeles medium named Tara Rand. Mrs Rand then entered into communication with the spirit of Agatha Christie who revealed to her that, "the secret of those eleven missing days was hidden in room 411 at the Pera Palace in Istanbul".

In 1979, during a spiritualist seance broadcast live on American TV, Mrs Rand even dictated, by telephone, the steps to be taken in room 411. A rusty key 8 centimetres in size was thus discovered hidden between the wooden floorboards and the concrete beneath. The medium announced that this key would provide access to Agatha Christie's diary, in which the writer discussed the eleven missing days. The matter then became even more complicated: the hotel manager wished to sell the key to Warner Bros, but the sum he was asking for was so exorbitant (he was hoping for enough money to pay for the hotel's desperately needed restoration) that the producers refused. The medium then gave a message from Agatha Christie stating that the mystery would not be elucidated until the medium held the key in her hand. In August 1979, the representatives of Warner Bros held a press conference in room 411 to announce that the mystery had been solved. Ultimately though, the project was abandoned more for political rather than medium-related reasons. At this time the employees of the Pera Palace embarked on a strike that became prolonged during the period of troubles preceding the coup d'état of September 1980. To complicate matters, a second key was discovered in 1986 in room 511, next door to room 411.

The first key is now held for safe keeping in a bank.

SOCIETÀ OPERAIÀ

Deva Çıkmazı (Deva cul-de-sac) nos. 2-5
Avenue Istiklal
Beyoğlu
• Tel: 0212 293 98 48
• www.iicistanbul.esteri.it • Email: iicistanbul@esteri.it
• Open weekdays 9am—5pm
• Tram: Odakule stop
• The society also has another main office: Hayriye cad. no. 12,
in Galatasaray

> *An old
> mutual
> aid society
> founded
> by Garibaldi,
> exiled in Istanbul*

Founded in 1863 by 41 Italian refugees under the aegis of Giuseppe Garibaldi, the Società Operaià di Mutuo Soccorso ("Workers' Mutual Aid Society"), with its marble bust of Garibaldi, has become a meeting place for the Italian-speaking and Italophile community of Istanbul.

Many Italians, mostly workers, took refuge and settled in Istanbul after the revolutionary events of 1848 in Italy.

Faced with the political radicalism of this group, which brought together revolutionary conspirators, the sultan showed complete indifference and perhaps even quiet complicity.

By making life difficult for the Austro-Hungarian Empire, the Italian nationalists were indirectly serving the interests of the Ottoman Empire.

The Turkish public accepted this new institution without difficulty, almost certainly mistaking it for a charitable religious organisation, without taking too much notice of its socialist and Garibaldian aims.

Although the Società Operaià had a strong ideological orientation (Mazzini, Garibaldi's companion in exile, was offered the honorary presidency of the society), it still functioned as a support institution that undertook charitable works, such as promoting the creation of an Italian primary school in 1901. The members' registers, society archives and book collection remain accessible in beautiful old bookcases.

THE PLAQUE OF THE CHURCH OF ST. MARY DRAPERIS

⓭

Avenue Istiklal caddesi, no. 215
• Italian mass Mon – Fri 8am, Sun 9am, 11.30am and Spanish Sun 5pm and 6.30pm
• Metro: Şişhane, Istiklal Caddesi exit

E rected in 1904 by the Italian architect Guiglielmo Semprini, the Church of St. Mary Draperis was built with the active support of Sultan Abdülhamid and the then mayor of Istanbul, Ridvan Pasha. In order to ensure the loyalty of the different minorities

> *A Catholic church indebted to an Islamic caliph*

within the empire, Abdülhamid regularly showed favouritism towards individual communities, as circumstances required.

Above the right side door, among the three doors leading to Avenue Istiklal, an inscription on the frontispiece serves as a reminder of this support which now seems sadly anachronistic.

The church owes its name to its very first benefactress, Clara Bratola Draperis, who donated a plot of land to the Franciscans in the 16th century, in the Galata/Tophane area. After a fire, the church was moved to its current site, where it suffered further fires and was subsequently restored and rebuilt. The icon of the Virgin adorning the main altar was entirely unaffected by the fire damage.

St. Mary Draperis is still occupied by the Franciscans, whose symbol sits above the central door, next to the inscription of gratitude.

THE ROOD SCREEN PORTRAITS OF THE CRIMEAN CHURCH

Crimean Memorial Church or Christ's Church
Serdar Ekrem Sokak Street, no.52
• Two masses daily at 9.00am and 6.00pm (except Sun: 10.00am).
• Metro: Şişhane, İstiklal Caddesi exit

> *Remarkable anachronistic icons*

Built in a neo-Gothic style between 1858 and 1868 to commemorate the English soldiers killed during the Crimean War (1853 – 1856), the Crimean Church, also known as the Crimean Memorial Church or Christ's Church, is the work of the architects William Burges and George Edmund Street (the latter is known for having built the Royal Courts of Justice in London).

Originally designed to display portraits of the British officers killed during the Gallipoli Campaign in 1915, the church's rood screen has been decorated with remarkable and anachronistic icons by the Scottish painter Mungo McCosh since 2005. In these icons, we find: Moses depicted with the features of one of the painter's Jewish friends and wearing a checked waterproof; a Sri Lankan St. Thomas (shown opposite), although this may be a way of commemorating his role in evangelising southern India; the Emperor Constantine and his mother St. Helena depicted with the features of current parishioners; and St. Joseph wearing the typical costume of a Turkish shepherd.

This pleasant procession of saints and Christian patriarchs is also set against the silhouette of the Islamic Historic Peninsula with its minarets and mosques, as a reminder that religions need not be hostile to one another. It was, after all, Sultan Abdulmedjid (1823 – 1861) who supplied this site (formerly a Greek cemetery) to the thriving British colony of Galata which lacked a local church.

Surrounded by a beautiful garden, the church was closed for worship in 1979, then restored and reopened in the middle of the 1990s on the initiative of Sri Lankan refugees who have since turned it into the largest centre for Protestant worship in Istanbul.

THE COLUMNS OF THE KILIÇ ALI PASHA MOSQUE ⓯

Avenue Necati Bey Caddesi
Kemankeş area
• Tramway: Tophane

Columns that warn of earthquakes

At the entrance of the Kılıç Ali Pasha Mosque, two narrow columns were placed at the corners of the walls by the architect Sinan. Although the columns appear at first sight to be entirely classical, in reality they have one extraordinary feature: in the event of a landslide or earthquake, the columns begin turning on their axis, thus indicating to the worshippers that they must end their prayers and leave the building. Indeed, the ground on which the Kılıç Ali Pasha Mosque was built is highly unstable since it was reclaimed from the sea.

The mosque was built in 1580 for the Ottoman admiral Ali Pasha (1519 – 1587), alias Giovanni Dionigi Galeni, a Calabrian who, after converting to Islam, made his career in the Ottoman navy. After becoming Grand Admiral of the fleet, he decided that he would build a mosque in the manner of any Ottoman dignitary wishing to be remembered by posterity. On expressing his desire to build a mosque, Kılıç Ali Pasha was told that as commander of the fleet, he would only be allowed to construct it on the sea, which was perhaps a discreet way of suggesting to him that an old pirate like him was not under any obligation to erect a mosque. Taking the advice literally, Kılıç Ali ordered the bay to be filled in and invited the architect Sinan to begin the works.

There are also columns designed to warn worshippers of earthquakes at the Şemsi Pasha Mosque, which is also built on unstable ground at the edge of the sea. Unfortunately, this system no longer works due to changes made to the structure of the mosque over the centuries.

KILIÇ ALI: AN ITALIAN SAILOR CAPTURED BY PIRATES WHO BECAME ADMIRAL OF THE OTTOMAN FLEET

The son of a poor sailor, Kılıç Ali or Uluç ali (known as Occhiali by the Europeans) was born in 1519 at Le Castella, near present-day Isola Capo Rizzuto in Calabria. Originally destined for the priesthood, he was taken prisoner by the corsairs of Hayreddin Barbarossa and served on the galleys. After several years of captivity, he converted to Islam and joined the Ottoman pirates. He enjoyed rapid success and became the intrepid leader (*rais*) of the Barbary Coast. He joined forces with the famous Dragut, Bey of Tripoli, and finally came to the attention of Piyale Paşa, admiral of the Ottoman fleet, who then gained the support of Kılıç Ali's ships during naval expeditions. In 1550 Kılıç Ali received official responsibility for the Aegean island of Samos and became Governor of Alexandria in 1565. In the same year, he participated in the Siege of Malta, in which Dragut died. Kılıç was appointed Bey of Tripoli to replace him. From this maritime base, he undertook numerous raids on the Sicilian coast, Naples and his native Calabria. In 1568, he was appointed Governor of Algiers, a province that became progressively more independent. In 1571, he commanded the left flank of the Ottoman fleet at the Battle of Lepanto, which marked the decline of Turkish naval power. During the rout, Kılıç Ali not only succeeded in gathering and evacuating eighty-seven Ottoman ships but also seized the flagship of the Knights of Malta and took their banner as war booty, which he then offered to the sultan. He was now known as "Kapudan Pasha" (commander of the Ottoman fleet). He continued his expeditions on the Italian coast, recaptured the Tunisian ports which had fallen to the Spanish and constructed a fort on the Moroccan coast opposite Spain. Kılıç Ali Pasha died in 1587 and was buried in a mausoleum situated in the courtyard of the mosque that he had erected at Tophane, Constantinople (see opposite).

DID CERVANTES PARTICIPATE IN THE BUILDING OF THE KILIÇ ALI PASHA MOSQUE?

Cervantes was taken prisoner on 26 September 1575, off the coast of Catalonia, by Algerian corsairs commanded by a renegade Albanian. He spent five years in captivity in Algiers, until a ransom was paid by his parents and the Trinitarian Order, which specialised in the redeeming of captives. This period of his life supplied the literary content for chapter XXXIX of *Don Quixote de la Mancha* (in which Kılıç, or Uluç, Ali Pasha is called "Uchali") and two plays whose action is set in Algiers: *El Trato de Argel* and *Los Baños de Argel*. Cervantes' period of captivity coincides curiously with the building of the mosque and opens the possibility that the captives in Algiers were in fact sent to Istanbul (all the more likely given that Kılıç Ali Pasha had been Governor of Algiers) in order to assist in building the mosque, leading some specialists to claim that Cervantes participated in the construction work as a prisoner of war.

THE SIGN OF THE CHURCH OF OUR LADY OF CAFFA

16

Church of Our Lady of Caffa (Panaghia Cafatiani)
Ali Paşa Değirmeni Sokak Street, no. 2
Kemankeş Mustafa Paşa Mahallesi area
Karaköy
• Tram: Karaköy or Tophane

The Autocephalus Turkish Orthodox Patriarchate: an endangered church

Although the last three remaining churches of the Autocephalus Turkish Orthodox Patriarchate in Karaköy (see opposite) have not held religious services since 2008, the façade of the Our Lady of Caffa church still bears the signs of its unusual status. Visible to the left of the entrance are the unusual coats of arms of the patriarchate: a red cross against a white background (Christian) and an Islamic star and crescent (the Turkish flag) in the top left corner.

The church, which was originally a Greek Orthodox church, was taken over by the Autocephalus Turkish Orthodox Patriarchate in 1924. In 1965, the devotees of this church occupied two other Greek Orthodox churches, also in Galata: Aghios Nicolaos (Saint-Nicolas or Aya Nikola in Turkish, Hoca Tahsin Sokak Street, no. 8) and Aghios Ioannis Prodromos (St John the Baptist or Aya Yani or Aziz Yahya in Turkish, Vekilharç Sokak Street, no. 15). Both of these churches remain under the authority of the Autocephalus Turkish Orthodox Patriarchate. The first is closed and the second is now rented out to Syriac Christians who celebrate their Aramaic mass there (see p. 170).

WHAT IS THE AUTOCEPHALUS TURKISH ORTHODOX PATRIARCHATE?

During the Turkish War of Independence (1921 – 1922) between the Kemalist government in Ankara and the occupying Greek forces, the Ankara government created an independent Turkish Patriarchate in order to reduce the influence of the Ecumenical Patriarchate of Constantinople, which it viewed as being in the pay of the Greek government. Since Asia Minor had a population of approximately 1.5 million Greek Orthodox at that time, including about 400,000 Turkish-speakers, the issue was very important. At the head of this new patriarchate, Ankara placed a Greek Orthodox pope who spoke Karamanlı (a Greco-Turkish dialect), Pavlos Karahisarithis, who took the name Eftim I. During the negotiations that led to the Treaty of Lausanne in 1923, the Turkish government used the newly-created Turkish Orthodox Church to demonstrate that the Ecumenical Patriarchate of Constantinople was no longer necessary and could therefore be transferred to Greece. The Orthodox of Turkish nationality now had their own national patriarchate, on the model of the Bularian and Serbian Orthodox, who have their own churches. Convinced by the Allies' promise that the Greek Patriarchate "would no longer become involved in any way in political matters and would confine itself to matters of a religious nature", the Turkish government finally consented to the continued presence of the Ecumenical (Greek) Patriarchate in Istanbul. The very existence of the Turkish national patriarchate thus lost all meaning. An almost fatal blow was then administered by the Convention Concerning the Exchange of Populations (based on religious affiliation), which had been signed in Lausanne in 1923. The Orthodox in Turkey (with the exception of those in Istanbul and the islands of Tenedos and Imbros) were obliged to leave Turkish territory for Greece (whose language they did not speak), and the Greek-speaking Muslims of Greece emigrated to Turkey. The population exchange brought an end to the Orthodox presence in Anatolia and dealt a fatal blow to this new church by removing its only potential source of members. By special permission of Atatürk, the Eftim family was permitted to remain in Istanbul, however. Eftim supplied a list of sixty-five people who settled with him, was given several buildings that had been abandoned by the Greeks who had moved to Greece, and finally attempted to secure the title of Ecumenical Patriarch by occupying the Greek patriarchal seat for seventeen days in 1923. In order to obtain a place of worship for his church, he also occupied the Greek Orthodox church Panaghia Cafatiani (Our Lady of Caffa, built originally in 1475 by Greek émigrés from Caffa in the Crimea) in the Galata area, which remains under their control to this day. As a survival measure, the Turkish national church, now reduced to a handful of families, began to allow its bishops and Patriarch to marry. When Eftim I died, he was replaced by his son, Eftim II.

RUSSIAN CHAPEL OF ST. ANDREW ⑰

Mumhane Cad., no. 39
Karaköy (Galata)
• Open Sun (mass 10am—12 noon) and Russian Orthodox holidays
• Tram: Karaköy

" *A Russian chapel on the roof*

In Karaköy, if you look up at the beautiful buildings you will see roof chapels built in typical 19th-century Russian style, the most famous being the Saint Andrew Chapel, located on top of the Aya Andrea Han, an old hospice dedicated to the saint.

After climbing the steep stairs of the building up to the 5th floor, you will enter a space that is not just a sanctuary but a remnant of 19th-century Russia, with magnificent frescoes covering every wall and life-size depictions of the saints of the Orthodox Church, including St. John of Damascus, who is shown in Arab dress in keeping with his origins.

The mass is full of worshippers. These are mostly Russians who have arrived recently to find work in Istanbul, but there are also several descendants of the émigrés who fled the Revolution of 1917 and Russians from Kars, a town in

eastern Turkey which was under Russian occupation from 1878 to 1917.

The chapel also serves as a meeting place for the Russian community and plays a role in the religious education of children, distributing prayer books and icons. The walls of the small meeting room, which is also used as a refectory, are covered in numerous photos illustrating the history of the institution.

The Church of St. Andrew is dependent on the Monastery of Vatopedi on Mont Athos.

TWO MORE RUSSIAN ROOF CHAPELS

There are two more Russian roof chapels located in the Karaköy area: St. Pantaleimon, located nearby (Hoca Tahsin Sokak Street, no. 19, Sun mass at 10am) and the now abandoned St. Elias (Aya Iliya, Karanlık Fırın Sokak Street, no. 6), which is located opposite the Turkish Orthodox church of St. Nicolas (Aya Nikola).

THE RUSSIAN LODGING HOUSES OF GALATA

In the 19th century, a number of hospices were constructed in Galata (present-day Karaköy): monasteries for accommodating both Russian pilgrims en route to Jerusalem or Mount Athos and Russian clergy visiting the Ecumenical Patriarchate. Ever since the signing of the Treaty of Kutchuk-Kaïnardji in 1774, the Russian Empire had enjoyed the right of protection over the Orthodox subjects of the Ottoman Empire, which included Greeks, Bulgarians, Serbs, Romanians, Albanians, Georgians and a handful of Arab Orthodox. Since land was in short supply and expensive at that time, these lodging houses/monasteries were constructed to a considerable height, in common with many of the commercial buildings in the area, and the chapels were placed on the rooftops. After the 1917 revolution, the lodging houses of Galata provided a refuge for Russians, and especially aristocrats, fleeing the Bolshevik regime. These buildings later fell into decay, as the Soviet Union had no real interest in funding their maintenance. Immediately after the Second World War, Stalin attempted to revive the Russian monasteries in the Middle East in order to fill them with KGB agents posing as monks. Strangely though, he showed almost no interest in the monastic institutions in Galata, despite their location in a country and city that were of major importance at this stage of the Cold War. Nevertheless, the Russian churches in Galata were faithfully maintained by a handful of descendants of the 1917 immigrants until a large number of Russians arrived in Istanbul following the break-up of the Soviet Union in 1991.

STATUE OF COUNT DE BONNEVAL ⓲

Palais de France – French Consulate in Instanbul
Nuruziya sokak Street no. 10
Beyoğlu
• Tel: 0212 334 87 30
• www.consulfrance-istanbul.org/
• Visits are permitted by appointment with proof of professional interest (historian, artist, architect, etc.) or during any of the numerous activities organised by the Consulate
• On 14 July, all French citizens are welcome to visit the magnificent gardens, provided they pre-register
• Metro: Şişhane/İstiklal Caddesi. Tram: Tophane

> **A French
> nobleman who was
> a Whirling Dervish**

The lavish Palais de France – the state's embassy to the Sublime Porte during the Ottoman era – is currently used as the residence of the French Consul General. Within the vast, beautiful gardens (open to any French citizen in Istanbul on 14 July), there is a highly unusual statue portraying Count de Bonneval as a Whirling Dervish.

During his eventful life (see opposite), Bonneval changed army and country twice, and religion once.

He was often accused of having faked his conversion to Islam in order to secure his position within the Ottoman bureaucracy. However, his affiliation with the order of Whirling Dervishes, the Mevlevi, points to a more sincere conversion on the part of this passionate man who, perhaps, finally found peace of mind in mystical experience.

Whatever the case, his membership of the Mevlevi order explains the costume worn by his statue in the garden of the Palais de France.

COUNT DE BONNEVAL: A FRENCHMAN IN SERVICE OF FRANCE, THEN AUSTRIA AND FINALLY THE OTTOMAN EMPIRE

Claude Alexandre, Count de Bonneval (1675 – 1747), a descendent of an old family in the Limousin region of France, joined the army at a very young age where he demonstrated brilliant abilities as a commander. Court-martialled for apparently causing offence to Madame de Maintenon (mistress of King Louis XIV), he fled and joined the ranks of the Austrian army. After forming a friendship with Prince Eugene of Savoy, Bonneval became a general and fought bravely against his own country and also against the Ottoman forces. Although an excellent soldier, Bonneval was temperamentally violent and unstable, which led him to quarrel with Prince Eugene, for which he was sentenced to death by an Austrian court-martial. The emperor then commuted his death penalty to a year's imprisonment and exile in Venice. On his release, Bonneval offered his services to the Sublime Porte, who enlisted him in 1729 for the purposes of reorganising the Ottoman artillery. Bonneval assumed the name Ahmed, was appointed pasha (general) and created the first modern school of artillery, where he taught mathematics lessons himself. Henceforth he was known as Humbaracı Ahmed Pasha, or Ahmed Pasha the bombardier. His defection to the enemy undoubtedly cost the Viennese government dearly. The artillery troupes formed by Ahmed Pasha contributed significantly to the Austrian defeat near Niš which led to the Treaty of Belgrade in 1739 in which Austria was forced to give up northern Serbia. Bonneval gave outstanding service to the sultan in his campaigns against Russia and Persia and was granted the governorship of Chios in return. Although Bonneval played an important role in Ottoman diplomacy, in the end his character forced him into exile in Kastamonu, near the Black Sea, although he was later recalled to Istanbul, where he died in 1747. The school of artillery that he founded did not long outlive him. It was closed under pressure from the reactionary Janissaries, who remained attached to the old methods.

Count de Bonneval's gravestone can be found in the shrine of the Whirling Dervishes of Galata, which is now a museum.
Avenue Galip Dede Caddesi no. 15 Tünel Beyoğlu (close to the "Tünel" exit).
Tues—Thurs 9am-7pm. Weekend: 9am—4.30pm. Closed Mon.

TULIP FOUNTAIN

19

At the junction of Avenue Şair Ziya Paşa Caddesi and Laleli Çeşme Sokağı
Street - Galata
• Metro: Şişhane

The "Tulip Fountain" (*Laleli Çeşme*) is a delightful, forgotten art nouveau
edifice designed by the Italian architect Raimondo d'Aronco (see p. 145). The
stylised flowers sculpted on the fountain are typical art nouveau features,
even if they do not look particularly like tulips.

FRENCH ROYAL COAT OF ARMS ⓴

Saint Pierre Han
Eski Banka Sokağı Street, no. 5 (parallel with Avenue Bankalar/Voyvoda Caddesi)
Galata
• Tram: Galata. Metro: Haliç

> *A rare French royal coat of arms that escaped the destruction of the French Revolution*

Although the French Revolution sought to destroy the symbols of royalty within France, starting with the mausoleums of the French kings at Saint Denis, near Paris, its reach did not extend as far as the Ottoman territories, where the Saint Pierre Han building displays the coat of arms of the Kingdom of France, adorned with fleurs-de-lys, as well as that of the Comte de Saint Priest, French ambassador to the Sublime Porte (1768-1784) who built this residential property between 1771 and 1775 to accommodate French merchants and their banking activities. Appointed Minister of the Interior by Louis XVI in 1789 and accused of treason, he only just escaped the guillotine. The Saint Pierre

Han building then became the head office of the new Ottoman Bank in 1863, until it moved in 1892 to its majestic headquarters on the Avenue of Banks, built by the architect Vallaury. The Han building subsequently became the location of the Bar of Istanbul, and then the Italian Chamber of Commerce. Neglected throughout the 20th century, it housed electrical equipment workshops before recently being given a new lease of life under the auspices of Bahçeşehir University.

A commemorative plaque affixed to the old Han building informs us that the poet André Chénier was born here. This is only half true: born of a French father who was a merchant in Istanbul, and a Greek mother, Chenier came into the world on 30 October 1762 in a building that was destroyed by fire and on the site of the current Saint Pierre Han. Chénier was executed by guillotine in France on 25 July 1794 at the age of 31. The architect Vallaury (see above), who was an admirer of Chénier, had the commemorative plaque installed.

HODIGHITRIA ICON OF CAFFA ㉑

Church of SS. Peter and Paul
Galata Kulesi Sokak Street 44, Kuledibi
• Metro: Şişhane. Tram: Karaköy

*A Black
Virgin
in Istanbul?*

Within the Church of SS. Peter and Paul, the icon of the Virgin Hodighitria (*hodighitria* is Greek for "guide") comes from the Genoese colony of Caffa in the Crimea, which was captured by Sultan Mehmed the Conqueror in 1475 and whose inhabitants (Genoese, Greeks, Armenians, and Jews) were forced to emigrate to Istanbul. The Hodighitria icon was initially preserved in a Catholic church intra muros, which was converted into a mosque allocated to the small number of married Janissaries, after which the icon was moved to the Dominican Church of SS. Peter and Paul. Though it miraculously survived the fire of 1640, the face of Mary was blackened; this gave her the appearance of a Black Virgin. For certain people there remains an element of doubt: was the icon intended to be a Black Virgin from the very beginning?

BLACK VIRGINS: VESTIGES OF PRE-CHRISTIAN RELIGIONS?

The Black Virgins are effigies of the Virgin Mary (sculptures, icons, paintings) which, for the most part, were created between the eleventh and fourteenth centuries. Their name refers quite simply to their dark colour.

Around 500 of them have been counted, mainly around the Mediterranean basin. Usually found in churches, some of them have been the object of major pilgrimages.

According to the Roman Catholic Church, there is no theological basis for the colour of these Virgins, although some experts have pointed to the passage in the Song of Songs (1:5), "*Nigra sum sed Formosa*", which can be translated as "I am black but beautiful".

Some other very simple reasons have been proposed to explain this black colouring: the colour of the material used (ebony, mahogany, or a dark local wood) or deposits of soot from votive candles. But the importance that this colour has taken over time (some images have even been repainted black during restorations) leads to the belief that a deeper force is at work.

Thus, for some, the colour of the Black Virgin is a reminder that the Virgin, like the Catholic religion in general, did not become established *ex nihilo*, but replaced other ancient faiths in Western Europe: the Mithraic cult (for more details on this fascinating cult which was fundamental in creating a European identity, see *Secret Rome* in this series of guides), Mother-goddess cults, the cult of the Egyptian goddess Isis bearing Horus in her arms, etc.

In these archaic contexts, tribute was often rendered to the Mother goddess, symbol of fertility, gestation, procreation, regeneration, and renewal of life in general, on which the peasantry relied to ensure a bountiful harvest.

As the Christian religion began to affirm itself, the Virgin, mother of Jesus, son of God the Creator, thus became associated with this Mother goddess.

In symbolic terms, the black colour of the Virgin naturally evokes that of the virgin earth as well as the maternal/regenerative side of life in the sense that feminine procreation takes place in the (dark/black) depths of the woman's uterus. And her dark colour may also have brought her closer to the peasants whose own skin darkened from working out in the fields in the sun.

So it is therefore no accident if similar inscriptions are found on certain statues of Isis as on many of the Black Virgins: "*Virgini parituræ*" (to the Virgin who will give birth).

Finally, although many of the Black Virgins are associated with miracles, it is interesting to note that these events are usually linked to the beginning of a new cycle or a new era, thus respecting the image of the Virgin as the giver of life, above all else.

ORGAN OF THE CHURCH OF SS. PETER AND PAUL ㉒

Galata Kulesi Sokak Street 44, Kuledibi
• Metro: Şişhane. Tram: Karaköy

> *An organ with multiple uses which escaped the rigours of papal regulations*

U nder the authority of the Italian fathers, the Dominican church of Saint Peter and Paul houses a magnificent organ able to produce numerous musical registers which has mysteriously survived the severe regulations made by the Vatican at the beginning of the 20th century concerning liturgical musical instruments.

Issued in 1903 by Pope Pius X, the motu propriu "Tra le Sollecitudini" on sacred music stipulated that, "the sound of the organ when accompanying singing must be in keeping with the inherent nature of the instrument; the use, in church, of the piano, as well as noisy or frivolous instruments such as the drum, bass drum, cymbals and bells, is prohibited".

Built in 1875 by Camillo Guglielmo Bianchi (1821-1890), who also built numerous organs in southern Piedmont and Liguria, the organ of the Church of SS. Peter and Paul incorporates registers imitating the sounds of instruments forbidden under the papal order. These registers still work perfectly today, as does the rest of the organ, which has only rarely required repairs in the century and a half of its existence. It appears that this church was unaware of the order issued by Rome (as is also the case with others throughout the world), and therefore did not destroy the registers so ingeniously created for this instrument, which gives it the impression of being a giant mechanical computer. Did the faraway location of this church in an Islamic country enable it to survive the papal injunction?

Although the current church was built in 1843 by the architect Gaspare Fossati, the origins of the Dominican community at Galata within the Genoese colony go back to the 13th century. After their first church had been transformed into a mosque in 1475 (the present-day Arap Camii), the Dominicans moved into a house donated by a Venetian located on the site of the current church. A monastery was established in the 17th century, under French protection and supported by Venice. This monastery suffered numerous fires and went through many renovations, producing the complex as it stands today. It also incorporates a beautiful library, which backs onto one of the last remaining sections of the Genoese wall.

VOYVODA HAN PLAQUE ㉓

Avenue Bankalar Caddesi, no. 19
• Metro: Karaköy station on the old metro (Tünel). Tram: Karaköy stop

**Is
Dracula's head
buried
in Istanbul?**

Voyvoda caddesi (Avenue Voyvoda), recently renamed Bankalar Caddesi (avenue of the banks), begins close to Karaköy Square. The former Avenue Voyvoda and the residential building still known as Voyvoda Han owe their name to the infamous Dracula, whose head is said to be buried under this street.

The word "*voivode*", which is of Slavonic origin, means commander or governor. Within the Ottoman administrative system, it referred first of all to the princes of Wallachia (a region situated in present-day Romania) and Moldavia, vassals of the empire, and subsequently to a minor administrative position.

Avenue Voyvoda takes its name from Vlad III, Prince of Wallachia, who inspired the film character Dracula. The actual historical figure had become famous, not because of his thirst for blood, but because of his preferred method of torture. His abundant use of impaling earned him the nickname "Tepes", the Impaler. An engraving even shows him dining unperturbed in front of men undergoing this torture (see illustration p. 202).

Wallachia had been placed under Ottoman suzerainty since the end of the 14th century. It was customary for the sons of the Wallachian prince, vassal of the Sublime Porte, to be sent to the Ottoman court as hostages, but also for the purposes of familiarising them with Turkish culture, as was the case for Vlad and his brother, Radu, in 1442. Their father was also assassinated by John Hunyadi for his complicity with the Turks. In 1448, Vlad received the crown of Wallachia from the Ottomans, only to revolt against them, in collusion with the Hungarians, in 1461. An Ottoman delegation led by Yunus Bey, the Greek secretary of Mehmed the Conqueror, and commander Hamza Bey was sent for the purposes of making the rebel see sense. The entire delegation was subsequently captured and impaled, along with many other victims of Turkish and Bulgarian origin. On approaching the site of the meeting between Vlad and the missing Ottoman delegation, the Ottoman army initially mistook this sinister collection of impaled corpses for a forest, in which one tree stood higher than the others. Out of respect for his hierarchical rank, Hamza Bey had been given a long stake to raise him above the other victims.

Mehmed the Conqueror soon realised he would have to command a military expedition against such an enemy in person. Vlad attacked the Ottoman camp in a night raid and almost succeeded in killing Mehmed himself in his tent. On his return to Istanbul, the Ottoman ruler placed Vlad's brother Radu on the Wallachian throne. Vlad then sought to make amends in an effort to recover his principality and sent a letter of supplication to Mehmed, which unfortunately fell into the hands of Matthias Corvinus, king of Hungary. Corvinus then had Vlad imprisoned in the fortress of Višegrad where he remained for twelve whole years. After Radu's death in 1475, Matthias offered to restore Vlad to power, on condition that the Orthodox prince embrace the Catholic faith. Wallachia turned out to be worth a Catholic mass, but his abjuration did not bring Vlad any good fortune. He continued to wage war against the Turks, aided by Stephen Báthory, grandfather of the Countess Báthory, who achieved fame for bathing in the blood of young women.

This collaboration undoubtedly contributed to Vlad's future reputation since he was eventually able to recover his throne. Nevertheless, two months after his enthronement, his decapitated corpse was discovered in the marshes of Vlăsia, close to the island monastery of Snagov, and buried by the monks. Two legends survived after his death. The first claims that, due to his apostasy, Vlad's soul was condemned to return to this world and wander among the living in order to torment them. According to the second, Vlad was decapitated by a Turkish soldier who, after disguising himself and slipping in amongst Vlad's lackeys to commit the deed, brought the head to Istanbul where it was put on public display and then buried in Galata, on a street that would subsequently be called Avenue Voyvoda.

WHERE IS DRACULA'S BODY?

Excavations undertaken at the church of the Snagov Monastery in the 1930s led to the discovery of a headless skeleton which was wearing the trappings of the Order of the Dragon to which Vlad belonged. At Nuremberg in 1408, Emperor Sigismund had indeed founded the chivalric Order of the Dragon into which Vlad II was initiated, taking the name Dracul ("dragon" in Romanian). His son, Vlad III, the Impaler, was known as the son of Dracul, (the Dracula made famous by Bram Stoker in his 1897 novel).

However, the recent discovery of a gravestone at the convent of Santa Maria Nova in Naples, next to the tombs of Vlad's daughter and son-in-law, has led some to believe that he might, in fact, be buried in this cemetery. Indeed, the bas-relief covering the stone features a dragon, an explicit allusion to Dracul, and a sphinx, the symbol of the town of Thebes (similar to "Tepeş", which means "the impaler" in Romanian). Some historians have suggested that Vlad's daughter, who was then at the court of Naples, paid the ransom demanded by the Ottomans in order to have her father sent to the city, where he later died.

For more about vampires in the Ottoman Empire, see the following double-page spread.

VAMPIRES IN THE OTTOMAN EMPIRE

Although an ancient Turkish etymology[1] has been proposed for the word "vampire", Ottoman culture was unacquainted with this bloody legend, despite its wide dissemination in the Balkan regions of the Empire. The religious authorities had been approached about cases of vampirism in the Balkans, especially in the area around Salonica (Greece) and Edirne (Turkey, on the Greek border), since the 16th century but had difficulty finding an Islamic response to the problem, so they turned to local custom. Nevertheless, one case of vampirism in the early 19th century merits closer examination due to its political context and some of its more humorous aspects.

The central authorities took this case so seriously that they published a report in the newly established official gazette of the empire, *Takvim-i Vekayi*. According to an article published in the gazette in 1833, vampires had appeared at Tirnovo, in present-day Bulgaria.

They attacked the houses after dusk, defiled food, tore cushions, pillows and covers and threw stones and pieces of pottery at people. They were invisible. The Tirnovo residents called on the services of a renowned exorcist called Nicolas who detected vampires by turning an icon on the tips of his fingers. This method led to the excavation of the tombs of Tetikoğlu Ali and Apti Alemdar, two former Janissaries (see p. 56) who had become bloodthirsty bandits and committed many crimes. The bodies in the tombs had not decomposed but had expanded by half their size, while their hair and nails had also grown significantly. Their eyes were covered in

blood. It was believed that the two bandits – having been spared execution out of respect for their advanced age and allowed to die of natural causes – were not satisfied with having lived a life of criminality and had begun to harass people after their deaths.

Although the advice given by the exorcist was followed – a pole was driven into the abdomens of the corpses and boiling water poured over their hearts – the problem persisted. Nicolas then instructed the townspeople to burn the corpses (which was done rapidly after religious authorisation had been obtained), after which Tirnovo was saved from the vampires.

Historians today treat this narrative as a fabrication by Mahmud II intended to vilify the Janissaries, even after their deaths, an entirely plausible theory given the sultan's brilliant political and propagandistic skills. However, one question still remains: how do we explain the fact that the bodies had not yet decomposed years after their burial if, in fact, this was really the case?

1 "Vampire" comes from Tatar ubyr ("witch") or from a root meaning to absorb or suck (öpmek, "to kiss" in modern Turkish).

JEAN-JACQUES ROUSSEAU, VAMPIRES AND THE SULTAN

Jean Jacques Rousseau, whose father had been the sultan's watchmaker, was also intrigued by vampirism. As the illustrious philosopher said, "If there is a well-attested history in this world, it is that of vampires. Nothing is lacking: official reports, affidavits from notables, surgeons, parish priests, magistrates. The legal proof is among the most complete. And with all that, who believes in vampires? Will we all be damned for not believing?"

FORMER GENOESE COURT OF CAPITULATION ㉔

Saksı Han
Perşembe Pazarı Caddesi
Bakır Sokak no. 2
Karaköy
• Tram: Karaköy

> **The remains
> of a remarkable
> special court**

Hidden among a quarter of hardware stores (Perşembepazarı), this old ashlar stone building with an attractive corbelled upper storey, currently used as business premises, was formerly the court of the Genoese colony of Constantinople, which was established during the Byzantine period and prospered during the Ottoman era. It had jurisdiction over the Genoese residing in Istanbul due to treaties concluded between Genoa and the Byzantine Empire, and subsequently with the Ottomans.

In 1261, the Genoese helped the Byzantines to reconquer their capital which had been occupied by the Crusaders, and in particular Genoa's traditional enemies, the Venetians, since 1204. Out of gratitude, Byzantium gave Genoa the entire area of Galata, which the Genoese colony then enclosed with a wall with the Galata tower as the keep. The court, which dates from the beginning of the period of Genoese domination, is located in the middle of this area.

Following the capture of Constantinople by the Turks, the Genoese handed over the keys of the gates to their city enclosure to Sultan Mehmed the Conqueror, who consequently enhanced the privileges they had held under the Byzantines. The court continued to function during the Ottoman period under the treaties of capitulation and has survived to the present day, although with considerable architectural damage. The buildings opposite are the former court prisons.

For further remains of the capitulation courts, see following double-page spread.

OTHER GENOESE REMAINS IN ISTANBUL

On the corner of Kartçınar sokak and Galata Kulesi sokak streets, the Genoese Palace ("Palazzo del Commune"), the colony's former administrative and political centre, has lost much of its original character. A few remains of the walls, which once had a circumference of 2.8 km, can still be seen: a 150-metre segment bordering the above-ground metro line; the Yanık Kapı Gate ("Burnt Gate") on Yanık Kapı Street, which dates from the 14th century; a marble plaque above this gate engraved with the coats of arms of its reigning doge, De Merude, and of the podestà of the Galata community, Rafaelo de Auria; and another section of wall with superimposed arches in the park connecting the Haliç metro station bridge with Avenue Tersane caddesi.

Several towers have also survived: the famous Galata Tower; the tower behind the library of the Convent of Saint Peter and Paul, which holds an icon from the Genoese colony of Caffa (see p. 196); and the tower at the corner of Lüleci Hendek and Revani streets, behind Lycée Saint Benoît.

The Genoese chapel of Lycée Saint Benoît (see photo) dates from the 14th century and is the oldest Catholic church in Istanbul. First the Jesuits, then the Franciscans, gave assistance there to prisoners of war incarcerated in the naval prisons, penal colonies and galleys. It houses the tomb of Ferenc Rákóczi (1676-1735), prince of Transylvania and Hungarian nationalist hero, who took refuge among the Ottomans and whose bones were recovered by the Hungarian government in 1906.

Although the moats have disappeared along with the walls, some of the Galata street names evoke their memory, such as Büyük Hendek (great pit), Küçük Hendek (little pit) and Lüleci Hendek (pipemakers' pit).

OTHER REMAINS OF THE CAPITULATION COURTS

French court

At the end of Tomtom Kaptan sokak Street.Tram: Tophane

Although the first treaty of capitulation between the Sublime Porte and France was concluded in 1535, the current building which forms part of the Palais de France complex dates from 1844 and is an outbuilding of the Lycée Pierre Loti.

Old prison of the English capitulation court Galata Kulesi Sok. no. 15 (61). Tram: Karaköy

The prison of the English capitulation court, where insolvent debtors and others were incarcerated, is now a pleasant café-restaurant (The Galata House/Galata Evi/Eski İngiliz Karakolu, piano after 8pm, Tel: 0212-245 18 61, http://www.thegalatahouse.com/info.htm).

Former Russian court of Narmanlı Han

Avenue İstiklal Caddesi no. 388-390. Metro: old "Tünel" line or new "Şişhane" line

The former Russian jail was built during the first half of the 19th century to serve as a chancery for the Russian embassy. Once the embassy had moved into its grand building in 1843, it housed the consular offices, including the capitulation court and its prison.

Following the collapse of the Tsarist empire, Narmanlı Han became a private property whose rooms were rented out to private individuals,

NARMANLI HAN
No 390

the most illustrious of whom was undoubtedly Ahmet Hamdi Tanpınar (1901-1962), the great novelist, poet and thinker. A disciple of Bergson in philosophy and Proust in literature, Tanpinar was forgotten after his death, then rediscovered in the 1990s. The Turkish public was enraptured by the depth of his thought and the issues he addressed: the perennial crisis of a Turkish society torn between East and West, social and psychological analyses and the full-fledged worship of the city of Istanbul.

THE CAPITULATION COURTS: A REMARKABLE SPECIAL COURT

In the Beyoğlu/Galata/Tophane area the remains of several former "capitulation courts" can still be found. These courts, which had jurisdiction over the subjects of their respective founding countries, thus constituted a special jurisdiction in relation to the Ottoman legal system.

They had their origins in the "treaties of capitulation" concluded between the Ottoman Empire and the European powers from the 16th century onwards. These treaties guaranteed Christian subjects living in an Islamic country the right to be exempted from the actions of local authorities and to remain under the jurisdiction of their own national authorities despite the general legal convention (the principle of territoriality) whereby a foreigner physically present in a foreign territory is subject to the laws and authorities of that country.

It is commonly accepted that the first treaty of capitulation was signed between the Ottoman Empire and France in 1535, even though it appears that there were precedents created with Italian maritime cities such as Genoa (see preceding double-page spread) and Amalfi. The Franco-Ottoman treaty of 1535 was followed by a range of treaties with other powers, such as Tuscany, England, the Netherlands, Austria, Poland, Russia, Sweden, Prussia, and the Kingdom of the Two Sicilies, which constituted a network of privileges maintained at the expense of the sultans' empire.

The capitulation provisions created important exceptions: foreigners were, in principle, subject solely to the jurisdiction of their consul in matters of litigation between them. In any disputes that they might have with Ottoman subjects, the Ottoman courts retained complete jurisdiction, on condition that they were assisted by a dragoman, an interpreter who also acted as an advisor. The jurisdiction of the capitulation courts extended even to criminal matters; it was a genuinely extraterritorial system which also established tax exemptions and the inviolability of the home.

Inevitably, abuses occurred: many Ottoman subjects became foreign nationals in order to benefit from these privileges. From the 18th century onwards, the treaties of capitulation also began to incorporate a most favoured nation clause, to the extent that the privileges granted in a treaty concluded with one European power also extended in practice to the others.

The empire tried many times, and without success, (notably in 1914, after war had been declared) to rid itself of this system that undermined both its economy as well as its prestige. After the empire had collapsed, the Turkish delegation sent to Lausanne to conclude the treaty that would become the birth certificate of the Turkish Republic received explicit instructions not to make any concessions in relation to the abolition of the capitulations. They won their case and the Treaty of Lausanne of 24 July 1923 ended the system of capitulations.

REMAINS OF THE OR HADASH SYNAGOGUE ❷❺

At the junction of Alageyik and Zürafa streets
• Tram: Karaköy or Tophane

*The former
synagogue
of the sex trade*

At the junction of Alageyik and Zürafa
streets, there stands a now ruined
building with a remarkable history. The
only visible remnant of this history, however,
is a Hebrew inscription.

The former Or Hadash Synagogue was an Ashkenazi synagogue which was
not only situated in the heart of an area known for prostitution (the famous
Zürafa Sokak, or street of the brothels), but was also established, funded,
managed and attended by those involved in the sex trade.

In 1854, during the Crimean War, the Russian prisoners of war of Jewish
origin captured by the European allied forces were freed in Istanbul but
obliged to live in the Galata area, on Avenue Yüksekkaldırım (literally
"high pavement" in Turkish). A number of them became involved in the
procuring of prostitutes, which had long been a highly lucrative activity in this
neighbourhood. They thus formed a genuine Ashkenazi colony, with roots in
Poland, Romania and Russia. Its members – not only the pimps but also their
families – lived entirely from this trade. Galicia and Romania thus became
significant trafficking sites for white women, and Odessa acted as a port for
exports to Istanbul and the wider world. The tentacles of the prostitution
trade reached even as far as South America, which is why many of the brothel
owners in Istanbul maintained close contact with similar institutions in
Buenos Aires.

The Sephardic community, which was dominant in Istanbul, viewed the
development of this "Little Poland", as it was now known, with horror, and not a
single Sephardic women was to be found there. As a minority within the Jewish
population, the Ashkenazi community suffered greatly in the circumstances,
as "Ashkenazi" became almost synonymous for pimp, to the extent that on
disembarking at Thessaloniki in 1910 David Ben Gurion was told by his
friends to hide his Ashkenazi origins and to describe himself as Sephardic, in
order to avoid being mistaken for a procurer.

The Sephardic community eventually closed the doors of their synagogues
to the newly-arrived Ashkenazi, who were obliged to build their own
synagogue in 1897. Its president, Michael Moses Salamovitz (nicknamed
Michael Pasha), was both a trafficker of prostitutes and a spy for the Ottoman
government. The very existence of the synagogue was intimately intertwined
with prostitution: its leaders, worshippers and funding were all dependent
on this trade. It is even said that the top floor of the synagogue was used as a
retirement home for old prostitutes.

The traditional Ashkenazi community eventually succeeded in closing this synagogue, but the Chief Rabbi Moses Levi (1872-1908) allowed the families living from prostitution (as many as 200) to reopen the synagogue on condition that they surrounded it with high walls. In 1915, the Istanbul Police Commissioner, Bedri Bey, at last put an end to the age-old activity of the Ashkenazi traffickers. Abandoned by its original members, the synagogue was then used for a brief period by Georgian Jews, before falling into ruin.

In common with the rest of the port area, Galata was, throughout its history, overflowing with inns and brothels which were very common in every part of Beyoğlu/Pera. There were even streets comprised solely of licensed brothels, under government control, such as Abanoz Sokak Street, which has now been sanitised and renamed Halas ("salvation" or "rescue"). The last remnant of these streets is Zürafa Sokak Street, where prostitution has been subject to strict policing and hygienic control during the Republican era. In 2009, there were still eighteen active establishments, with 120 prostitutes, providing services to 5000 clients every day.

A PLAQUE IN HONOUR
OF THE AUSTRO-HUNGARIAN EMPEROR

(26)

Ashkenazi Synagogue
Avenue Yüksek Kaldırım caddesi, no. 27
Karaköy
• www.turkyahudileri.com
• Visiting: contact synagogue Rabbi, Mendy Chitrik (mendy@
rabbimendy.com) or the Chief Rabbinate (tel: 0212 2938794 - email:
seheratilla@yahoo.com)
• Tram: Karaköy. Metro: Şişhane, İstiklal exit

> **When
> the German
> and Austrian
> monarchs
> supported the Jews
> of the Ottoman
> Empire**

At the entrance of the Ashkenazi Great Synagogue of Istanbul, a black marble plaque, written in German, states that the building was erected in 1900, "to commemorate the fifty-year reign of His Serene Majesty, the Emperor and King Franz Joseph the First". (The plaque bears an identical text on the other side, for unknown reasons.) The Ashkenazi community of Istanbul had indeed collected the funds necessary for its construction from Austrian Jews, with the indulgence and financial support of the Emperor.

Throughout the 19th century, the German and Austrian rulers actively

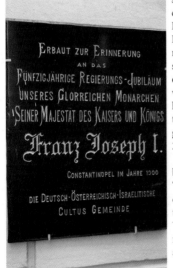

supported the Ashkenazi communities within the Ottoman Empire, particularly in the Holy Land, considering them to be representatives of Germanic culture, since they spoke Yiddish, a language of Germanic origin suffused with Hebrew, Aramaic and other local languages. This sympathetic treatment is all the more remarkable given the subsequent history of the 20th century.

The synagogue was designed by the Venetian architect Cornaro. The Torah ark, made of delicately carved wood in an Ottoman style, is the work of the sculptor Fogelstein. With its two balconies reserved for women, the building is able to accommodate up to 400 people.

THE ROMAN CAPITAL OF KURŞUNLU HAN ㉗

Kardeşim Sokak Street, no. 26
At the junction with Avenue Kürekçiler. Behind the Galata Bedesteni, at
the end of Kürekçiler Caddesi, where the post office is located
Perşembe Pazarı
Karaköy
• Tram: Karaköy

*A Roman
capital
transformed into
the coping of a well*

Although it is not unusual to find ancient building materials salvaged and reused in more recent buildings, the late Roman (or perhaps early Byzantine) capital of Kurşunlu Han has been put to an unusual use. It has not only been overturned to be used as the coping for a well but also bored through with an old pump, which still works today and is used to hose down and clean the Han yard (a former caravanserai). The Kurşunlu Han derives its name from the metalworking that has been practised there for centuries (Kurşunlu means "made of lead" in Turkish). Also known as Rüstem Paşa Kervansarayı, the caravanserai was built in 1550 by the architect Sinan for Rüstempaşa, who also built the mosque of the same name. Now occupied by hardware stores and metal workshops, as is common throughout the neighbourhood, Kurşunlu Han stands on the site of a Genoese cathedral dedicated to St Michael, which was already in ruins by the mid-16th century.

THE SECRET TOMB
OF MAKBUL İBRAHIM PAŞA?

(28)

Bilgin Han
Avenue Fermeneciler Caddesi, no. 32
Perşembe Pazarı (Thurs market)
Galata/Karaköy
• Tram: Karaköy. Metro: Haliç

> *A saint
> who would calm
> children down*

The tomb of holy Koyun Baba, also known as Koyun Dede ("father" or "grandfather sheep"), cannot be found by chance. In the Bilgin residential building, you must ask the building doorman to take you – through a dark and narrow corridor filled with boxes of merchandise – to the sanctuary. Located in a tiny vaulted cell into which light enters through a small window, the sarcophagus is covered with scarves patterned in decorative writing and crowned with a marble inscription, which tells us that Koyun Dede was buried in the Galata prison and that his commander restored the tomb in 1773. A tower situated next to the tomb, which formed part of the walls of Galata, was previously used as a prison.

Although we cannot be absolutely sure of the saint's affiliation with Sufism, a pin attached to the wall makes us think of the brotherhood of the Rifa'i, certain followers of which would stick pins into their cheeks when in a state of mystical ecstasy to show their insensitivity to pain. Like his Fatih namesake, holy Koyun Baba was visited by parents who brought their unmanageable children to him in order to calm them down.

THE SECRET SEPULCHRE OF THE GRAND VIZIER İBRAHIM PAŞA?

According to another theory, the tomb is held to be the secret sepulchre of the Grand Vizir İbrahim Paşa, executed by order of Suleiman the Magnificent in 1536.

Born of humble Italian, Albanian or Greek parents at Parga, in present-day Greece, Ibrahim Pasa was kidnapped by pirates who sold him to an old lady at Manisa. There he was noticed by the crown prince, the future Suleiman the Magnificent, who brought him to Istanbul to become part of his retinue. Ibrahim became an advisor, confidant and friend of the sultan and received every kind of honour from the civil and military bureaucracy. After becoming Grand Vizier, he married the sultan's sister. A great polyglot, man of letters and musician, Ibrahim showed his innate talent for diplomacy and established the great principles of the Empire's foreign policy towards the European powers, and the Holy Roman Empire in particular, whose emperor enjoyed formal equality with the Grand Vizier – and not with the sultan.

Ibrahim soon attracted the jealousy of the court, who incited the sultan to order his execution. During Ramadan 1536, he was invited to an end-of-fast dinner (*İftar*) after which four deaf-and-dumb executioners strangled him. His corpse was buried at an unknown location, out of fear that his tomb would become a symbol and an attraction for visitors. It had been rumoured that his remains were buried secretly in the Sufi tekke of Canfeda, near the Yağkapanı Mosque. These buildings have since been replaced by Koyun Baba, near the mosque erected by Ibrahim Paşa, in the middle of the fish market.

Local residents also claim that Koyun Baba used to attract a large number of Albanian visitors: was this as a sign of solidarity with the Pacha's origins? Certain people even claim that the very choice of the name "Koyun Dede" for hiding his remains could be a message, alluding to the sacrifice of the pasha ("like a sheep whose throat is cut") and used to indicate that his tomb is located here.

The history of Ibrahim Pasha constituted an important episode in the very popular Turkish television series Muhteşem Yüzyıl ("The Magnificent Century").

MASONIC SYMBOLS ON THE FACADE OF THE AGRICULTURAL BANK

㉙

Branch of Ziraat Bankası (Agricultural Bank)
Avenue Rıhtım cad., no. 1 Place Karaköy
• Tram: Karaköy. Metro: Haliç

On the facade of this branch of the Ziraat Bankası (Agricultural Bank) which looks out on the Golden Horn, there are two statues depicting an old man and a young woman, surrounded by children. They are both holding a mallet and a chisel, familiar Masonic symbols.

Hiram, architect of the Temple of Solomon in Jerusalem

According to certain sources, the young woman represents the Biblical Jael (Book of Judges 4:17-22), who killed Sisera, commander of the army of Jabin, the oppressor of Israel. Defeated on Mount Tabor by Barak, the Hebrew general, Sisera took refuge in the tent of Jael, who had offered him hospitality. Once Sisera had fallen asleep, "Jael, Heber's wife, picked up a tent peg and a hammer and went quietly to him while he lay fast asleep, exhausted. She drove the peg through his temple into the ground".

The other figure is apparently Hiram, architect of the famous Temple of Solomon in Jerusalem. The Bible tells us: "King Solomon sent to Tyre and brought Hiram whose mother was a widow from the tribe of Naphtali and whose father was from Tyre and a skilled craftsman in bronze. Hiram was filled with wisdom, with understanding and with knowledge to do all kinds of bronze work. He came to King Solomon and did all the work assigned to him" (1 Kings 7:13).

Although the depiction of Hiram does not really require any further commentary due to its Masonic symbolism, the presence of Jael is probably explained by the fact that the tools she used to kill Sisera are identical to the Masonic symbols of the mallet and chisel.

The statues are most commonly attributed to Midhat Pasha, founder of the Agricultural Bank (1873) and an acknowledged Freemason. The instigator of two coups d'état, Midhat Pasha was murdered by strangulation in his prison while exiled in Ta'if, in the Hejaz (present-day Saudi Arabia), in 1884.

The current building, built in a neoclassical style, only dates from 1912. It was originally the main office of the Bank of Vienna (Wiener Bank Verein).

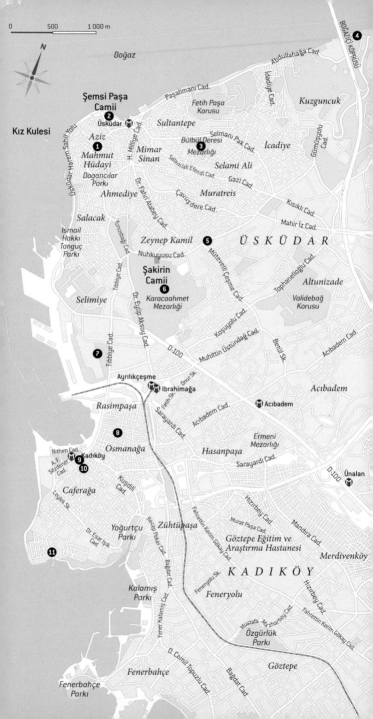

ÜSKÜDAR - KADIKÖY

ALMS STONE OF THE IMRAHOR MOSQUE ❶

2 Avenue Doğancılar Cad., Üsküdar
• Metro: Üsküdar

Remains
from the Islamic
charitable tradition

In the courtyard of the Imrahor Mosque in Üsküdar, an ancient porphyry column, which was previously located on Doğancılar Avenue, is surrounded by anachronistic mosaics. It is still used today as an alms stone, a historical relic of Ottoman charity.

Usually found at the entrance or near mosques, shrines (such as saints' tombs) and charitable institutions, alms stones are blocks of stones that are generally ancient columns in marble, porphyry or granite. They often have a hollow part at the top or a hole in the actual column shaft where visitors could leave coins, food or old clothes to be passed discreetly on to the poor.

Donations were often made in the following way: on their way to the evening prayers, several hours after sunset, the faithful would place coins on the alms stones. After prayers, the needy left the mosque last and took coins equal to the daily price of bread before disappearing into the night. In this way, neither the donors nor the other worshippers knew who had need of this money, nor how much had been taken.

"PLAY THE PIANO LIKE A GOOD MUSLIM WHO GIVES ALMS"
Although Islamic piety mandates almsgiving, it also seeks to avoid humiliating the poor and making the rich proud. The Islamic principle thus ensures that while giving alms, the left hand of the donor must not know what the right hand is doing. Thus, to make fun of a bad pianist, Turks still today say that he plays the piano like a good Muslim giving alms: his left hand does not know what his right hand is doing.

Alms stones were also situated near the tombs of executioners.
Although Ottoman society despised these professionals, it nevertheless provided for their families after the executioners had died.

OTHER ALMS STONES IN ISTANBUL

There are other beautiful alms stones near these mosques: Mehmet Ağa (Fatih), Sümbül Efendi (Kocamustafapaşa), Hakimoğlu Ali Paşa (Kocamustafapaşa), Laleli (see p. 20), Süleymaniye, Nuruosmaniye, Yenicami (Eminönü), Sultanahmet, Arap Camii (the Arab Mosque, Karaköy), Kemankeş Mustafa Paşa (Karaköy), Aşçıbaşı (Üsküdar) and next to the Kazlıçeşme fountain (see p. 132). This list is not exhaustive.

SEISMOGRAPHIC COLUMNS OF THE ŞEMSI PAŞA MOSQUE

❷

Şemsipaşa (Şemsi Paşa Camii or Kuşkonmaz Camii), Şemsipaşa Square, Üsküdar pier
• Metro Marmaray: Üsküdar. Bus: Balaban

> *An earthquake-proof mosque*

Inside the Şemsi Paşa Mosque, the mihrab (recess) of the main altar is flanked by two remarkable little columns made of dark green marble. Resembling the columns at the entrance to the Kılıç Ali Paşa Mosque (see p. 28), which was also designed by the architect Sinan, these columns rotate on their axis. They were designed to warn the faithful in the event of an earthquake or a landslide occurring during prayers.

Sinan built this mosque on behalf of Şemsi Paşa, Governor General of the Balkan provinces of the empire, and later *musahib* (groom of the chamber) for sultans Selim II and Murad III. Constructed a little before the death of the great architect and overlooking the sea, the mosque is also highly susceptible to the repeated action of the waves and the infiltration of sea water. Sinan is thus alleged to have used a special mortar to absorb the vibrations caused by the waves.

THE MOSQUE WHERE BIRDS NEVER LAND

Another unique characteristic of the Şemsipaşa Mosque is that birds never land on the dome, thereby giving rise to its alternative name, "Kuşkonmaz" (The bird does not land). Şemsi Paşa was concerned that birds would defile his shrine with their droppings; Sinan therefore suggested that the mosque should be built at this precise location on the Bosphorus, where the southerly and northerly winds, which meet at this very point, are so strong that birds do not venture here at all. This phenomenon can still be observed today.

A different explanation is that the continuing vibrations caused by the waves are condensed inside the dome, creating infrasonic vibrations that keep the birds away. The older people in the area recall that in the 1940s, a whole family of seals found refuge in the small sea cave situated under the Şemsi Paşa Mosque. This cave, which perhaps acts as part of the mechanism transforming the sound of the waves into infrasound, is now hidden by a thick layer of concrete that is used as a promenade along the Bosphorus.

MUALLIM
ŞEMSİ EF.
ATATÜRKÜN
HOCASI

SABBATEAN CEMETERY OF BÜLBÜLDERESI ❸

Bülbülderesi Mezarlığı,
Avenue Selmanipak CaddesiMetro: Üsküdar

Spread out over a slope populated with cypress trees, the Sabbatean cemetery of Bülbülderesi (literally, "nightingale river"), which is officially Islamic, has some strange tombs that bear little resemblance to traditional Muslim graves. We thus find tombs that have not been turned towards Mecca, numerous sarcophagi that are completely enclosed (a rare phenomenon in Muslim societies), gravestones hewn into the shape of an obelisk, others displaying esoteric or Masonic symbols (certain tombs are flanked by Masonic Jachin and Boaz columns) or stones placed on the tombs by visitors, as in Jewish cemeteries. The tomb inscriptions rarely refer to a given religion, but there are many poems that are full of sadness, death, oblivion, tragedy, pain, separation, and so on. We often find the inscription "I have hidden, I have not mentioned my concern, I have put it to sleep," which probably refers to the clandestine practice of the occupants' religion.

> *Unusual graves of a crypto-Jewish community*

The cemetery, which was originally orthodox Muslim, has, in fact, become that of the crypto-Jewish community of the Sabbateans, who began to bury their dead there in the 1920s. Thus we find the names of great families of intellectuals, industrialists, politicians, as well as the gravestone of Şemsi Efendi, teacher at the primary school attended by Mustafa Kemal Atatürk, founder of the Republic of Turkey who was born in Thessaloniki. Any Turkish pupil who paid attention at school knows that Atatürk's mother wanted to send him to the nearby Koranic school, whereas his father, a customs officer, favoured a modern western education and had his son enrolled in the private school of Şemsi Efendi, alias Shimon Zvi, a Jew who was not only Dönmeh (see p. 225) but also, we are told, a Kabbalist.

To find out more about Sabbateanism, see the next double-page spread.

WHAT IS THE ORIGIN OF THE NAME SELANIKLILER SOKAK (STREET OF THE SALONICANS)?

The street next to the cemetery of Bülbülderesi is called Selanikliler Sokak (Street of the Salonicans) in memory of the deportation of the Muslims and Sabbateans of Salonica in 1923 (see p. 224).

WHAT IS SABBATEANISM?

Sabbatai Zevi was born in Izmir (Smyrna) in 1625. Within the Izmir Jewish community, which was mostly Sephardic, he received a solid Jewish education and was attracted to the Kabbalah. In 1648, at the age of 23, he began to style himself as the new, long-awaited Messiah and publicly defied some of the major prohibitions of Judaism, such as pronouncing the Tetragrammaton (the sacred name of God which cannot be spoken according to the Bible. See Exodus III 13–14: story of the burning bush). He was eventually banished by the Izmir community, went with his disciples to Istanbul and visited Thessaloniki, Alexandria, Athens and Jerusalem, attracting disciples during the course of his travels. In 1665 he returned to Izmir, where he solemnly declared himself to be the Messiah and subjected the local community to his authority. His following, which also included renowned rabbis, grew in Europe where messianic movements were flourishing among both Jews and Protestants. Decimated by massacres, most notably in Poland, European Jews were in a state of despair, thereby intensifying the expectation of a new Messiah. Moreover, many Christian theologians considered the year 1666 to be the year of the Apocalypse prior to which, according to the Bible, a new Messiah would appear (666 is the Number of the Beast in the Apocalypse of John). According to one less common interpretation of the Talmud, Zevi began to abolish certain sacred duties; the Messiah had come and the old law was now repealed. In 1666, either voluntarily or due to pressure from the official authorities in Izmir, he went to Istanbul where he was arrested on the orders of the Grand Vizier. He was initially imprisoned in Istanbul and then in a castle on the Dardanelles that he transformed into a full-fledged royal court, and from which he continued his mission. He enjoyed the support of the Jewish communities of Europe but also attracted a strong response from rabbis who rejected his claims and warned the Ottoman authorities of the danger that Zevi represented for public order. He was therefore taken to the sultan's court at Edirne, where the sultan's physician, a Jewish convert, suggested that he convert to Islam in order to save his life, which was hanging by a thread. In the presence of the sultan, Zevi removed his Jewish clothing and placed a turban on his head as a sign of his conversion, assuming the name of Aziz Mehmet Efendi. The satisfied sultan offered him a sinecure in the palace. Along with Zevi, 300 families who belonged to his sect embraced Islam, thus creating the nucleus of the community that would later be known as the Dönmeh. The latter called themselves "*ma'minim*" ("believers" in Hebrew: see opposite). While pretending to be devout Muslims, Zevi and his followers nevertheless continued to practise Judaism in their own fashion. Caught in the very act of singing psalms with Jews, Zevi was exiled to the Albanian port city of Dulcigno (Ülgun in Turkish, the modern Montenegrin town of Ulcinj), a real centre for piracy at that time, where he died in 1676.

THE DÖNMEH

The followers of Zevi (see opposite) settled in the great cities of the Ottoman Empire, and especially at Thessaloniki, where they formed an unusual community of crypto-Jews that was regarded with general suspicion. The Muslims never considered them to be part of the Umma (the universal community of Muslims) and the Jews treated them as heretics disguised as Muslims. In an astonishing twist of fate, in 1923 they were sent to Turkey along with all the Muslims of Thessaloniki under the 1923 Treaty of Lausanne, which made provision for the exchange of the Christian Orthodox population in Turkey and the Muslims in Greece, without distinguishing their particular characteristics. In Thessaloniki, the Dönmeh had their own districts, mosques, organisations and separate cemeteries. They practised endogamy (marriage within their group) and constituted a closed community that scrupulously observed the rule of silence, so that we know relatively little about their theology and religious practices, giving rise to all kinds of gossip, including stories of ritual orgies. It appears that the Dönmeh movement incorporated a type of syncretism in which Kabbalah coexisted with Sufism, the views of certain Dönmeh coming close to the latter.

The Dönmeh were economically powerful and, towards the end of the empire, participated actively in political life, and especially in revolutionary Thessaloniki, which gave birth to the constitutionalist movement that finally succeeded in deposing Abdülhamid II. The strong representation of Dönmeh among the leaders of the Young Turks (Committee of Union and Progress), which guided the empire to its destruction, gave rise to conspiracy theories: it was claimed that the Dönmeh, after ruining the Ottoman Empire and the caliphate, were now attempting to control the Turkish Republic economically and politically. To strengthen the legend, it happens that the Dönmeh actively supported the new secular regime, which did not discriminate against different faiths, and that the founder of the Republic had had a Dönmeh teacher (see p. 223). As at Thessaloniki, the Dönmeh were economically successful in the Turkish Republic and were highly visible in the press and in the field of education – yet another reason for suspecting them of being involved in any number of conspiracies. The witch hunt, which continues today, sometimes takes astonishing forms: intellectuals are sometimes denounced as crypto-Jews based on their family name after they have declared themselves openly to be Jewish.

Even though Sabbateanism survived in parts of Europe (in the 18th century, western Europe experienced a partial resurgence of the movement under the leadership of Jacob Franck [1726–91], another self-proclaimed Messiah), the failure of Sabbatean messianism was a shock for European Jews who, tired of the disillusionments associated with the mystical movements, began to look for more secular solutions to the Jewish problem. As a result, certain commentators believe that the Sabbatean crisis was one of the causes of the emergence of Zionism.

STATUE OF SULTAN ABDÜLAZIZ ❹

Beylerbeyi Palace
Avenue Abdullahağa Caddesi
Beylerbeyi-Üsküdar
• Open daily 8.30am–5pm except Mon and Thurs
• Metrobus: Boğaziçi Köprüsü

Unique statue of a sultan-caliph

In the great state room of the Beylerbeyi summer palace, the statue of Sultan Abdülaziz (reigned 1861–76), who commissioned and unveiled it in 1865, has the distinction of being the only existing statue of a sultan-caliph, given that human images are a source of controversy within Islam. If the Koran considers statues to be an "abomination invented by Satan" (5:90), the context makes it clear that it was referring to idols worshipped by the polytheists. Another verse (34:13) reports that engineers "built for him [Solomon] as many works as he wished, palaces, statues" etc. without any negative comments about him. The human images forbidden by a plethora of hadiths also appear to refer to images that may be used for idolatry. This was the interpretation adopted by the Umayyad dynasty (661–750) whose palaces were decorated with all kinds of images. It was under the Abbasids (751–1258) that a new broader interpretation of the hadiths led to the prohibition and destruction of all images of living creatures. A parallel may be observed with the iconoclasm that emerged at the same time in the Byzantine border provinces of the Islamic Empire.

The first Muslim ruler to commission his own portrait was an Ottoman. Mehmed the Conqueror (reigned 1451–81) had invited the Venetian painter Gentile Bellini to paint the portrait now hanging in the British Museum. Nobody dared to oppose the powerful sultan, whose palace was teeming with European and Byzantine scholars. It was his son and successor Bayezid II who expelled the painters and destroyed the paintings. Any existing portraits of earlier sultans by European painters were painted after these rulers and their authenticity is uncertain. From the 16th century onwards, Ottoman miniatures depicting the sultans became commonplace.

While portraits of rulers are rare in Sunni regions (even if one image of the Mamluk Sultan Qansuh al-Ghawri is extant), the Iranian and Mongol traditions produced beautiful miniatures that may be likened to genuine portraits. It was during Abdülaziz's journey to Europe in 1867 – the first peaceful European expedition undertaken by an Ottoman sultan – that he noticed that it had become the custom for rulers to commission statues of themselves. On his return, he began to test the waters by ordering two dozen animal statues to beautify the Beylerbeyi Palace.

He subsequently asked the sculptor Fuller to make an equestrian statue depicting the sultan in official dress, but also wearing a loose-fitting, hooded raincoat, which he liked to wear during his frequent excursions into the

city, in defiance of protocol. The statue of the sultan–caliph did not provoke any religious controversy; in any case, it was situated within the palace and inaccessible to the general public, who were aware of its existence but unable to see it. Besides, those who had access to the palace were already familiar with the European style and way of living, whereas the portraits of Sultan Mahmud II in the public offices, barely thirty years earlier, had caused full-blown insurrections in the Arab provinces. Mahmud had learned from his diplomats that in modern kingdoms the image of the ruler was placed within public institutions in order to strengthen monarchical authority and project an impression of paternalistic protection.

This initiative formed part of a programme of administrative modernisation and centralisation that was highly successful in those provinces already affected by westernisation. However, for the ultra-conservative Arab provinces, these human portrayals, unheard-of for a millennium, were clear proof of the impiety of the Ottomans, who now had to be removed.

ŞAKIRIN MOSQUE

5

2 Avenue Nuhkuyusu Cad., Karacaahmet
• Bus or dolmuş from Kadıköy on Üsküdar Square. Get off in front of Karacaahmet *tekke*

O pened for Islamic worship in April 2009, the Şakirin Mosque impresses both the faithful and visitors with its modern architecture that breaks with more traditional local customs regarding places of worship: glass-covered side walls in the nave,

A "feminine" mosque?

aluminium composite dome (instead of the lead used in Ottoman mosques), gently rising stairways, chandelier composed of elements shaped like drops of water (symbolising divine grace falling on the faithful like rain, water being associated with divine mercy in Islam, a religion born in the desert), minbar (pulpit where the imam preaches) strewn with dried flowers covered in a transparent protective layer, and so on. Even though we find the traditional Islamic 99 names of God and the sura "Nur" (Light) from the Koran on the circular chandelier, the mosque still surprises.

In addition to its revolutionary architecture, the building has been the subject of heated controversy. Although the overall plan was the work of a man (Hüsrev Tayla), the decoration and internal architecture were partly designed by a woman (Zeynep Fadıllıoğlu), who is more accustomed to designing chic restaurants or luxury villas in London and Istanbul than places of worship. This is the first time that she has helped to design a mosque. She describes her work as follows: "Rather than simply designing a monument, I have been careful to introduce more emotion, to take account of how one feels there, to encourage meditation and communion with God. This is perhaps what makes the mosque more 'feminine.'"

Financed by the Şakir family, renowned for their charitable and philanthropic work, the mosque is dedicated to those who praise the Lord, with a discreet reference to the name of its sponsors (in Arabic, *chakir* means "he who thanks God").

Constructed on a 3,000 m^2 site, in the middle of a 10,000 m^2 garden, the Şakirin Mosque has two 35-metre minarets and can accommodate 500 worshippers during communal prayers. Located on the edge of the immense Karacaahmet cemetery, it is intended to become the "ceremonial" mosque on the Asian side of Istanbul, for the funerary prayers of leading figures.

HORSE TOMB ❻

Karacaahmet cemetery
To the left of the Karacaahmet *tekke*
Junction of Nuhkuyusu and Gündoğumu avenues, Üsküdar
• Bus or dolmuş from Kadıköy on Üsküdar Square; get off in front of
Karacaahmet *tekke*

*Vows
for a horse*

Within Karacaahmet cemetery, a large elliptical tomb is venerated as being that of the legendary Karaca Ahmet, the son of a Turkmen commandant from Khorasan and sheikh of the Bektaşiye brotherhood, which established its *tekke* (spiritual retreat) here in the 14th century as a sort of outpost prior to the conquest of Istanbul. He gave his name to the largest cemetery in Istanbul, which is also one of the largest in the world.

The horse tomb is covered by a dome resting on six graceful granite columns, and is clearly visible from Gündoğumu avenue. Popular religious devotion has led to the installation of a sort of fireplace in which candles are lit. Another practice, designed to ensure that wishes are granted, consists of sticking stones or coins on the columns. In ancient times, children who had walking difficulties were led around the tomb. The ritual was completed by throwing grains of barley on the ground and cutting a sheep's throat as a sacrifice.

Some sources claim that the horse in question did not belong to Karaca Ahmet, but to Ebul-Derda, the Prophet's companion who participated in the first siege of Constantinople and whose honorary cenotaph is located just next door (his real tomb is in Eyüp).

Beyond the traditions and beliefs accumulated over the centuries, historians argue that the tomb in question is, in fact, that of Rum Paşazade Nişanci Hamza, a statesman of the late 16th century. His epithet ("son of the Greek Pasha") presents a curious parallel with the presence of the remains of Byzantine columns around the tomb. These columns appear to have been recovered from older buildings – yet more evidence of the smooth transition from the Byzantine to the Ottoman empire, in both the architectural and aristocratic spheres.

We simply do not know how belief in the horse tomb and its related practices began. Whatever the case, it is not the only horse tomb in Istanbul: Sultan Osman II (1618–21) had his favourite horse buried in Kavak Palace, near Karacaahmet. After the suppression of this palace, the horse's gravestone was transferred to Topkapı Palace (see p. 59). Another horse tomb, belonging to Suleiman Pasha (early 14th century) is located at Gelibolu (Gallipoli) on the Dardanelles, close to the mausoleum of its master.

Another horse tomb has been preserved inside Topkapi Palace (see p. 59).

HAYDARPAŞA BRITISH CEMETERY ❼

Next to the entrance to the Gata Haydarpaşa Eğitim Hastanesi military
hospital (Selimiye Mh.), Üsküdar
• Open daily 9.00am–dusk
• Metro: Kadıköy
• From Kadıköy pier, turn left and go over the railway bridge and up
Avenue Tıbbiye Caddesi. When you reach the traffic lights, turn left and
walk towards the sea.

> *A little-known and moving place*

Hidden among the medical and military complexes of Haydarpaşa, and most easily seen from the boats on the Kadıköy line due to its monumental obelisk, the Haydarpaşa British cemetery is a relatively unknown and moving place.

The cemetery was established for English soldiers (mostly cholera victims) who had died during the Crimean War (1853–56) in the military hospital established by Florence Nightingale in the English barracks of Üsküdar. On her initiative, the British government persuaded Sultan Abdülmecid to give the land to the British crown, on the site of the former summer palace.

The cemetery then continued to receive soldiers from every part of the Commonwealth who had been killed during the First World War, in which the Ottoman Empire and Great Britain were on opposing sides.

The cemetery thus housed the remains of Indian Muslims, which were buried in this site strewn with Christian crosses with all the respect due to their religion, as well as the ashes of Hindu soldiers.

During the Allied occupation of Istanbul (1918–22), the bodies of British soldiers killed by the Turkish resistance were also buried there. During the Second World War, the bodies of British (and sometimes even American) soldiers, including many airmen, killed close to Turkey were buried there.

The cemetery, which is well maintained, is managed by the Commonwealth War Graves Commission, whose head office is in Berkshire, UK.

SIR EDWARD BARTON: AN ENGLISHMAN WHO FOUGHT WITH THE OTTOMANS AGAINST THE CATHOLICS

Sir Edward Barton (1533–98), Queen Elizabeth's ambassador to the Ottoman Empire, established the first permanent Embassy of Her Britannic Majesty and sought Ottoman support against Spain. Full-fledged supporter of an anti-Catholic alliance, he accompanied Sultan Mehmed III in his campaign against Hungary and fought bravely in the Ottoman ranks in 1596. In order to escape the plague that had broken out in Istanbul in 1598, he took refuge in Heybeliada, where he died and was buried in the Greek cemetery. His funerary stele, which was moved to Haydarpaşa in the 1970s, bears his family coat of arms and also cypress bas-reliefs, a typical decoration on Turkish gravestones.

HOBART PASHA: AN ENGLISHMAN WHO WAS THE FIRST FOREIGNER TO BE MADE A FIELD MARSHAL IN THE OTTOMAN ARMY

After completing his career in the British navy, Augustus Charles Hobart-Hampden (1822-86), known as Hobart Pasha, enjoyed a life of adventure, which included participating in the American Civil War. He finally entered service with the Ottomans in 1867 and obtained command of a fleet as rear admiral. He succeeded in suppressing the Cretan uprising in 1869, which earned him the title of Pasha. During the Russo-Turkish War of 1877–78, he enforced a merciless blockade on the Russian ports of the Black Sea. In 1881 he was appointed field marshal, thereby becoming the first Christian to receive this title in the Ottoman army. He died in Milan, where he had gone to receive medical treatment. Sultan Abdülhamid dispatched a boat to transport Hobart Pasha's remains to the Haydarpaşa cemetery, since the pasha had expressed the wish in his will to be buried on Turkish soil.

HEMDAT ISRAEL SYNAGOGUE ❽

61 Izzettin Street, Yeldeğirmeni, Kadıköy
• Tel: 0212 2938794
• www.turkyahudileri.com/index.php
• Email: seheratilla@yahoo.com
• Visits by permission of the Chief Rabbinate
• Metro: Kadıköy

> *A synagogue dedicated to a Muslim sultan*

Situated in a lush, green garden, the Hemdat Israel Synagogue is notable for its wonderfully light and spacious interior, decorated with ornamental frescoes characteristic of the era; it has two entrances to the north and south, in accordance with Sephardic tradition. The interior space is dominated by a majestic *ehal*, a recess oriented towards Jerusalem used for storing the Torah whose doors symbolise the passage from the material to the spiritual world.

The synagogue, which owes its existence to the personal intervention of Sultan Abdülhamid, astonishingly bears a name that refers discreetly to that of the sultan.

During the 1890s, the small Jewish community of the Kadıköy district lost their synagogue in a fire and wanted to construct a new one at the location of the current synagogue. However, they encountered violent opposition from the Greek community, which formed a majority in the district and sought to build a church at the site in question. Sultan Abdülhamid, who heard of the incident through Elias Pacha, his personal ophthalmologist, sent a detachment from the Selimiye barracks to suppress the unrest. The sultan placed the construction of the synagogue under his august protection via a *firman* (imperial decree) of 14 January 1896. The synagogue was inaugurated on 3 September 1899 with speeches given by prominent Jews of the city, in highly culturally-significant languages: Turkish, Judaeo-Spanish and French.

Abdülhamid continually sought to maintain a certain balance between the different religious communities of the empire. On the other hand, promoting the Jews to the detriment of the Greeks might also be interpreted as sending an indirect message in view of the deterioration in relations between the Sublime Porte and the Kingdom of Greece, which led to outright war in 1897. It is also possible that the Jewish community of the district was the sole legitimate owner of the ground and that the sultan was simply playing the role of arbitrator.

Whatever the case, the Jews were extremely grateful to the sultan and wished to leave a lasting mark of their gratitude; thus they named their new synagogue Hemdat Israel, which means "compassionate to Israel". Significantly, the Hebrew word *hemdat* comes from the same Semitic root as the Arabic word *hamid* (which means "praiseworthy"). Thus the phonetics of the synagogue name subtly continue to evoke Sultan Abdülhamid.

CHURCH OF ST EUPHEMIA   ⑨

27 Avenue Yasa Cad., Kadıköy
• Open for Sunday mass from 10.00am and on Orthodox holidays, in
particular St Euphemia (16 Sept)
• Metro: Kadıköy

> *St Euphemia, location of the Council of Chalcedon in 451*

Built in 1832 in a neo-Byzantine style, the Church of St Euphemia has a remarkable picture to the right of the vestibule. This represents a scene from the Council of Chalcedon that took place in 451. In it we see 343 bishops (the number present at the council) seated in their golden robes and two Monophysite prelates (see opposite) depicted in black. The prelates (who were banished and expelled) have their Greek names inscribed above their heads: Eutyches and Dioscorus, Patriarch of Alexandria, deposed by the council but acknowledged as Patriarch and canonised by the Coptic Church and the other Monophysite churches. The two prelates are also marked with the epithet "Monophysite".

In the centre of the painting lies the body of St Euphemia, martyred at Chalcedon in 303 under Emperor Diocletian for refusing to deny her Christian faith. Her role was crucial: during the council, documents were placed in her tomb summarising the two opposing doctrines of Monophysitism and Dyophysitism. Three days later, the tomb was reopened: the saint was found holding the text of the Orthodox confession in her right hand, while the Monophysite text was resting at her feet, as the icon shows. Thus the saint had chosen her camp. The presence of this painting at St Euphemia is far from accidental. According to legend, the church was constructed on the site of an ancient church of the same name, which had been the location of the Council of Chalcedon in 451. The church housed the relics of St Euphemia, currently preserved in the Patriarchal Church of St George. Some archaeologists, however, maintain that the original church, destroyed in 1555, was located in Haydarpaşa.

Chalcedon is the ancient name for Kadıköy.

THE COUNCIL OF CHALCEDON: MONOPHYSITISM BEHIND THE SCHISM OF THE ARMENIAN, SYRIAC AND COPTIC CHURCHES

Summoned by the Byzantine Emperor Marcian, the 4th Ecumenical Council of Chalcedon (after those held in Nicaea in 325, Constantinople in 381 and Ephesus in 431) established the Dyophysite doctrine of Christ that is accepted today by the traditional Orthodox, Catholic and Protestant churches. According to this doctrine, Christ has a "double nature", both human and divine. It was in the wake of this council – which condemned the Monophysite doctrine of Eutyches, according to which Christ has only one nature (divine), his human nature having been somehow absorbed by the divine – that one of the first Christian schisms (after that of the Nestorians in 431) occurred, giving rise to the Oriental Orthodox churches established in Syria, Armenia, Egypt and Ethiopia. These churches, also described as "pre-Chalcedonian", include the churches from the Armenian, Syriac, Coptic and Abyssinian liturgical traditions. It should be noted that the Armenian Church, which was not present at Chalcedon, did not join the schism until 506.

PONTOS'UN AĞZINDA
MEGARALILAR TARAFIN-
DAN KURULMUŞ OLAN
KHALKEDON VE BİR KÖY
OLAN KHRYSOPOLİS VE
KHALKEDONLAR TAPINA-
ĞI BULUNUR. VE DENİZ-
DEN BİRAZ İÇERDE İÇİN-
DE KÜÇÜK TİMSAHLARIN
BESLENDİĞİ BİR PINAR
VARDIR.

COĞRAFYA
ANADOLU KİTAP XII
STRABON M.Ö 63-M.S.21

KADIKÖY CROCODILE 🔟

At the junction between Muvakkithane and Mühürdar avenues
• Metro: Kadıköy

> *A crocodile in memory of Strabo, geographer of antiquity*

Since 2007, the small square of Kadıköy market has been decorated with an astonishing monument consisting of a great marble plinth laid on the ground, in the corner of which a small bronze statue of a crocodile takes pride of place.

The inscription engraved on the marble is a direct quotation from the book *Geographica* by the Greek geographer and historian Strabo (book XII.4 – Bithynia) according to which "here upon the mouth of the Pontus is situated Chalcedon, founded by the Megareans, the village Chrysopolis and the famous temple known as the temple of Chalcedon. In the country, a little above the sea coast, is a fountain, Azaritia, which breeds little crocodiles."

We should note that Chalcedon is the earlier name for Kadıköy and that Chrysopolis subsequently became Scutari before assuming its current name, Üsküdar. Strabo was a Greek geographer and historian of the Hellenistic era (58 B.C.–A.D. 21–25) from Amaseia, present-day Amasya in Turkey. Although his monumental 43-volume *Historical Memoirs* have been lost, his *Geographica* continues to provide an accurate portrayal of the ancient world,

in the midst of its transition from the Hellenistic era to the Roman Empire. In its passages dealing with Turkey, the *Geographica* provides several surprising details, including information on the crocodiles of Chalcedon/Kadıköy, which stimulated a lively debate after the statue had been erected. Zoologist fossil experts maintain that there have never been any crocodiles in the Istanbul area and that those mentioned by Strabo were, in fact, large lizards. All that remains of the controversy is this remarkable monument, which is a pleasant and unexpected reminder of the ancient history of the area.

SACRED SPRING OF KOÇO RESTAURANT ⓫

265 Avenue Moda Caddesi, KadıköyTel: 0216 3360795
Service: Mon 9.00am
• Tramway T3 Kadıköy-Moda from Kadıköy Square: "Moda" stop

A sacred spring in an old restaurant

Underneath Koço restaurant, which is highly regarded by Istanbulites, who even come from the European side to taste its mezze and fish, there is an *agiasma* (sacred spring of Greek or Byzantine origin) dedicated to St Catherine.

In 1924 Greek fishermen discovered a freshwater spring in Moda at the back of a sea cave where they often took refuge. They decided to turn it into an *agiasma*. According to legend, during the work they even found the foundations of a church and an icon of St Catherine, to whom they naturally dedicated the underground *agiasma*.

In 1950 Constantine Corondos opened an open-air café-restaurant on the site of the *agiasma*, which rapidly became famous due to the quality of its food and the generosity of its owner. After his death, the restaurant was managed for a long time by Greeks from the island of Imbros (Gökçeada, birthplace of the current Patriarch, Bartholomew).

Even though the management has changed, the head waiter, Athanasius, is still a Greek from Imbros who has worked there since the 1950s.

The head chef, Halil Bey, has also been there for a long time. Despite the changes in management, the restaurant is still called "Koço" in memory of its founder, Constantine.

At Koço, piety involves love of good food and vice versa. To pray in the *agiasma*, you must go through the restaurant and out into the restaurant garden.

As with all the *agiasmas* of Istanbul, St Catherine of Koço is also visited by Muslims who light candles there and participate in the service celebrated by the priest, who comes from the Metropolitan Church of Kadıköy (Chalcedon) on Mondays.

AGIASMAS: HOLY WATER SPRINGS IN THE GREEK ORTHODOX TRADITION THAT ARE VENERATED BY TURKISH MUSLIMS

Agiasma (spelt ayazma in Turkish) comes from Greek (h)agios (αγιος) which means "holy". It is a term that refers to a sacred spring to which healing and spiritual properties are attributed within Greek Orthodox tradition. Widespread throughout Istanbul, they continue to attract visitors and have given their name to a number of places including streets and rivers. There is even an *agiasma* mosque (Ayazma Camii) in Üsküdar, which is almost certainly located on the site of an old *agiasma*, as is evident from the large cisterns on the site.

Although the *agiasmas* attract the largest crowds of visitors on the feast days of the saints to whom they are dedicated, they may nevertheless be visited on any day of the week. An *agiasma* can be an isolated sanctuary or form part of a complex associated with a church or monastery.

As the Greek community of Istanbul has been much reduced in size, these churches are not always open. It is therefore best to visit on a Sunday, when the church will be open for mass. Note that in some churches, mass is no longer celebrated on Sundays due to the disappearance of the local parishioners and limited number of clergy. At the church of Saint-Dimitri of Kuruçeşme, however, famous for its Byzantine-era *agiasma*, a pope does come to say mass every Saturday (see p. 155).

Visitors of every religion and denomination come to plead for healing, to make a request for exorcism or simply to pray for spiritual support. The water from the *agiasma* plays the central role in these rituals. It is thought to remove both physical and metaphysical troubles and can be taken away in a bottle. Vials (unfortunately in plastic) bearing an image of the saint are sometimes available and make for excellent gifts (especially for friends in Greece). The water from the Balikli *agiasma* (see p. 129) is particularly sought-after.

The *agiasmas* are sometimes located on the site of former pagan shrines relating to the worship of aquatic deities, such as the Nereids, although certain springs were dedicated as *agiasmas* at a much later period. The early 19th century, for instance, saw the creation of a plethora of new *agiasmas*, with the tolerance, and sometimes even sympathy, of the Ottoman authorities. Turkish Muslims were, and indeed still are, frequent visitors to the Greek Orthodox *agiasmas*, whose rituals nevertheless appear to be somewhat incompatible with orthodox Islam. Could this be a subconscious recollection of the sacred rivers and springs of shamanism?

NORTH BOSPHORUS

THE TOWER OF OVID ❶

Uskumruköy village
European shore of the Black Sea
• By car: travel to Sarıyer and follow the signs for Kilyos, then head for Uskumruköy
• Public transport: get off at last metro station (Hacıosman) and take the bus or Kısırkaya minibus (every 15 mins), which serves Uskumruköy village

In the footsteps of the great Latin poet on the road to exile

In the village of Uskumruköy (literally, "village of the mackerel"), although the old square tower known as the "Tower of Ovid" dates from the 13th or 14th century A.D., the large minutely-adjusted ashlar blocks at its base, which contrast with the small irregularly-arranged stones in the upper parts, appear to bear witness to its Roman origins, leading back to the poet's own era (43 B.C. – 17 A.D.).

Ovid is said to have been detained in this tower, which was rebuilt either by the Byzantines or Genoese as a surveillance point for the entrance to the Black Sea.

Ovid did indeed stop in this area before reaching his place of exile,

now located in modern Romania.

In 8 A.D. he was sent by the Emperor Augustus into exile in Tomis (north of present-day Constanţa) on the shore of the Pontus Euxinus (Black Sea), for reasons that remain obscure.

Was it the immorality of his *Ars Amatoria*, an amorous adventure with Julia, the daughter of Augustus, or the claim that Ovid had caught Augustus in a delicate situation with a young man that got him sent away?

THE POMPEY COLUMN

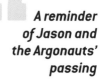

Rumelifeneri
• Bus no. 150 at Hacıosman metro exit

Next to the restaurant on the Rumelifeneri quay, a steep path leads to the summit of a rock on which stands a marble column of Greek origin that was reused by the Roman general Pompey. A Latin text is engraved on the column, which is

> *A reminder of Jason and the Argonauts' passing*

also decorated with bucrania (ox skulls), a form of decoration typically found in classical Greek architecture evoking the oxen whose heads were displayed on temple walls after being sacrificed. Pompey's Column appears to be the last remaining Greek antiquity in the city. It has, moreover, remained intact and in its original position. Yet it was Jason who made this place famous. To the north, the Bosphorus ended in rocks, known as the Cyaneans (from the Greek *kyanos*, "dark blue"), which, according to the ancient poets, previously floated on the water and had been destined by the gods to defend the entrance to the Black Sea against the curiosity of the profane. (There is a grouping of rocks situated on the Asian side that end in sharp points which are continuously submerged and uncovered by the movement of the waves: this is likely the cause of

this illusion.) During the Argonaut expedition, Jason resorted to subterfuge to allow his ship, the Argo, to pass between the rocks, which threatened to close up again while the vessel was travelling through. He first sent a dove, which only just succeeded in passing between the rocks. The Argo then exploited the short pause before the gap between the rocks closed for the second time. Apparently surprised by Jason's trickery, the rocks let his vessel pass.

The sorceress Medea, who was pursuing Jason, poisoned the spring where the Argonauts (who included Theseus, Orpheus, Castor, Pollux and Hercules) quenched their thirst. Forewarned, the goddesses Hera and Athena intervened, transforming the spring into a therapeutic spring named Therapia (modern Tarabya).

TOMB OF SARI SALTUK

③

Rumeli Feneri Lighthouse
Rumelifeneri
• Open daily 9am-5pm (ring to contact the lighthouse keeper)
• Bus no. 150 at exit to Hacıosman metro

> *The tomb of a "saint in a lighthouse"*

Constructed between 1855 and 1856 to provide an easier passage for the French and English fleets travelling to Crimea (Crimean War: 1853 – 1856), the Rumeli Feneri Lighthouse houses the tomb of Sarı Saltuk, (or rather one of the many tombs traditionally ascribed to the saint – see opposite) in a quite remarkable fashion. The entrance to the crypt leading to his tomb is located to the right of the stairway to the lighthouse. The date placed at the head of the saint's coffin (1204 of the Hegira, or 1789-1790 in the Julian calendar) contradicts certain popular traditions which claim that the tomb was discovered when a villager's dream revealed the site to the builders. Although nothing is known about the tomb prior to that period, legend has it that the first attempts at building a lighthouse, undertaken by a French company, were unsuccessful as the structure was said to have collapsed for no apparent reason. Could the saint's tomb, located on this site, have had something to do with this failure? In the absence of any certainty, a decision was taken to construct a small mausoleum to cover the tomb, after which the construction of the lighthouse resumed without any further difficulties.

The village of Rumelifeneri was devastated by repeated shelling from the sea during the Balkan Wars (1912) and the First World War, while the lighthouse, despite being a strategic target of crucial importance, remained intact. All the while, the lighthouse keepers would be sure to leave wooden clogs near the tomb so that the saint could perform his ablutions in preparation for evening prayers. Sometimes the clogs were found mysteriously wet the next morning.

Besides this phenomenon, which has been reported at many other saints' mausoleums, the keepers who climbed the stairs of the lighthouse also believed that they could hear the saint chanting. Sarı Saltuk thus became a sort of patron saint for the village fishermen, who would ask for his blessing before taking to the ocean. Healing properties were also attributed to the tomb and the small spring that surfaced close to the lighthouse. This provides a curious parallel with the tomb of Sarı Saltuk in Romania, which is flanked by a fountain with healing powers, and also with this saint's biography (the *Saltuknâme*), which relates that he made water flow miraculously from the earth.

SARI SALTUK: A MYTHICAL WARRIOR DERVISH WHO POSSESSES 12 DIFFERENT TOMBS

Venerated especially within the heterodox Alevi and Bektashi communities, Sarı Saltuk was a legendary dervish warrior who played an important role in the conquest and Islamisation of Anatolia and the Balkans at the close of the Middle Ages. Although his warlike exploits took place mostly in the 13th century, most of his tombs are located in the Balkans, whose conquest did not begin until the early 14th century. Saltuk belonged to a group of Turkmen charged by the Byzantine Emperor Michael VIII with protecting the northern marches of the empire in the 13th century. Although most of the Turkmen returned to Anatolia after the death of Saltuk, some remained in Dobruja (a region of Romania on the Black Sea) and converted to Christianity, thereby creating the Gagauz community, a Turkish-speaking Orthodox community which has survived to the present day, mainly in southern Moldova.

According to the mythological biography of Sarı Saltuk, the famous *Saltuknâme* composed in 1480 and which blurs the line between the supernatural and the real, the saint supposedly has twelve tombs. Sarı Saltuk had predicted during his lifetime that, "kings and lords would wish to own his tomb". Accordingly, in his will he ordered that eleven empty coffins be prepared so they could be given to those who required them. Each lord who received a coffin believed he possessed the body of Sarı Saltuk and was burying him in his kingdom. After naming the kingdoms of Tartary, Wallachia, Moldavia, Russia, Hungary, Poland, Bosnia and Croatia, which all requested coffins, the *Saltuknâme* explains that the real coffin was buried at Babadag, in Romanian Dobruja, although, obviously, at present there are more than a dozen tombs claiming to be the authentic one, including those at Babaeski, near Edirne, İznik (Nicaea), Diyarbakır, Tunceli, Bor (Niğde), Alaşehir in Turkey, Ohrid in Macedonia, Kruja in Albania, Blagaj in Bosnia-Herzegovina, and in the wonderful Sufi tekke by the source of the Buna River.

Both Muslims and Christians visit the tombs of Sarı Saltuk, which bears witness to the omnipresent religious syncretism to be found in the Balkans and Anatolia. Certain Balkan traditions even identify him with St. Spyridon, as at Corfu in Greece.

TELLI BABA MAUSOLEUM ④

On the cliff, on Liman Caddesi, between Sarıyer and Rumelikavağı (not to be confused with Rumelifeneri)
• Open daily 9am-6pm
• Bus: Telli Baba

The saint of the golden threads

Perched on a cliff overlooking the Bosphorus that offers a wonderful view towards the Black Sea, the strange mausoleum of Telli Baba, which is reached by walking down a narrow stairway, houses a sarcophagus covered with a thick layer of golden threads left there by visitors. Telli Baba is visited in particular by young women dreaming of marriage and young couples who travel there on their wedding day to ask for a long life, prosperity and happiness. The ritual – which does not sit easily with orthodox Islam – consists of taking a golden thread from the saint's sarcophagus. Once the wish has been granted, the visitor returns to deposit his or her golden threads as an expression of gratitude. It is said that the shorter the thread is, the more rapidly the wish will be granted. The saint's origins are highly disputed. Some commentators maintain that Telli Baba was an imam named Abdullah Efendi who served in Mehmed the Conqueror's army and was martyred during the siege of Constantinople. His tomb is said to have been discovered eighty years after the conquest in the wake of a revelation offered by a sick girl who saw him in a dream and was miraculously restored to health. Others claim that the saint was a young Byzantine nun who fell in love with a Turkish fisherman and subsequently drowned while attempting to swim away from her convent. Golden threads were placed on her tomb, as would have been done with her hair if she had succeeded in marrying. Over time, the tomb has become completely covered with threads and it is no longer known whether the saint was male or female.

THE FOUR SPIRITUAL PROTECTORS OF THE BOSPHORUS STRAIT

According to seafaring tradition, Telli Baba is one of the four spiritual protectors guarding the entrance to the Bosphorus and whose tombs may easily be seen from the sea. Southern entrance: Aziz Mahmud Hüdai at Üsküdar and Yahya Efendi at Ortaköy. Northern entrance: Telli Baba and Yuşa (Joshua) (see p. 250). Although the guardians of the southern entrance are clearly-identified historical figures, those in the north evoke old traditions dating back to antiquity.

THE TOMB OF JOSHUA ❺

Hill of the Giant (Yuşa Tepesi)
Located at the northern entrance to the Bosphorus, on the road between Beykoz and Anadolukavağı.
Go to Beykoz, in the northern part of the Asian side of the Bosphorus, then take a taxi. The bus ride is very long. Another option is to go to Sarıyer, in the northern part of the European side of the Bosphorus, then go to Anadolukavağı by boat, which would allow you to visit this beautiful village and Genoese (or, more accurately, Byzantine) castle. From there, take a taxi.

> **Is this really the burial site of the prophet Joshua?**

The second highest hill on the Bosphorus after Çamlıca, at 198 metres, the Hill of the Giant provides a breathtaking panoramic view. To the south, it is possible to see as far as the historic peninsula of Istanbul in good weather, and to the north, the northern entrance to the Bosphorus and the redoubtable and yet seductive vistas of the Black Sea.

The Hill of the Giant derives its name from an impressive tomb, nearly six metres in length, which is alleged to be the tomb of Joshua, the Old Testament prophet. In the Bible, Joshua appears both in the Book of Exodus and the eponymous book of Joshua, where he is depicted as a military leader of great courage and an excellent strategist who led his troops to a succession of victories, his most famous conquest being that of Jericho.

The tomb is also a place of pilgrimage for Muslims. Islam recognises the figure of Joshua under the name of Yuşa. Joshua is thus referred to implicitly in the Koran in sura al-Kahf as the servant of Moses (18:60).

The site was also sometimes identified as the bed of Hercules, or that of the giant Amykos, who was killed by Pollux during the Argonaut expedition.

In antiquity, an altar dedicated to Zeus was located on the site of the current tomb of Joshua. During the Byzantine era, Justinian ordered the pagan sanctuary to be transformed into a church dedicated to St. Michael. The sacred enclosure was Islamicised in the Ottoman period and a dervish lodge was added to the mosque in 1755 and again in 1863-64.

The tomb is also said to possess healing powers. Every year, numerous pilgrims visit in the hope of curing their diseases, even though they are kept at a distance by the surrounding railings.

Although Joshua is occasionally described as a giant in the rabbinical literature, certain historians are deeply sceptical regarding the claim that Joshua was buried on this site. Some see the confusion as resulting from a mix-up between the names of Jesus and Joshua (a Christian legend states that this is the place where the devil tried to tempt Jesus), while others believe that the word Joshua is the result of confusing the Hebrew name of the prophet (Yehoshua) with the fact that Phoenician navigators used the Hill of the Giant as a landmark signalling the entrance to the Bosphorus. In a sense, the hill thus "saved" (also Yehoshua in Hebrew) them from the dangerous waters in the area.

"'T is a grand sight, from off the Giant's Grave / To watch the progress of those rolling seas / Between the Bosphorus, as they lash and lave / Europe and Asia…", Lord Byron, *Don Juan* (1819).

THE TUNNEL OF THE YPSILANTI PALACE ⁶

Lycée Pierre Loti campus
Avenue Haydar Aliyev caddesi no. 128 Tarabya
• To visit, contact the school on 0212 299 94 00 or by email:
secret@pierreloti.k12.tr
• Bus: Marmara Üniversitesi (it is possible to take the metro to the last
station, Hacıosman, and then take the dolmuş)

*A haunted
yalı where
the Greek revolt
began*

The great pink-coloured wooden building on the road that borders the Bosphorus between Tarabya and Kireçburnu is all that remains of the formerly magnificent yalı that previously belonged to the Phanariot Ypsilanti family, who claimed to descend from the Byzantine imperial dynasty of the Komnenoi. Some of the members of this family attained recognition through their involvement in the Greek revolutionary movements. The great polyglot Alexander Ypsilanti (1726-1806) enjoyed a brilliant career within the Ottoman government as the principal dragoman (official interpreter) to the Sublime Porte (1774). He subsequently became the voivode (governor of the autonomous principalities) of Moldavia (1787) and then Wallachia (1794), where he began to orchestrate a plot against the Ottoman Empire that would later lead to the Greek revolt. Taken prisoner by the Ottomans during the Russo-Turkish War of 1787, then pardoned and restored to his various offices, he later resigned, was arrested for high treason and finally died in prison. His son Constantine replaced him, becoming the principal dragoman, and then voivode of Wallachia. Relieved of his duties in 1806 because of the influence of General Sebastiani, the French ambassador, he was forced into exile in Russia. His son, also called Alexander, would play a decisive role in the Greek nationalist movement, and in the uprising in the Balkans in general. Enticed by Sebastiani's offer of an alliance with Napoleon, Sultan Selim III gave the yalı to the famous soldier and diplomat as a gift, in 1807, to serve as a summer residence for the French embassy. The yalı suffered continually from the rigors of the north wind (the Poyraz) which blows in from the Black Sea, and the main building was destroyed by a fire in 1913. The present buildings, which date from the mid-19th century, are merely the annexes that were used as the offices of the first secretary and dragomans of the embassy. It is still rumoured that Alexander Ypsilanti's ghost haunts the gardens and buildings of his former palace. The buildings, which provide splendid views over the Bosphorus and Black Sea, have a melancholic charm. In a corner of the garden, next to the sea, the tunnel that was allegedly used by the Ypsilanti to dispatch their secret correspondence and arms deliveries may still be seen (see photo).

By the palace entrance, go back up towards the north for a short distance and stop at Kireçburnu, to the left, in order to taste the delights of a traditional bakery (Tarihi Kireçburnu Fırını), or to the right, close to the sea, to savour the grilled fish at Set restaurant, well-known for its original seafood hors d'œuvres.

FIELD MARSHAL VON DER GOLTZ'S TOMB ❼

German War Cemetery of Tarabya
Almanya Sefareti Tarabya Yazlık Rezidansı
88 Avenue Yeniköy Caddesi
Tarabya
• Contact the German Consulate
• Tel. (0 212) 334 61 39 - (0 212) 299 26 61 • info@istanbul.diplo.de
• Open weekdays 8am-3pm

I nside the German War Cemetery of Tarabya, the gravestone of von der Goltz, the Prussian Field Marshal who served under the Ottoman flag, attracts the attention of curious visitors. The large stone cross, with a small Teutonic cross engraved at the top, is encircled by a bronze garland, which is itself

When Islam and Christianity lived in harmony

surmounted by the star and crescent, symbols of the Turkish flag. There is also an inscription in Ottoman Turkish at the base of the cross. Here we find a rare example of the mixing of Christian and Islamic symbols, a reminder that these two religions have not always been opposed, as some claim.

Born in 1843, Colmar Freiherr von der Goltz enrolled in the Ottoman army in 1883 with the intention of reforming its educational system. After returning to Germany and being promoted to the rank of field marshal in 1911, he was sent back to the Ottoman General Staff to take command of an army in Mesopotamia. He died of typhus in 1916 after encircling a British army corps at Kut, which eventually surrendered en masse to Halil Pasha, who replaced him. The bronze garland was donated, "on behalf of the Ottoman army, to Mushir [Field Marshal] von der Goltz" in recognition of services rendered to Turkey. A discreet, non-confessional prayer wishes him eternal rest.

NEARBY

THE VON MOLTKE OBELISK

In the same cemetery stands a monumental obelisk dedicated to Helmut von Moltke, a Prussian officer invited by Sultan Mahmud II to modernise the Ottoman army during the 1830s. After returning to Prussia, Moltke advanced rapidly through the ranks, becoming Chief of Staff in 1857. He was notably the architect of Prussia's victory over France in 1870, which paved the way for the unification of Germany in 1871. He left behind wonderful letters from Turkey which turned him into a genuine literary celebrity. This great intellectual also considered waging a second military campaign in order to raze Paris, which risked becoming a centre of resistance. While in Istanbul, Moltke lived at the residence of an Armenian bureaucrat, whose large waterfront mansion made of dark red wood has miraculously survived to the present day (5 Arnavutköy Caddesi in Kuruçeşme).

Another Helmut von Moltke, great nephew of the first, travelled to Istanbul at the end of the Second World War to negotiate a separate peace with the Allies, as part of a plot against Hitler.

THE YALI OF THE SHARIFS OF MECCA ❽

Şerifler Yalısı
Emirgan Mektebi Street no. 7
Emirgan
• Tel: 0212 323 31 32 • info@tarihikentlerbirligi.org
• To visit, contact the "Union of Historical Towns" (Tarihi Kentler Birliği)
• Bus: Emirgân/Çınaraltı

In the footsteps of Lawrence of Arabia

Seat of the great Arab dynasty of the sharifs of Mecca, who played a decisive role in the insurrection orchestrated by Lawrence of Arabia, the sharifs' yalı (Şerifler Yalısı) has become the headquarters of the Union of Historical Towns (Tarihi Kentler Birliği), a member of Heritage Europe, which specialises in the protection of architectural heritage. It is possible to make a booking to visit this magnificent palace on the shore of the Bosphorus which was originally built at the end of the 18th century by Antoine Ignace Melling (1763-1831), a native of Alsace who served the Ottoman dynasty for eighteen years as an architect, jeweller, fashion designer, painter and engraver. In 1803, he also published a book in Paris entitled *Voyage*, which led to his appointment as the official landscape painter to Empress Joséphine, on the recommendation of Talleyrand.

The yalı was purchased in 1894 by Sharif* Abdullah Pasha, Emir of Mecca. After the death of the Prophet Muhammed, the task of protecting the holy places of Islam was entrusted to his descendants and the "sharifs of Mecca" became the guardians of the city. They continued to fulfil their role, if only nominally, after the holy places of Islam had been conquered by the Ottoman Empire, which selected the Emir of Mecca from the sharifs.

Towards the end of the 19th century, in the wake of the nationalist movements that had already begun to dismantle the empire, the situation of the sharifs of Mecca became more insecure. In order to ensure their loyalty, Sultan Abdulhamid II invited them to Istanbul, where they were showered with gifts and honours and subjected to a forced residency, under the strict surveillance of the sultan's secret police. Hussein bin Ali was thus born in Istanbul in 1852 and lived in the sharifs' yalı before participating in the events of the Arab insurrection. He became sharif of Mecca in 1908, in the midst of the revolution precipitated by the Young Turks, whose extreme Turkish nationalism drove him to embrace the cause of Arab nationalism. At the beginning of the Great War, Hussein remained outwardly loyal to the Sublime Porte while simultaneously undertaking secret negotiations with the English, from whom he demanded recognition for an Arab caliphate and Arab state, of which he would be the king. The great Arab revolt against the Ottoman Empire began in 1916, with the support of Lawrence of Arabia.

Frustrated by the imposition of British and French mandates on the Arab territories at the end of the war, Hussein finally declared himself caliph in 1924, two days after the caliphate had been abolished by the Turkish parliament. The Saudis refused to recognise Hussein's caliphate and seized the holy places of Islam. Abandoned by the British, Hussein was forced to flee to Cyprus before settling in Jordan, where his son Abdullah had become king. After his death in Amman in 1931, Hussein was buried in Jerusalem.

* Sharif: descendant of Muhammed

BORUSAN CONTEMPORARY ❾

5 Baltalimanı Hisar Caddesi.
Rumeli Hisarı
• http://borusancontemporary.com/anasayfa.aspx
• Contemporary art collection open Sat and Sun 10am-8pm
• Bus: Rumelihisarı

Borusan is an industrial group specialising in steel, logistics and energy that has adopted an approach that is rarely found in the world of commerce. Since 2011, its headquarters have been located in the Yusuf Ziya Pasha Mansion (see below),

> *A museum of modern art haunted by ancient ghosts*

which is open to the public every weekend, once the employees have left. On Friday evenings, the office equipment is removed to make way for cutting-edge contemporary art exhibitions. The museum has a cafe, an "ArtStore" and an outside space with very beautiful views overlooking the Bosphorus.

THE FAIRY MANSION

Built from 1910 as a residence for Yusuf Ziya Pasha, aide-de-camp to the Khedive of Egypt, a vassal state of the Ottoman Empire, the Yusuf Ziya Pasha House is also known as the Perili Köşk ("haunted house" or "fairy mansion", in Turkish). In fact, the building's construction was interrupted by the First World War and the second and third floors remained uninhabited for many years, giving rise to several legends about Yusuf Ziya Pasha's first wife. As she was a woman of great beauty, and highly susceptible to the charms of certain young officers, her husband was forced to lock her in the house. The recluse, who according to the Turkish expression was, "as beautiful as a fairy", nevertheless continued to attract amorous young men. Tired of fighting, Yusuf Pasha took her to Egypt, where she died. In keeping with her will, bricks were removed from the building's tower to be used for her tomb in Egypt.

Yusuf Ziya Pasha concluded a second marriage with Nebiye Hanım and lived in his mansion until his death, in 1926. His three daughters continued to live there until 1993. Throughout the 1990s and 2000s, Borusan carried out sophisticated restoration work, which included ordering reproductions of period bricks to be sent from England. However, the project also encountered substantial difficulties: the workers, who came from the heart of Anatolia where superstition is still very much a part of life, often stopped working due to their fear of the ghosts that haunted the house, which still contained a piano and a mirror dating from the time of the pasha and his first wife. Legend has it that whoever dares to look straight into this mirror will see the pasha's wife staring back.

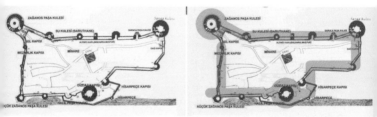

THE RUMELIHISARI GROUND PLAN ❿

42 Yahya Kemal Caddesi, Bebek
• Bus: Rumelihisarı

> *The ground plan of a fortress that reads "Muhammed" in Arabic when seen from above*

The Rumelihisarı Fortress was built by Mehmed the Conqueror prior to the siege of Constantinople in 1453 in order to prevent the besieged city from receiving any military reinforcements from the Genoese colonies in the Crimea or the Greek Empire of Trebizond, in the Black Sea. Its extremely rapid construction for military reasons is the subject of a legend that was directly inspired by that of the foundation of Carthage.

According to Evliya Çelebi (1611-1682), author of the *Seyahatname*, a wonderful collection of stories relating to travel and history, a Byzantine monastery was located on the site at Rumelihisarı. One day, the abbot of the monastery, who had secretly converted to Islam, informed Sultan Mehmed that he would be the conqueror of Constantinople and recommended that he construct a fortress on the Bosphorus. Following the abbot's advice, the sultan asked the Byzantine emperor for permission to build a hunting lodge on the site. The latter granted permission, provided that the surface area of the lodge was no greater than that of an ox's hide. The ingenious abbot then suggested to Sultan Mehmed that he have the ox hide cut into thin strips and that the fortress should be constructed in the space defined by the resulting ribbon. The abbot then fixed the layout of the fortress in such a way that, when seen from above, it resembled the word "Muhammed/Mehmed" written in Kufic Arabic characters, with a double reference to the Prophet Muhammed, who had predicted the fall of Constantinople (in a Hadith), and the sultan of the same name. Once the building had been completed, the emperor accused Mehmed of having violated the agreement. The sultan sent him the ox hide cut into strips, invited him to measure the dimensions of the fortress and promised that he would demolish the excess part, which would, in fact, not be necessary.

Was Mehmed the Conqueror, who was able to read the ancient authors in the original sources, inspired by another legend with a similar theme?

In the 9th century B.C., when Princess Dido sought to establish a Phoenician colony in present-day Tunisia, King Iarbas granted her as much land, "as could be contained in the hide of an ox". Dido had an ox hide cut into extremely thin slices. Placed end to end, they marked out the boundaries of a city, which became Carthage.

In the *Aeneid*, Virgil speaks of, "great walls and the rising citadel of the new city of Carthage, […] a piece of land called the 'Byrsa', the animal's hide, as large an area as they could include within the hide of a bull" (1/365).

A CABBAGE-SHAPED FOUNTAIN ⑪

In front of the police station
12 Çengelköy Halk caddesi
Çengelköy
• Bus: Çengelköy

> **A reminder
> of the Cabbages
> club's sporting
> competitions**

I n Çengelköy, in front of the police station on Halk Caddesi, a small column used as a fountain is adorned with a remarkable ball sculpted in the shape of a cabbage.

In fact, this is one of the commemorative columns erected by the Cabbages sports team during the period when they competed against the rival Bamyas (also known as "okra" or "gumbo", see p. 81). Although these competitions generally took place in the garden of the Topkapı Palace, they were sometimes held in other locations by the Bosphorus, and in particular here, as this cabbage fountain testifies.

NEARBY

A similar monument can also be seen a bit further to the north, on the public square behind the bus stop in the Paşabahçe area. The square fountain, also surmounted by a cabbage, is unusual in that it is also decorated with a crescent and star, symbols that appeared on the Ottoman flag after 1844 and which are still seen on the flag of the Turkish Republic, although they were somewhat altered by a law passed in 1936.

For more information regarding the historic competitions between the Cabbages and Bamyas, see p. 80.

Küçükçekmece

Bağcılar

Eyüp

Beyoğlu   Beşiktaş

İSTANBUL

0-3

Bahçelievler

Fatih

Zeytinburnu

0-100

Bakırköy

0-100

D-100

✈ Atatürk
Havalimanı

Marmara Denizi

N

0   5   10 km

PRINCES' ISLANDS

UNDERWATER REMAINS OF THE VORDONISI MONASTERY ❶

Location: between the island of Kınalıada and the Bostancı pier, marked by two lighthouses. The Bostancı-Kınalıada boat passes close to Vordonisi, which is also visible from the boat linking Sirkeci/Kabataş with the Princes' Islands

An island engulfed by an earthquake

The group of rocks known today as Vordonisi are all that remains of a previously inhabited island, which was engulfed by an earthquake in the 10th century. We know about Vordonisi in part thanks to fishermen who spoke of "monastery rocks" as well as to Byzantine religious history and ancient maps which, in addition to the nine existing islands close to Istanbul (Büyükada/Prinkipo, Heybeli/Halki, Burgaz/Antigoni, Kınalı/Proti, Sedef, Tavşan, Kaşik, Sivri/Oxya and Yassı/Plati), identify a tenth, Vordonisi. These maps (oriented towards the east) show it in the middle of the strait formed by the Asiatic shore of Istanbul to the north and the Princes' Islands to the south, between the two images of sailboats.

Following a preliminary exploration in 1965, a group of divers then explored the site in 2004 and discovered ruins that fully corroborated the religious history of Byzantium. After removing a thick layer of seaweed and mussels, they discovered mosaics and the ruins of the monastery where the Patriarch Photios had ended his days. A further surprise resulted when the plans of the Vordonisi Monastery were compared with those of the Monastery of Satyros, on the opposite shore, at Küçükyalı, near to the Bryas Palace which the Emperor Theophilos (829 – 842) had built on the model of the palace of the Abbasid Caliphs of Baghdad. The layout of the two monasteries was shown to be almost identical.

Today, the island of Vordonissi is being investigated not only by historians but also by seismologists seeking to draw lessons from the disappearance of Vordonisi; a major seismic fault line that passes to the south of the

Princes' Islands is probably the very line that caused Vordonisi to disappear. Such investigations are especially important when we recall the deadly earthquake in 1999, which devastated the eastern part of the Marmara region.

THE VORDONISI MONASTERY : A TERRIBLE RIVALRY

The Vordonisi Monastery was built by Photios, appointed Patriarch after the deposing of Ignatios in 858. Showing no hesitation in excommunicating Pope Nicolas I, ostensibly over the *filioque** controversy, but more probably due to a conflict relating to jurisdiction over the Slav dioceses, Photios was himself unseated for protesting against the Emperor Basil who had obtained the imperial throne by murdering his predecessor. An anathema was accordingly pronounced against Photios at the Council of Constantinople in 869-870 and he was replaced with Ignatios. An interesting character, Ignatios was the son of the Emperor Michael I Rangabe. After the deposing of his father in 813, he had been castrated to thwart any claim to the throne, which was forbidden to eunuchs, and sent to the Princes' Islands where he established monasteries. He was a devout churchman, canonised by the Orthodox church and also recognised by the Roman Catholic church. When he initially ascended to the patriarchal throne, his castration caused several problems due to the prohibitions of canon law. In 873-877, Ignatios, now Patriarch for the second time, built a shrine dedicated to Saint Michael on the site of a Satyr temple, close to present-day Küçükyalı, which was called the "Monastery of Satyros", according to ancient toponymy. During that time, Photios lived within the Vordonisi Monastery which he had founded, and was then recalled to act as schoolmaster for Prince Leon. On Ignatios' death, he became Patriarch again. He improved his relations with the Church of Rome, but fell into disgrace under the new Emperor Leon VI and was once again exiled to Vordonisi until the end of his life, in 893. Following the example of Ignatios, Photios was eventually canonised. The island of Vordonisi, where he had founded his monastery, outlived him by a few more years: it was engulfed by an earthquake that occurred at the beginning of the 11th century.

* *Filioque*: theological divergence of opinion regarding the Holy Spirit, whom the Orthodox believe proceeds only from the Father, but proceeds from the Father and the Son according to the western churches, who add the phrase *Patre filioque procedit* to the Nicene Creed.

MONASTERY OF THE TRANSFIGURATION OF CHRIST

❷

Kınalıada
- Mass celebrated at the church on Friday at 9.30am • Free entry
- On other days, opening is at caretaker's discretion.
- For the boat or seabus, consult: http://www.ido.com.tr
- Please note the winter and summer timetable changes

Little-known wonders

On the hill to the south of Kınalıada (the first of the Princes' Islands reached after Istanbul, hence its Greek name, Proti, meaning "the first"), the Monastery of the Transfiguration of Christ is a little-known place, which is nevertheless accessible to the public and contains wonderful post-Byzantine icons as well as decorative inscriptions in a mixture of Greek and Turkish/karamanlidika (Turkish dialect spoken by the Orthodox Turkish speakers of Anatolia and written in Greek characters).

Of special interest, on the right wing of the iconostasis, is a beautiful icon of the Metamorphosis (Greek name for the "Transfiguration"*), executed in a Byzantine style in which the influence of the Renaissance can barely be discerned. The faces of the Apostles are particularly expressive. To its right there is an impressive Saint John the Baptist.

In the garden, we find several Greek gravestones from the Ottoman period and beautiful decorative inscriptions in Greek on the façade of the church, although it is possible to make out several references in Karamanlidika. The benefactor of the monastery, whose statue and tomb are seen at the entrance, elsewhere bears a name that sounds Karamanli: Siniossoglou.

Still in use during the Ottoman era, the monastery became a battlefield in 1804 between the troops belonging to the fleet of the English admiral Duckworth and the Turks. The large monastery building is almost deserted in winter but in summer is transformed into a school for the children of the Greek community in Istanbul. Several Byzantine cisterns have been blocked up to prevent the pupils from falling into them.

The Emperor Leo V, the Armenian, was also buried in this monastery, after his murder in the Basilica of Saint Sophia on Christmas Day 820, in the midst of the iconoclastic controversies. His body parts, which had been mutilated by axe blows, were gathered together and buried by his four sons, who had all been castrated to prevent them from claiming the throne.

Kınalıada means the island (ada) of henna (kına), in reference to the colour of the earth on the island, which contains iron.

WHERE IS THE TOMB OF THE BYZANTINE EMPEROR ROMANUS LOCATED?

According to some sources, the monastery housed the tomb of Romanos IV Diogenes, the Byzantine Emperor who was defeated by the Seljuk army at the battle of Manzikert in 1071 (Malazgirt in Turkish), close to Lake Van. This marked the beginning of Turkish sovereignty in Anatolia and the beginning of the end for Byzantium.

On returning to Constantinople, Romanos Diogenes was deposed by his son-in-law Michael VII Doukas, who exiled his mother, the Empress Eudokia, and later had his father-in-law's eyes gouged out; the latter was then incarcerated in a monastery on the island of Kınaliada, where he soon died of septicaemia and was buried.

Although we do not know the exact location of the tomb of Romanos IV Diogenes, beneath the wooden iconostasis there is a beautifully tiled floor of Byzantine mosaics, which seems to indicate that the current 19th century church is built directly over the ancient church.

THE CELL OF THE PATRIARCH METHODIUS ❸

Church of St John the Baptist
Burgazada/Antigoni Island
Takımağa Meydanı Sokağı Street, no. 19, Burgazada
• Tel: 0 216-381 1401
• Open Sundays (Sunday mass in summer from 10.00am) and Orthodox holidays
• For the boat or seabus, consult www.ido.com.tr
• Please note the winter and summer timetable changes

> *The cell of a victim of the iconoclastic crises of the 8th century*

On the island of Burgazada, the Orthodox parish church of Saint John the Baptist (Saint John Prodrome in Greek) is home to a strange cell inside its crypt. This cell is a testimony to the horrors of the iconoclastic crises that shook Byzantium during the 8th and 9th centuries. Access is found on the left hand side, after the entrance door. Go down a narrow stairway until you come to a tiny room whose low ceiling makes it impossible to stand upright; this is where the prisoners were incarcerated. Among the prisoners held here was the Patriarch Methodius, a protagonist in the iconoclastic controversies that divided the society and theologians of the time over the question of whether sacred images should be venerated. This controversy, which assumed a political nature, gave rise to numerous conflicts between imperial power and the ecclesiastical authorities, who often changed their doctrine. The iconoclasts (opponents of the cult of images) thus started to vandalise all kinds of "lifeless images", which explains why it is now so rare to find Byzantine icons dating from before the 9th century. During a period in which the iconoclasts were in the ascendancy, Methodius the Confessor, Patriarch of Constantinople and passionate iconodule (supporter of the veneration of icons), was thrown into a sepulchral chapel on the island of Antigoni (Burgazada) after being flagellated and tortured. He spent seven years there, along with two bandits who had been placed there to keep him company. After one of them died, the body was left to rot there in order to increase the prelate's suffering. Methodius was eventually freed by the efforts of the Emperor Theophilos, after which he restored the cult of images in 842. The present day church, built in a neo-Byzantine style and dedicated to Saint John the Baptist, was designed by the architect Dimadis, who in 1899 constructed the Phanar Patriarchal Great School, on the ruins of the ancient church erected by the Empress Theodora.

At the entrance to the church there is a fire engine that was used by the roving firemen of the parish.

At the beginning of the 2000s, the church acquired a reputation for being haunted. Strange noises were heard there on summer nights at a precise time and the area around the church became a sort of theatre with the crowd waiting for the sounds to be repeated. In the end it was discovered that the noises were being made by birds.

AN ALCHEMIC SYMBOL

4

Coping of the well of the Heybeliada orthodox seminary
At the top of the Ümit Tepesi hill, close to the island's port
• Open daily 8.30am—4.30pm

> ## *The only visible alchemic symbol in Istanbul?*

On the island of Heybeliada, from the door of the chapel of the Halki orthodox seminary (Heybeliada Ruhban Okulu), walk to the right and along the walls of the sanctuary to reach the coping of a well, in the middle of the garden, bearing two inscriptions in Karamanlı Turkish (see p. 168) and Armenian, dating from 1792. These inscriptions state that the coping is a gift from the banker Hadji Nicolas, a native of Eğin, a town in eastern Anatolia. According to experts, it is highly likely that the latter belonged to the now extinct community of the Hay-Horom (Armenians affiliated to the Greek Orthodox church).

In the middle of this inscription is a strange sign that is reputed to be the only alchemic symbol visible in Istanbul. According to the alchemist Johann Christoff Sommerhoff (1701), this symbol represented the *lapis magnes* ("philosopher's stone") while other alchemists believed it was the hermetic symbol for arsenic, derived from the magical seal of Saturn.

Although alchemy was widespread in Byzantium and the Islamic world (the word itself comes from the Arabic *el kimiya*), the presence of this alchemic symbol is still surprising. Could Hadji Nicolas have been a practitioner of alchemy?

ALCHEMY

Most religious orders of the Middle Ages and the Renaissance considered alchemy (from the Coptic term *Allah-Chemia*, or divine chemistry) as the art of the Holy Spirit or royal art of the divine creation of the world and man. It was connected to Orthodox Catholic doctrine.

The followers of this art divided it into two principal forms. Spiritual alchemy exclusively concerns the inspiration of the soul, transforming the impure elements of the body in the refined states of spiritual consciousness, which is also called the Way of the Repentants. Laboratory alchemy, called the Way of the Philosophers, reproduces the alchemical universe of the transmutation of nature's impure elements into noble metals, such as silver and gold, in the laboratory. These two alchemical practices are generally followed in combination, thus becoming the Way of the Humble, where the humility is that of man faced with the grandeur of the universe reproduced in the laboratory (in Latin *labor* + *oratorium*); the alchemy of the (interior) soul is expressed exteriorly in the laboratory. Those who practise Laboratory alchemy with the sole purpose of finding silver and gold, and thus neglect the essential aspects of the betterment of the soul, will fail and become charlatans, who might have a wide-ranging culture but certainly not the required moral qualities. To avoid becoming a charlatan (it was this heretic form that was condemned by the Church), followers must balance the heart and soul, culture and moral qualities, penitence and humility, to become a true philosopher.

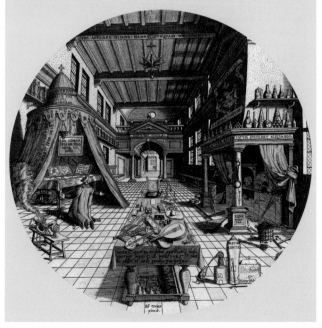

ΕΞΗΡΑΝΘΗ Ο ΧΟΡΤΟΣ ΚΑΙ ΤΟ ΑΝΘΟΣ ΑΥΤΟΥ ΕΞΕ
ΤΟ ΔΕ ΡΗΜΑ ΚΥΡΙΟΥ ΜΕΝΕΙ ΕΙΣ ΤΟΝ ΑΙΩΝΑ

KANGELARIS MAUSOLEUM

5

Garden of the Monastery of Saint George
Oruç Reis Sokak Street, no. 27
Heybeliada
• Open Sundays and Orthodox holidays
• Monastery's special feast day: 23 August
• The mausoleum can be seen from the street without entering the garden

> *A man who killed his wife but still lies next to her...*

L ocated in the garden of the Monastery of Saint George, within a ruined octagonal pavilion, the mausoleum of Mr and Mrs Kangelaris consists of an obelisk with a truncated top. Posted as British Consul to Kios (Gemlik), in the southern part of the Sea of Marmara, Spyridon Kangelaris was madly in love with his extremely beautiful wife Sevasti. He killed her out of jealousy in 1865. No doubt benefiting from diplomatic immunity, he remained at liberty and was able to have this tomb erected in 1866 with imported Carrara marble used to construct the obelisk. He had candles lit there regularly until he joined his wife five years later.

On the southern façade, facing the entrance, there is a bas-relief in which the deceased is described as, "an intelligent, pious, beautiful wife and life companion for her husband, an excellent mother who cared for her children, who was charitable to the poor and merciful, born in Istanbul in 1817 into a noble family, died in Heybeliada in 1865, a source of eternal grief and bitter tears". The bas-relief portrait of the couple is found on the eastern façade, surrounded by garlands of poppies (symbol of eternal rest) and laurel. An inscription there reads, "The flower has withered, the grains are scattered, but the word of God will endure for ever and ever". The western façade bears a figure symbolising the night, a dish from which fire spurts out (symbolising hope), a phoenix (symbolising the promise of resurrection) and a pelican (symbolising maternal love and sacrifice – according to the ancient belief that it feeds its children with its blood). On the northern façade, we see the god of sleep (Hypnos).

According to the pupils of the neighbouring military school, the deceased ("Sarıkız" – the blonde girl) would sometimes wake up on winter nights in order to go into the dormitories and cover up the pupils whose covers had fallen.

NEARBY

Hanging from the main door of the iconostasis of the monastery church, a rare picture (another exists in Basel Minster, in Switzerland) shows the Christ in the centre of a Star of David. Apart from the fact that this symbol, the star hexagram, is not exclusively Jewish (see p. 30), Monsignor Nektarios, hegumen of the monastery and the Orthodox Patriarchate of Jerusalem's representative to the Constantinople Patriarchate, explains that the Star of David also invokes the word David in Greek, which begins and ends with the letter delta (Δ). Two overlapping deltas, one of which is reversed, thus form the Star of David. According to the genealogies given in the Gospels of Matthew and Luke, Jesus is also the descendant of David, who reigned in Jerusalem. Finally, the Monastery of Saint George is a metochion (embassy church) of the Patriarchate of Jerusalem.

THE RUSSIAN MONUMENT
OF THE MONASTERY OF SAINT NICHOLAS

6

Aya Nikola Manastırı (Selvili Batmış Manastırı)
Avenue Yılmaz Türk Caddesi
Karacabey Mevkii
Büyükada Yolu
• Tel: +90-216-382.61.12.

An enchanting place

Situated on the eastern shore of Büyükada, among the pine trees, the towering Monastery of Saint Nicholas (Aghios Nikolaos in Greek / Aya Nikola in Turkish) is an enchanting place that previously housed a large community of which there now only remains a single, friendly monk from Mount Athos (Greece), who exchanged his philosophical first name, Socrates, for the monastic name Bartholomew. In the garden, a marble obelisk surmounted with a Russian cross has been erected in honour of the Russian soldiers taken prisoner during the Crimean War (1853 – 1856), and who were interned and subsequently died in Büyükada. It is interesting to note that although the double-headed eagle bas-relief, a political symbol adorning the obelisk, was destroyed by unknown people at the beginning of the First World War, when the Ottoman Empire declared war against the Russian Empire, the funerary monument itself has remained intact, out of respect for the religion of the deceased. It should also be noted that the Russian Monument to Saint Stephen (Ayastefanos) at Yeşilköy was destroyed at the same time, in the Istanbul suburb where the victorious Russian army arrived in 1878 (the demolition of the monument was the subject of the first film shot in Turkey).

There is another monument to the memory of the Russian soldiers at Heybeliada.

A SUNKEN BELL TOWER?

The Monastery of Saint Nicholas is also known as the sunken or buried monastery. One explanation is that the original 14th-century monastery was buried in the ground by an earthquake in 1509; another explanation is that this is the second monastery, dating from the Ottoman period, which collapsed into the water along with its bell tower during the earthquake of 1894. The fishermen of the island say that during storms the bells can be heard tolling from the depths of the Sea of Marmara, where the bell tower and its bells remain intact.

The current building was erected after the 1894 earthquake by a banker called Stefanovic, using the remnants of the material used in constructing the Orthodox seminary of Halki/Heybeliada. Although it is located on the island of Büyükada, the Monastery of Saint Nicholas is not answerable to the archdiocese of the Princes' Islands, but directly to the Ecumenical Patriarchate.

THE BÜYÜKADA GREEK ORPHANAGE   ❼

Aşıklar Yolu Sk, Nizam - Büyükada
Visiting the inside is not permitted for safety reasons
• Garden visits are sometimes possible if one asks the caretaker nicely
• For the boat or seabus, consult: http://www.ido.com.tr
• Please note the winter and summer timetable changes

> **The largest wooden building in the world?**

On the island of Büyükada (Prinkipo in Greek), the Greek orphanage is a spectacular wooden building that backs onto the Hill of Christ (Hristos Tepesi). Once the boat has landed, do not walk up the main avenue, Çankaya Caddesi, on the right, but go up the big slope opposite, Kadıyoran Yokuşu ("The slope that tires the judge"). You will find the orphanage on the romantic Aşıklar Yolu ("Lovers' Way"). The orphanage, which can be seen from the boat, impresses because of its huge size; some claim it to be the largest wooden structure in the world.

The company Grands Hôtels d'Europe began to construct this building in 1898, according to the plan drawn up by the architect Vallaury, with the intention of using it as a hotel-casino. However, Abdülhamid II, the reigning sultan-caliph, was not pleased when he heard about this and forbade the opening of this highly conspicuous den of iniquity right in the middle of the Sea of Marmara. The hotel project was therefore quickly abandoned since it would not have been profitable without a casino.

The famous Turkish writer Ahmed Rasim was the first to come up with the idea of transforming the building into an orphanage, after which it was bought by a rich Greek woman named Madame Hélène Zarifi, who then donated it to the Greek Patriarchate, on condition that it be used for this purpose.

The orphanage was inaugurated by the Patriarch Joachim III in 1903. The sultan sent him a telegram of praise, had 146 gold coins distributed to the Greek orphans and gave them a daily allocation of 7.5 oka, or ten kilos, of meat.

During the First World War, the Kuleli Military School moved into the orphanage while its occupants were sent to the Greek business school of Heybeliada (Halki). The ultra-Germanophile Minister of War, Enver Pacha, even used it to accommodate his Prussian friends. Following the Germano-Ottoman defeat, the British occupying forces used it to lodge Russian aristocrats, before returning it to the Greek orphans in 1920.

The Cypriot crisis that erupted in the 1950s poisoned Greek-Turkish relations and the orphanage was closed in 1964, "for violating legislation relating to fire prevention". The Patriarchate eventually filed a petition with the European Court of Human Rights which, in 2008, confirmed its property rights.

In order to thank Izzet Pacha, Abdülhamid's *éminence grise* who secured the necessary authorisation, the Patriarchate presented him, in Büyükada, with the Blacque Bey Pavilion (French diplomat, journalist and official in the service of the Sublime Porte, 1824-1895).

THE MASONIC SYMBOLS
OF THE SABUNCAKIS PAVILION

8

Avenue Yılmaz Türk Caddesi, no. 23
Büyükada (The Princes' Islands)
• Not open to visitors

> *A greek
> businessman
> turned freemason*

Built in 1904 for George Sabuncakis,
a Greek businessman who turned it
into his family's summer residence,
the Sabuncakis Pavilion displays several
Masonic symbols on its façade as reminders
of its founder's affiliation with Freemasonry
including: a set square and compass over the entrance; an Eye of Providence
on the pediment; and, on the golden bas-relief above the pediment, acacia
branches (a Masonic symbol associated with the memory of Master
Hiram since his three assassin companions planted one on his tomb) and
a bee (which symbolises the work carried out in the lodge and adorns the
Freemasons' apron).

Originally from Crete, the Sabuncakis began as soapmakers (as their name
indicates), who cultivated the flowers they used in their soapmaking. After
emigrating to Istanbul in the 1870s, the Sabuncakis then made their fortune
by establishing a chain of flower stores, which stretched as far as Thessaloniki.
Their business expanded rapidly during the republican era, as the ceremonies
of the new regime required many flowers for their garlands.

The Sabuncakis company enjoyed significant privileges, including a special
car on the Istanbul-Ankara express and a building in the very centre of the new
capital, given to them on Atatürk's personal instructions.

The central lounge, originally octagonal in shape, was capped with a
wooden dome that symbolised the sky and depicted various deities recognised
in Egyptian, Assyro-Phoenician, Greco-Roman and Hindu mythology. This
building was destroyed by fire in 1971.

In the local area, the building has been nicknamed "the bridge house", "the
eye house" or "the bee house" because of its architecture and symbols.

THE ACACIA: A FREEMASON SYMBOL OF IMMORTALITY

The acacia branch, adopted universally by Freemasonry, alludes to the
Master Mason, Masonic initiation and immortality.

The word acacia is derived from the Greek *ake*, meaning "point", having a
sharp end, (this gave rise to *lanke*, the lance). The ancient word for this
thorn tree was *akantha*, which means the plant with thorns: the acanthus,
the acacia, hence akakia, a term derived from ake. These thorns represent
the painful trials that the initiated encounter and must overcome on their
way to achieving the grade of Perfect Master.

ALPHABETICAL INDEX

ALPHABETICAL INDEX

Acknowledgements

Prof. İlber Ortaylı, Prof. Baha Tanman, Prof. Nurhan Atasoy, Prof. Kimberley Patton, Prof. Adam Seligman, Jean-François Pérouse, Giovanni Scognamillo, Saro Dadyan, Father Claudio Monge, Yusuf Altıntaş, İlhan Eksen, Hülya Benlisoy, Yorgo Benlisoy, Cenk Keskin, Aylin Tekiner, Orhan Türker, Katina Proku Türker, Eti Varon, Gözlem Gazetecilik Basın Yayın A. Ş., Father Yorgo Kasapoglu, Bora Keskiner, Burak Çetintaş, Prof. İsmail Taşpınar, Father Vağarşag Seropyan, Father David Neuhaus, Father Giuseppe Gandolfo, Win Dayton, Bleda Kurtdarcan, Sinan Kuneralp, Deniz Akkuş, Holta Vrioni, Rita Ender, Mgr. Stéphane, Father Bartholomée, Mete Boybeyi, Çağrı Yalkın, Mustafa Alpsoy, Peter Wolrich, Lale Ayşe Platin, Malik Can Baki, Sedat Bornovalı, Prof. Haluk Dursun, Alexandre Toumarkine, Constantin Belalidis, Athanase Belalidis, Father Tatoul Anoushian, Mgr. Elpidophoros, Kabataş school, Mgr. Nektarios, Father Minas Moskalli, Laki Vingas, Valentin Retornaz, Olivier Bouquet, Muriel Domenach, Betül Sözen, Şule Sökücü, Nurullah Özdem, Sait Süsin, Zeki Demir, Rabbi Mendy Chitrik, Prof. Remzi Sanver, Colonel İlyas Gürtaş, Colonel Zekeriya Türkmen, Colonel-Major Ömer Faruk Arslan, Kansu Şarman, Murat Serdar Saykal, Ensar Karagöz, Şule Gürbüz, Cansu Baş, Neslihan Şen, Maître Yiğit Okur, Pierre Gentric, Dominique Cornil, Serdar Güneysu, Alp Varanok, Bikem Ibrahimoglu, Manuela da Corta, Prof. Berlingeri, Mustafa Cambaz, Tuğçe Uğurlu, Süleyman Ertaş, Gökhan Karakaş, Matthieu Bardiaux, Saadet Ersin Arikgil, Sébastien de Courtois, Stefano Siviero, Paolo Girardelli, Owen Matthews, James Halliday, Pascal Cariou, Mgr. Klaus Wyrwoll, Ioannis Volanakis, Birol Özalp, Mustafa Alpsoy, Mikhail Paşa.

Special thanks go to Neslihan Sen and Cansu Bas at the Ciragan Palace Kempinski Istanbul.

Bahadir Kaleagasi, Murat Topaloglu, Olivier Hennebert, Olimpia Cavriani, Karin Paquay, Odette Swinnen, Oznur Koc, Marco Cespa. Memduh Ogur, His Excellency Mr. Murat Ersavcı, the Turkish Ambassador and his wife, Alexandre Varlik.

Texts pages 30, 35, 197, 273 : VMA

Photography credits

Mesut Tufan : p. 16, 17, 18, 20, 25, 26, 27, 28, 32, 33, 34, 41, 44, 46-47, 48-49, 50-51, 52-53, 58, 59, 60, 61, 62-63, 64, 65, 66, 69, 71, 73, 75, 79, 84, 86, 88-89, 90, 94-95, 100, 102, 104, 105, 106, 107, 108, 109, 110, 114, 115, 116-117, 120, 124, 125, 126, 128, 130, 132, 136-137, 138, 139, 142, 144, 147, 148, 150, 152, 154, 160, 160-161, 162, 163, 165, 166, 167, 168, 169, 171, 172, 174, 176, 181, 183, 184, 186, 192, 193, 194, 195, 196, 201, 209, 210, 212, 219, 222, 227, 230, 232, 233, 236, 237, 238, 247, 252, 254, 257, 258, 262, 269, 272, 274, 276, 277, 278, 282.
Letizia Missir : p. 22, 23, 38, 39, 76, 97, 99, 113, 122, 140, 175, 178, 185, 188, 189, 190, 191, 198, 204, 206, 214, 220, 228, 240, 244, 245, 248, 251, 270, 280.
Olimpia Cavriani : p. 36, 40, 41, 42, 43, 44, 45, 46, 92, 209, 211, 234, 279.
Fresco by Boris Delchev (2007), inspired by Melling's panoramas of the Bosphorus (18th century) - Ciragan Palace Keminski Hotel.

Maps **Cyrille Suss** - Layout design: **Roland Deloi** - Layout: **Stéphanie Benoit** - English translation: **Johanna Louw** - Proofreading: **Derek Linzey, Jana Gough** and **Kim Bess**

© JONGLEZ 2016

Registration of copyright: July 2016 – Edition: 01

ISBN: 978-2-36195-102-3

Printed in Turkey by Eray Basim